Compliments of
Passenger Traffic Department
Pittsburgh & Lake Erie R. R.

GRAND CENTRAL

Books by David Marshall:

GRAND CENTRAL

MODEL RAILROAD ENGINEERING

DAVID MARSHALL

GRAND CENTRAL

Whittlesey House
McGRAW-HILL BOOK COMPANY, INC.
NEW YORK: LONDON

GRAND CENTRAL

PUBLISHED BY WHITTLESEY HOUSE
A Division of the McGraw-Hill Book Company, Inc.

Printed in the United States of America

For JOHN

First-born of my nine
sons and daughters

PREFACE

THIS BOOK is supposed to be a portrait—but a portrait pieced together, as it were, of facts. Against a background of schemes and men, of great events and fateful decisions, I have traced the interlacing stories of stone and steel and people: of the Concourse and its great star-studded ceiling; of tracks and famous trains; of the clockmaster, the stationmaster and the men who throw the signal levers; of red caps, ticket sellers, information clerks and gatemen; and of the "wild" rush of commuters hurrying home each night to the suburbs. I have attempted to bring all their many stories into a single focus, for Grand Central Station is all of these and all of these together are Grand Central Station. I have attempted, not too solemnly, I hope, to tell their many stories—and let the final portrait emerge from the mixed mosaic.

The facts call for a certain explanation. Some of the most fantastic I have seen and heard and, perhaps, been a part of. But many more I have had to accept on the authority of others. Too, I have had to weigh an unusual number of contradictory sources one against another, and if this were a doctoral thesis, I could have sidestepped much responsibility, I suppose, by decorating every other sentence with an array of footnotes and "authorities." Instead I have taken the decisions and trusted that the completed story will show by its own integrity whether I had the sow by the right ear. Again, I have described as happening all within a single day events I witnessed over a period of many weeks; and, in some cases, I have described them as occurring in order rather than haphazardly. Finally, I have taken the liberty to omit some facts—I have not labored over things that ought to be obvious, nor have I exposed the reader to long and elaborate descriptions merely to verify the picture postcards.

Let us say, then, that I have selected facts, and arranged them; but facts they still remain, and the only moral is that facts alone, without any straining and without any sugaring over, can sometimes make a story—or a portrait. Anyhow, this is supposed to be a mosaic of facts; perhaps even a fantasy of facts.

Ichabod stands apart. He represents one of the most interesting of New York's minority groups, the noble breed of amateur railway and locomotive historians; and without him or one of his fellow spirits forever poking about, Grand Central would hardly be the place it is today. But he also takes up from time to time the role of narrator; so I have treated him less as one of the facts, more as a device for exhibiting the facts. In his person I have combined three different railway historians, of whom two are schoolteachers and the third a civil engineer. Thus, though I may not say that Ichabod is an actual person, perhaps I can argue that he is real.

But argue is the last thing I should wish to do. My simple intent has been to make this a good book, a revealing book, and a pleasing book, particularly to those who know and love Grand Central. The reader will find it too, I hope, a good companion—a readable book for the fireside, the slippers and the pipe.

Officially, of course, it's Grand Central Terminal, with all possible emphasis on that last word. The railroad publicity department insists upon this; and it's the mark of all New York Central publicity that it can, and does, insist like anything. Also the department has had for a whole generation now the volunteer aid of that battalion of unpleasant persons who go about insisting on everybody's calling everything by its official name, whether or no the official name happens to be the true name. Nor have these authoritarian spirits been the only ones. Their point, though, is absurd. I have taken a number of polls, mainly among newspaper men, and invariably the results have indicated that to 80 or 90 per cent of the people of New York it's Grand Central *Station*. And so I have called it in this book—on the principle of *Securus judicat orbis terrarum*.

Over the months I have had many interesting and always informative interviews with Ernest B. Moorhouse, the assistant terminal manager and former terminal engineer; Frederick H. Judd, the present terminal engineer; and Patrick F. Solan, the engineer in charge of structural maintenance. I am grateful to all three of these for checking on the engineering data and on a great host of straightforward facts and figures. I am further indebted to Mr. Moorhouse for having given me carte blanche to interview and quote whomever I pleased among the terminal employees.

For checking on a few obscure points of railway history, I have to thank two old friends, Walter A. Lucas of *Railway Age* and Henry Comstock of *Railroad Magazine;* and I must acknowledge, too, a debt to Freeman H. Hubbard, also of *Railroad Magazine,* who recommended me for the contract to write this book. For technical advice in the field of astronomy, I must thank Professor Roth of the Hayden Planetarium and James C. Hickey of *The New York Sun.* For spending hours and hours at Grand Central, listening to the crowds and jotting down their precise words, thus helping fix their tone and temper, I have to thank Miss Hannelore Kamnitzer, many of whose musical criticisms, signed H. K., have appeared in the *Sun.* And for setting before me virtually everything that was ever published about Grand Central Station, I must thank Charles Stolberg, head of the reference library of the *Sun.* For ransacking a score of books in quest of one little fact—when found, it spoiled a good story—and for help in other ways, I must thank Mrs. Margaret Fansler, librarian, and Mrs. Dora Burghardt, Mrs. Ida Crissey and Miss Helen Johnston, assistant librarians, all of the Public Library, South Orange, New Jersey. And for reading the manuscript in certain highly experimental forms, for checking on the passage of time and, above all, for liking Ichabod, I have to thank my good friends and neighbors, Irwin W. Thompson of Maplewood, New Jersey, and Theodore Gnagey and W. Freeman Crawford, both of South Orange.

D. M.

South Orange, New Jersey,
October 1, 1946.

CONTENTS

Preface vii
Heart of New York 1
Dawn 12
No Place for a Railroad 18
Kissing Gallery 27
Clockmaster 35
Yankee Railroad 39
Morning Rush 45
Train Departure 49
Waiting Room 54
The Old Man 58
Seats in the Gallery 72
Dispatcher 78
Red-cap Chief 88
The Merchantry 92
Information Service 102
Red-cap Preacher 111
Station Musician 115
Stationmaster 118
Luncheon for 10,000 121
Police Captain 131
Back of the Ticket Windows 143
Lady Ticket Seller 154
"The Public be Damned!" 159

Scars upon the Marble 168
Riddle of the Gates 175
Evening Rush 185
Departure of the "Century" 189
Gandy Dancer 196
Tower Work 203
Leverman 208
Train Protection 211
Tenor 218
Night Clerk 224
Tardy Arrival 230
Civil Engineer 237
Ten Years' Excavation 252
Three Architects 257
Glory to the Men of Old 267
Index 277

GRAND CENTRAL

HEART OF NEW YORK

OF ALL THE railway stations in all the cities of the world, the most famous is Grand Central. And that's the end of superlatives—for the rumor is false, and Grand Central is not, and never was, the biggest railway station in the world. Nor is it the busiest. And whether it's the most beautiful is for someone else to say; in New York you hear only contradictions on that point. But it is the world's most famous station.

It's one of the landmarks of the world, like the Marble Arch of London, the Etoile of Paris. It's a railway terminal, of course; but it's also a kind of crossroads at the heart and center of New York. It's known to everybody, open to everybody; and its splendid Concourse is everybody's meeting place. "I'll see you at the Golden Clock at Grand Central." In New York, of course, you take these words for granted. But you hear them in San Francisco too, occasionally; and you hear them on trains all over the United States. You hear them in the hotel lounges of London, and in happier days, when travel was for pleasure, you heard them in Paris, Geneva, Rome, Cairo, Bombay, and Hongkong. You heard them, sometimes, in the mouths of people who had never been to America, but who understood that, once arrived, they could surely find each other beside the four-faced Golden Clock at Grand Central Station.

It's a big place, of course. But it's less remarkable for its daily average of six hundred trains and 180,000 passengers; more remarkable for its daily average of 370,000 people who simply walk through the Concourse, or meet there, without any intention of purchasing a ticket or boarding a train. Anywhere else in the world the figures would hardly be credible, but this for more than a generation has been the mark of Grand Central—this multitude of people passing through, of whom only a minor fraction are railway passengers.

The rest? They're just people, and they exceed two hundred million every year—people who use the Concourse as a short cut to and from their offices and homes; people who patronize the station restaurants or the Terminal Newsreel Theatre; people who go shopping in the little stores that line the station corridors; people who come to hear the organ recitals in the Concourse or the carols at Christmas time; or suburbanites from Jersey who are simply fond of Grand Central and would consider a day in the city incomplete unless they visited the Concourse, with its acre of marble pavement, its marble staircase and balconies, and its great blue ceiling in which Pegasus and Orion and all the constellations of the winter zodiac twinkle with light.

They're just people. But in the end, of course, it's that everlasting throng of people who have made Grand Central famous. In a sense, they have taken possession of it and made it their own. Is a German plane, the *Bremen*, the first ever to fly westward across the Atlantic? The *Bremen* remains for many months on exhibition at Grand Central where it hangs, absurdly small, from the ceiling of the East Balcony (1927 and 1928). Does Bishop Manning call for ten million dollars to complete the building of Saint John's Cathedral? A campaign is launched at Grand Central; the Bishop speaks from the North Balcony, and silence falls upon the crowded Concourse as the people listen to his words (December 10, 1931). Or does the nation call upon New York for ten billion dollars to prosecute a war? Again a campaign is begun at Grand Central, and the crowds hear the voice of Secretary Morgenthau (December 14, 1941). The crowds are nearly always at Grand Central; but the point is that they have impressed their own character upon it. They have lifted it above the status of a simple railway terminal. They have made it a kind of unofficial Community Hall of New York.

And, when all is said, it lies at the heart of things. . . .

Outside, in Forty-second street, the city seethes and roars, and the clangor of streetcars mingles with the shouting of taximen and the hoarse bellowing of newsboys. Out here it's bitter cold in January, blustery in March, blazing hot in July. And it's noisy all the time; for this is one of the two or three busiest points in all New York.

To the south, directly in front of Grand Central, is fine old Murray Hill, still redolent of the days when men built marble mansions in the city. To the east is Lexington avenue, with its Chrysler Building, third or fourth tallest in the world. And to the north is residential Park avenue where rents are high and living is, in theory, gracious. The best of Park avenue, from Forty-sixth to Fifty-second street, is—strictly speaking—part and parcel of Grand Central Terminal; for all these buildings, Park avenue itself, and the grass plot down the center of Park avenue, stand cellarless upon a vast bridge that spans the railroad tracks.

Fifth avenue lies to the west, little more than two hundred yards from Grand Central. Just across the Avenue is New York's Public Library; and two blocks beyond the library—fittingly, perhaps, the blocks are long—glittering Broadway asserts her shuffling, shambling sway. Time was, back in the early 1920s, when a Methodist preacher conceived the idea of building on Broadway a combination church and skyscraper. To finance the venture, he raised a cry of "Buy Bonds and Let God Come to Broadway," and even Broadway was shocked. But Broadway never faltered in the slick performance of her chosen task, which is to welcome the stranger and take him in.

Three blocks away from Broadway (which is Theaters), a single short block from the Avenue (which is Shopping), and islanded about by skyscrapers (which is Business), Grand Central stands—but inwardly remote from all the fury and turmoil—close to the heart of New York.

It stands, to be precise, at No. 89 East Forty-second street; and—curious though it may seem in the case of a railway station—the number appears in gold letters upon the transom over the main doorway.

It stands, too, at the center of a regular spider's web of underground arcades and corridors that reach out from the Concourse and give direct access to eighteen surrounding buildings. In all the rest of New York—in all the world, perhaps—there's nothing to compare to those corridors, which make it possible, without ever stepping out into the weather, to go from the Concourse to any of a score of banks, hotels and private clubs, to any of two dozen restaurants and bars, to any of two hundred retail stores and shops, to any of 14,000 offices.

It's a point often insisted upon by visitors that the most celebrated parts of New York are those that are least like New York; that the elegance of Park avenue, for example, is not New York at all, but Paris—Paris on a bigger scale, perhaps; enlarged, elaborated, ever so slightly puffed up, but Paris just the same. We may as well concede the point; for when all is said, Grand Central is Paris too.

The exterior is the last word in Flamboyant French architecture; and, curiously, this was the last important building in New York designed in that style. The interior, however, is Modern French; it was New York's first example of that form, and it remains one of the best. Modern French dates from the first five years of the twentieth century; it came about when the Parisian schools turned away from the Flamboyant (which was Renaissance gone florid and flabby), back to the pure Classic, and attempted a further simplification of even that. The result, of course, was wholly French in spirit, but it captivated the minds of men everywhere, and everywhere it gave rise to new movements. It marked a great turning point in the history of architecture, and out of it, in direct line of development, came our present-day Functional design, exemplified by the Empire State Building and the various structures that make up Rockefeller Center. But Functional, of course, came later on; and, combining in herself the first of the Modern French and the last of the Flamboyant, Grand Central stands, in respect of her architecture, precisely where she stands in respect of the calendar. She was ten years abuilding, from 1903 to 1913, and she belongs essentially to those ten years.

Do you want to know what that Flamboyant exterior is like? Imagine a restaurant, a small restaurant, on the Boulevard des Capucines; not ravishing, but pleasing to the eye. And imagine that restaurant expanded several times over, and distorted in the process; so that nothing is left of that loveliness of proportion that the French are so conscious of. Then cap the structure with an excessively Flamboyant clock embedded in a mass of clumsy concrete "sculpture." That's Grand Central as she rears today above the brow of Murray Hill. Elmer Davis once called it "kolossal," and said in cold print—in the columns of *The New York Times*, July 4, 1928—that if the Germans had only blown it up in the First World War, New York would have been a better and a happier town.

Another day, of course, it may be different; for Grand Central was designed as a twenty-story building, and the additional fourteen stories may soon be added to it, transforming its appearance. But till that day it's going to be hard to look upon it from the outside without being irresistibly reminded of one of those precious little restaurants in Paris; or a squared-off wedding cake with white icing.

The fact is, however, that relatively few people ever see the exterior of Grand Central, and its shortcomings are redeemed by the interior, which millions know; above all, by the Concourse, which is, of its kind, one of the impressive things of New York. This, and not the Waiting Room, is the great hall of Grand Central Station. Including alcoves below the balconies, it forms a chamber 120 feet wide by 375 feet long; and the open floor, enclosed between four rows of pillars, is 108 feet wide by 185 feet long. The balconies look down upon the floor from three sides. The square pillars rise to a height of 97 feet to support the great barrel-vaulted ceiling. And the ceiling, rolling upward from either side, achieves a crest 117 feet above the center of the floor. It's a big place, to be sure, but not tremendous.

In more senses than one, perhaps, the night-blue ceiling ablaze with golden fire is the crowning feature of the Concourse. The Tennessee-marble floor and the lavish use of Botticino marble in staircase, balconies, and wainscoting—in everything that hand can touch—give it an air of uncommon splendor and richness. It's a mistake to think of the Concourse, however, in terms of all this marble. The dominant tone is set by the ceiling and the high, buff-colored walls—coursed ashlar walls in which random use is made of darker and lighter slabs. Buff-colored would seem to be the best general description, but for those who know the various shades of building stone there is an exact word—Caen. You remember the French city of Caen; in a notable victory that closed the battle of Normandy in the summer of 1944, the British captured Caen, famous for its stone quarries. In color and texture, as well as outline, the Concourse at Grand Central is very French.

The effect is heartwarming to an unusual degree; and New Yorkers have looked upon it for more than a generation without tiring of it. Artists and architects and the critics generally prefer, it is true, the more austere beauty of Pennsylvania Station with its Classic lines, its vast interior, its towering heights. And these, be sure of it, are things to take your breath away. But the immense majority of New Yorkers dismiss Pennsylvania Station as a cold barn of a place and turn gratefully to the warmer tones of Grand Central with its comfortable distances and its friendly, buff-colored walls. Often you see them linger affectionately in the Concourse: "Nice place, know what I mean?"

Its pavement lies a full story below street-level, and the restaurants and the Waiting Room and the stores that face on Forty-second street all stand between it and that noisy thoroughfare. Orderly and quiet, and always comfortably warm in winter, always comfortably cool in summer, the Concourse is a grateful refuge from the city. Its calm is magnificent; and what effect this works upon people you quickly realize if you listen to the crowds:

". . . such a thrill in my life as when I arrived here from Providence as a young man . . ."

"Know how I felt? On the train I was worried, first time I came to New York. But the minute I saw this, all the worry fell off me. I felt like *I'm taken care of*. Everything was so serene . . ."

". . . in the history of the ages, there's never been a place like this!"

Forthright and final, this last was the judgment of one who ought to know—for, as he presently explained, he was not only a sailorman, quartermaster aboard the *Lady Jane Grey*, out of Liverpool, but he was an Irishman from Tip, and therefore a man of erudition, and he had been everywhere, he had seen everything. With appealing dignity he added: "I know where the stars rise and set in every quarter of the globe." In which case it may be added that all the world comes trooping through Grand Central—men of every trade and calling, men of every color, men of every land, from Chinese aviators and Russian traders to great-hearted sailormen from Tipperary. And they all speak well of these buff-colored walls.

As the "history of ages" goes, of course, these walls are not old, though they stand—at the heart of the New World metropolis—upon the earth's oldest land. But neither are they new; and who is to say they have no storied past?

For as long as the Grand Central Depot shall stand
The Commodore still will haunt it.

It would be well to say, perhaps, that these walls have been a part of New York for as many years now as anybody cares to remember, and the New Yorker doesn't breathe who isn't stirred by their associations. They saw the end of the old America, when Taft was President and Horatio Alger was still a prophet; when *Progress* was in the air and *Equal Opportunity* was the watchword, and the leitmotiv of a glad, confident future was the daily clangor of a hundred thousand schoolbells. They heard the city singing "The Trail of the Lonesome Pine," and they heard that last of the older songs die out before the harsh new cacophony of "The International Rag." They saw the horned gramophone give place to the Victrola and the Victrola give place to radio. They saw the coming of the Federal income tax, the Woman Suffrage Amendment and the popular election of United States Senators. They saw the beginning of the First World War, they heard the shouting of the newsboys late that night in April, 1917: "War Extra! Wilson Calls for War on Germany!" They saw the troops pass through, saw thrones collapse and empires die. They looked upon the monstrous farce of Prohibition, poison liquor and unleased lawlessness. They saw the rise and fall of a fabulous prosperity; and after that they heard the whispering of former Wall street clerks and brokers, asking (in strict confidence) whether there was not some way of earning a free ticket back to the old home town. And now they've seen the troops pour through a second time, on their way to an immensely greater war. Each day for years they've seen 550,000 people pour in and out; and that's a greater population than dwells in the whole city of Cincinnati, Newark, or Kansas City.

Amid the murmur and the bustling, they've heard the groan of Age and the laughter of Youth. They've seen acts of mercy and, occasionally, heroism. They've witnessed, and more than once, the blind stupidity of crowds and the wilful stupidity that gets men into trouble. They've heard the "Wedding March," they've seen the funeral corteges pass through, and they've looked upon the lines of men chained wrist to wrist, and ankle to ankle, as they shuffled along in lock-step on their way to prison. They've looked upon flirtations, innocent and guilty; some that have led to high romance, and some that have led to tragedy. Human sorrow, human joy have never been absent from the Concourse; and Death itself is no stranger to these buff-colored walls—which in their day have also witnessed, and many a time, the everlasting mystery of Birth.

From the day it was first conceived by William J. Wilgus in a "sudden flash of light"—one afternoon in the late September of 1902—all this was meant to be a previously unheard-of thing, a profit-making railway terminal; and so the retail shops at Grand Central are not an afterthought but elements of a carefully integrated scheme. From restaurants and drugstores to millinery, lingerie and clothing stores, you count them by the dozens. There's a story, not altogether false, that between them all they can supply every temporal need of man; and there's another story, indignantly denied, that once a man evaded the police for two years by never leaving Grand Central in all that time.

"Grand Central Terminal," the company spokesmen say, "has everything but an undertaker's parlor." Let them say so. Grand Central has a morgue—where a young lady, victim of a Prohibition-day cocktail, was said to have found herself when she woke up. It also has a hospital with wards, nurses and a resident physician. And it has a police station complete with bar, desk and blotter. Every member of the Grand Central Terminal Police Department carries a commission signed by the commandant of the State Police; and under State supervision the department has the same general status as any municipal department. It keeps the same records in the same way; it files the same reports in the same place in Albany.

Three times a week religious meetings are held at Grand Central; and it is, after all, one of the few stations in which to hear an organ concert. (The organist is believed to be the only one in New York, perhaps the only one in America, forbidden to play "The Star-Spangled Banner.") It has a newsreel theater, a television studio and a famous art gallery. Oddly, Grand Central has a fabulous living room, a reproduction of the great hall of a Florentine palace, where a wealthy couple who live in the suburbs entertain their friends in the city.

"But where are the trains?" The question is asked perhaps a hundred thousand times a year, to be answered briefly: "Out of sight." Time was when the smoothly spoken gentry made a regular thing of "selling" Grand Central to rich but not cautious farmers; they said it was the latest thing in business properties, with railroad passenger service "right into our cellar," and in 1914 alone, the story goes, they "sold" Grand Central thirty-six times. In which case it may be stated that Grand Central is no ordinary railway station.

Indeed, you can sometimes forget that Grand Central is the New York terminal of the *Fast Mail*, the *Empire State Express*, the *Water-Level Limited*, the *Lake Shore Limited*, the *Wolverine*, the *Knickerbocker Express*, the *Twentieth Century Limited*—these and a score of other trains that are famous in the railway history of the world. The *Fast Mail*, which began running in 1875, was America's first "flyer," and the *Empire* was once believed the fastest train on earth; she made her greatest runs, hauled by locomotive No. 999, in the spring of 1893, and—

"And No. 999 did *not* exceed a hundred miles an hour!"

Have it so. In the early May of 1893 the *Empire State Express* was publicly stated and widely believed—

"No. 999 began to vibrate at seventy miles an hour! She'd have shaken herself to bits if she ever—"

Anyhow, the golden age of American railroading, which began in the post-Civil War period, came to an abrupt close on the tenth of May, 1893, when the *Empire State Express* flew over the rails at the debatable speed of—

"The tip-off is that Charlie Hogan, the engineman, would never say to a reporter what the speed was."

Grand Central Station, it may be asserted, is a favorite gathering place of large numbers of railroad fans, including members of half a dozen railway historical societies. They're a grand lot of men—teachers, business men, lawyers, journalists, bricklayers, doctors—all sorts of men. But they are, occasionally, a bit technical. You find them at every turn at Grand Central. On the subject of railway history they are unmerciful precisionists; and to know the unvarnished facts about Locomotive No. 999 makes, to them, all the difference between ignorance and culture.

It's a valid point of railway history, perhaps, that back in 1913 that great star-studded ceiling at Grand Central—the crowning feature of the Concourse—was proclaimed (with a fine contempt for Michelangelo) the "most beautiful ceiling in the world." Thousands upon thousands of people came to New York especially to see it in the spring and summer of that year. They supposed it was the work of Paul Helleu (as, in some measure, it really was), and Paul Helleu was then at the height of his fame as a painter and etcher. It was he who began the craze for cathedral interiors. It was he whose portrait of a beautiful woman captured the hearts of all Europe and America. (And that woman was the American-born Duchess of Marlborough, the former Consuelo Vanderbilt.) Crowds came pouring in to see the great ceiling he designed for Grand Central.

It was a painted ceiling; simply painted blue and gold. Some sixty-odd major stars were lighted up; and against a background of dark cerulean—the cold blue of a December night sky in the Mediterranean—the lesser stars were in gold leaf. In gold leaf, too, were the ecliptic and the celestial equator, crossing at the vernal equinox; and ten flaming figures out of ancient mythology, which embraced and tied together the stars of ten constellations. In all, there were nearly 2,500 stars on a field of 25,728 square feet. There were the six constellations of the winter zodiac: Aquarius, Pisces, Aries, Taurus, Gemini and Cancer. And there were four other constellations: Pagasus, Triangulum, Musca and Orion. It was forty feet from Orion's toe to the tip of his club; and, seen from the marble pavement below, the constellations were not far from "life size." In line and color, their presentation was beautiful; and there was no denying that the whole effect was majestic.

Inevitably the ceiling was recommended as a kind of still planetarium, to which students might come to study astronomy. And students came, along with all the others. The amateurs went into raptures. The brighter ones were puzzled. The professors conferred with one another in shocked whispers. And the station authorities turned their attention elsewhere and found other aspects of the terminal to center their praises on. The story—officially denied—was that the lights went out, the ceiling was for years and years left dark.

The story goes that the painter's bill alone came to forty thousand dollars. But the stars, alas, were all put on backwards and Pegasus came charging from the west instead of the east.

It's a curious phenomenon and one of the unexpected things about Grand Central and about that painted sky above the Concourse. Few people know about it, for it can happen only ten or so times a year, and even then the weather outside must be favorable; which it usually is not.

Ichabod—that, of course, is not the fellow's true name—claims to have seen it happen three or four times in the course of thirty years. There may be some who have seen it oftener; not many though.

To see it, you stand at about the center of the West Balcony and face the east. . . .

DAWN

IT WAS THE twentieth of January, a little before sunrise. Outside, the weather was crisp and clear, and over in the west the morning star was becoming brighter and brighter. It was 6:51 A. M. The stars were going out in the east.

Inside, the Concourse was still a little hushed; if you listened sharply, you could hear the ringing of the rails as early commuter trains approached the portals at Ninety-sixth street. The minutes passed. The Concourse was vaguely stirring. The lights were beginning to pale now; and now you heard the rumble of trains roaring down the tunnel. In a minute or two the sun would be coming up—red and dancing on a day like this.

So, as you stood at the middle of the West Balcony, you fixed your eyes upon the painted ceiling at Grand Central. You saw it slowly flush with crimson as the upward-slanting rays of the sun poured through the seventy-foot east windows; you saw the painted sky take on life, as it were, sharing and participating in the sunrise.

"Kinda like nature, ain't it?"

"Wha' do you know!"

"Some sight!"

"Is it like this every day?"

Ichabod answered the question.

"Only when the rising sun shines up Forty-third street—twenty-second of November and the twenty-first of January, plus two or three days before and after these dates. Ten months out of the year the sun rises too far north . . . or Forty-third street slants too far to the southeast.

"Due east is 90 degrees," said Ichabod, "and southeast is 135 degrees. The center-line of Forty-third street has a bearing of 119 degrees, 1 minute and 36.3 seconds; so it runs a great deal closer to southeast than to east. . . . You begin to understand a great deal about New York when you realize that."

Ichabod, of course, is a schoolteacher; that's why—or that's one reason why—we call him Ichabod.

"This Concourse," he went on to say with a wave of his hand, "is centered upon a point established by a Revolutionary soldier before the invention of the steam locomotive. At the center of the Concourse is the circular Information Desk; at the center of this desk is the Golden Clock you've heard so much about (which isn't gold at all, but highly polished bronze); and just above the dead center of the clock . . . the center-line of Forty-third street crosses the center-line of Park avenue —latitude, 40 degrees, 45 minutes, and 9.681 seconds north; longitude, 73 degrees, 58 minutes, and 39.457 seconds west.

"Folks like to know *all* the facts about a place like this," the tall fellow added.

"There," he continued, "you have a few of the fundamentals. A great deal follows. . . . Take the ceiling, for example. . . . The crown-line of that cylindrical ceiling follows the center-line of Forty-third street, dead above it; so that, if it should ever become necessary, Forty-third street could be carried on bridgework straight through the Concourse. The middle windows at the east and west, you'll notice, are already street-wide. They'd become open arches. The Concourse would be bridged over, fifteen feet or so above the floor . . . and Grand Central, then, would straddle Forty-third street as the Municipal Building straddles Chambers street today.

"It won't ever happen, the chances are. But the engineers who built Grand Central were as sure as anything, back in 1903, that New York would never stop growing. They figured the day would come when Forty-third and Forty-fourth streets and Park avenue, all three, would have to be 'cut through' the station, and Grand Central was designed on that assumption. It gave us, meanwhile, a magnificent Concourse."

Ichabod paused for a moment, then added briskly: "I'd better show you how Grand Central lies.

"We're on the West Balcony, roughly at street-level. The doorways back of us lead to Vanderbilt avenue and Forty-third street. The stairway ahead of us leads down to the Concourse. There's a pile of facts you haven't heard yet about the Concourse. . . .

"If we take our dates from the blueprints, Grand Central was the first railway terminal in the world in which the concourse was placed inside the 'head house'—that is to say, inside the station itself. . . . Every terminal has a concourse, but normally it lies outside the station, under the train-shed. It lies between the station and the bumper-line, where the tracks end. It lies at right angles to the peninsular train platforms; it's a kind of connecting platform that makes the others accessible to the station and ties them together in a single system of platforms. But here, as I say, the Concourse was brought indoors.

"Consequently, the train platforms at Grand Central open directly out of the station itself. Instead of gates, you have that long line of doors along the north wall of the Concourse, under the North Balcony —a pair of doors, a vestibule and another pair of doors for each pair of platforms. . . . The attendants are called 'doormen,' officially. But the generality of New Yorkers still call them 'gatemen'; and that's all to the good too," said Ichabod, "for it was here at Grand Central—rather, it was at the original Grand Central, built in 1870—that the gateman, a well-known figure in the history of railroading, made his first appearance on the American railway scene.

"Anyhow, they brought the concourse inside when they built the present-day Grand Central; and the ticket offices were built facing the concourse instead of the waiting room. This again was something new in railway history. . . . The concourse became the main element of Grand Central Station, became so important that we raised it from a common to a proper noun, and spelled it with a capital C."

The tall fellow with the green eyes paused here to consult his watch. It was a genuine "railroad man's watch," made to endure the lurch and sway of a locomotive; and the chain was decked with an array of golden railway charms—a tiny lantern, a four-wheeled caboose, crossed flags enameled red and green, a semaphore blade, an antique locomotive. Ichabod is nothing if not all-out in his enthusiasm for this strange hobby of his; or this mass of related hobbies, for Ichabod's capacious interest embraces everything from railway history to locomotive design and the noble art of model railroading.

"It's seven o'clock," he announced. "In twenty minutes from now No. 44 ought to be in on Track 39. . . . But she won't be. . . .

"As I was saying: The Concourse is the main thing at Grand Central, and the Waiting Room is secondary. The Waiting Room is there to the south; it lies between the Concourse and Forty-second street, somewhat below street-level, somewhat above the level of the Concourse. From the main entrance at Forty-second street and Park avenue, you come down a ramp to the Waiting Room . . . and from the Waiting Room you come down a second ramp to the Concourse.

"It's well below street-level," said Ichabod. "How far, it's hard to say . . . because we're on a hill here and the land falls away to the north and to the east more sharply than most people realize. Actually, the Concourse floor is forty-four feet three inches above the mean high-water mark of the East river at Forty-second street . . . possibly sixteen feet below Vanderbilt avenue at Forty-third street. . . .

"And below the Concourse in turn—downstairs, directly under it—is another one called the Lower Concourse. The tracks are double-decked at Grand Central; this is the only terminal in the world where the trains come and go on two levels, one above the other. . . . And both levels are below the ground.

"You have seventeen tracks on the lower level, thirty-one on the upper level. That makes forty-eight in all. The story that Grand Central has sixty-seven terminal tracks is not true, though you see it repeated year after year," said Ichabod, "in a lot of those sophisticated magazines. . . .

"Now the Lower Concourse," he went on to say, "is a railway station complete in itself—you've got to understand that. It's the suburban station, with seventeen tracks, its own ticket offices and its own information desk. . . . The idea was, originally, that all the commuter trains and suburban trains generally would use the lower-level tracks; and that the long-distance trains, the 'main-liners,' would have the upper-level tracks to themselves. True, it worked that way only for a little while, and ever since the First World War the overflow of commuter trains have been crowding their way onto upper-level tracks—during the rush hours, anyhow. . . . But that doesn't alter the fact that the Lower Concourse, with its benches around the walls in lieu of a waiting room, is a railway station all of itself; a complete and separate entity.

"In the same sense, the Concourse is a second railway station. This is the main-line departure station. . . . A specialized-purpose station they called it when Grand Central was new. The idea was that all outgoing liners would depart from the Concourse, that no trains would ever arrive there. The second half of the rule has broken down, and one of the causes, strangely, was the stream-lining of trains; though that's another story—I'll tell you about that later. But the first half of the rule still stands, and the Concourse is still the main-line departure station.

"And there's a third railway station at Grand Central," said Ichabod. "That's the Arrival Station, spelled with a capital A and a capital S. It used to be called the 'Kissing Gallery.' Back in 1913 the newspapers made a great deal of fuss about the Kissing Gallery."

Ichabod again consulted his watch, studied it in that very precise way of his, and then abruptly dashed on with his dissertation.

"The Arrival Station lies on the other side of Vanderbilt avenue. From the northwest corner of the Concourse, you go through the corridor below the West Balcony; then cut off to the northwest, diagonally, across that other corridor that lies below Vanderbilt avenue—that's how you reach it from the Concourse.

"Upstairs, above the Arrival Station is the Hotel Biltmore . . . across the street from Grand Central Station, most folks believe. Actually," said Ichabod, "Vanderbilt avenue is a bridge; the Biltmore is the upstairs portion of the Arrival Station; and the Biltmore, straddling two levels of railroad track, forms a single structural unit with Grand Central Station. . . .

"The point I wish to make, though," the tall fellow said, "is that the Arrival Station is quite far distant from the Concourse—and it remains what it was meant to be from the beginning, a one-purpose station. No trains depart from the Arrival Station. They only arrive. And their crowds don't clash with the crowds hurrying into the Concourse to catch out-going trains. . . .

"And now," said Ichabod, "I'll have to tell you one thing more about the physical layout at Grand Central. . . .

"Downstairs, below the Arrival Station . . . below the Biltmore . . . are the five arrival tracks. These are the most westerly of the thirty-one upper-level tracks. They're somewhat lower down, though; and, unlike the twenty-six others, they do not terminate in bumpers. They continue on below the floor of the Arrival Station. They curl eastward, combining as they go. They all come together in a single loop track that swings around three sides of the Lower Concourse and comes out in a yard that lies to the east of the Concourse tracks—below the skyscrapers along the west side of Lexington avenue.

"That," said Ichabod, "explains why five arrival tracks can handle so much traffic. Incoming trains stop just long enough to discharge their passengers, then pull forward round the loop and into the yard, thus clearing the way for the next train in. And that, too," he added, "is why the Lower Concourse is smaller than the Upper Concourse; it ies within the fold of the upper-level loop track.

"On the lower level there are two loop tracks. The second was built n 1929 by blasting through solid granite below the Lexington avenue skyscrapers—by undercutting their foundations and shoring them up as he work was carried forward. . . . It took an awful lot of engineering vork," said Ichabod, "it took an awful lot of daring and cold nerve to out Grand Central together. . . .

"Perhaps, though, you now see the lie of things. . . . You have three eparate stations at Grand Central; most folks don't seem to realize hat. At the center of everything is the Concourse. Directly under that s the Lower Concourse. And well over to the northwest is the Arrival Station with its own taxi-stand below the pavement of Forty-third treet. . . .

"There's a hotel, the Biltmore, upstairs above the Arrival Station; nd there's another hotel, the Commodore, that stands above the loop racks just beyond the southeast corner of the Concourse. . . . The Vaiting Room lies south of the Concourse, sandwiched between it nd the stores and restaurants that face on Forty-second street. And traddling fifteen departure tracks and nine platforms, directly north f the Concourse, is the eight-story Terminal Office Building. . . .

"All in all," said Ichabod, "it's a big place. But you'll miss the whole oint if you judge it by its bigness. . . ."

NO PLACE FOR A RAILROAD

"THE REMARKABLE thing about Grand Central," said Ichabod, "is not that it's so big; the remarkable thing is that it's so compact, that so much has been tucked away into so little space. You'll be all the more impressed by that the more you see of Grand Central.

"There's a reason, of course; and the reason," said Ichabod, "is granite. Grand Central was built upon granite. But it was also hedged in by granite . . . and men were pitted against the granite for the better part of a hundred years. Do you know what the granite of New York is like?"

The tall fellow took advantage of the question—which nobody present could have answered anyhow—to look again at his watch.

"It's eleven minutes after seven," he said. "I can tell you this briefly Then I'll show you round the three stations at Grand Central. . . .

"But first you have to understand what the granite is like. *Manhattan schist* is the name the geologists have given it. It belongs to the archaeozoic granite of the Appalachian Highlands, believed to be the oldest of present-day dry land. It's very hard and tough; it is not affected by exposure to the air; it forms a solid mass that goes down into the earth nobody knows how far. The Catskill water tunnel was cut through it . . . down to a depth of 750 feet. And still they had not found the bottom.

"When you realize that," said Ichabod, "you begin to *understand* Grand Central. I'll tell you what I mean. . . ."

It begins with the street design of New York. And so, in a way, it goes back to Lafayette and the American Revolution; for Lafayette was not alone when he came here from France. As he presented himself to Washington, there stood beside him a follower, a young civil engineer called Pierre L'Enfant. L'Enfant become a major in the Cont nental Army, and when the war was over, threw in his fortune with America. He designed the city of Washington. And a few years later he drew up the "gridiron plan" of streets and avenues for the city of New York.

That was in 1811. With a build-up area, then, of possibly one square mile, New York lay almost wholly south of Chambers street. Next year, in 1812, the new City Hall would be completed, a surprisingly beautiful structure built of white marble on three sides, brownstone at the rear; and as to the brownstone there was even at this moment a sharp difference of opinion. But the Mayor defended the economy by declaring that nobody would notice the brownstone anyhow, for nobody walked in Chambers street, back of the City Hall, and no considerable number of people would venture so far north for a hundred years to come. And on this point, it would seem, everybody was in cordial agreement; in any case, nobody arose in that year of grace, 1811, to contradict the Mayor.

Yet it was in that same year that the old Major L'Enfant completed his survey of the New York that was, and drew up his plan for the New York that was to be. They cheated him out of his fee. In lieu of cash, the Common Council offered him a tract of land up in Chelsea, and the testy-tempered old fellow rejected it. But they took his plan just the same, a plan embracing most of the twenty-seven square miles of Manhattan island; and they solemnly adopted it as the "Official Map of the City of New York." It was somewhat of a gesture, of course; the gesture of a little seaport town showing off before the big city of Philadelphia. But it fixed the fate of many things, once New York began to grow; and a hundred years beforehand—such are the things that history is made of—it determined the character as well as the site of the present-day Grand Central Terminal.

On the Official Map, all the streets and avenues were laid out with admirable precision; but, except in theory, only a handful of those above Chambers had any existence. One we are especially interested in. It had no name as yet. However, it ran north-and-south. Therefore, it was an avenue; and, counting from the east, it was the fourth of eleven avenues. So, with a fine flourish of Gallic penmanship, it was lettered on the map: "The *fourth* Avenue." It was a broad, imaginary highway through farming country as far north as Murray Hill, and through a wilderness beyond that—through a tumbled country of sharply tilted granite hills and mud flats. It was an impossible highway along the very spine of the island, where Manhattan's bedrock, as if in torment, broke surface and reared above a bottom land of alluvium and drift. People shook their heads in 1811; said the fourth avenue would never be cut through. And in our own day the Chief Engineer of the Borough of Manhattan, Mr. Dean G. Edwards, is of opinion that, in the ordinary course of events, the city might not have tackled the job much before 1925, the natural obstacles to road-building were so great.

But even in 1811 a new order of things was aborning in England; and, though New York might stubbornly deny it, the railway age was coming in. In England, of course, railways had been operating for two hundred years; private railways owned by the mining companies whose coal they carried. But eight years ago, in 1803, the Surrey Iron Railway, near London, was opened as a public freight carrier, and there was even talk of a public passenger railway. That was the point; it was the *public* railway that was coming into existence, open to anybody to ship his merchandise by it if he paid a tariff, or to travel by it if he paid a fare. And side by side with this development—though not a part of it, by any means—was the fascinating business of the steam locomotive.

In the next few years English books and magazines came pouring into New York, telling of the work of Richard Trevithick, George Stephenson, possibly half a dozen others. They had not yet mastered the problem of the locomotive. It was a difficult problem; there was good running as long as the steam lasted, but the steam would always give out, and the iron horse, easily winded, would have to stop. At times it had the look of a problem that never could be solved. It amounted to this: Boiler and firebox had to be small enough to fit upon a chassis; but—impossible contradiction, perhaps—boiler and firebox had to evaporate water fast enough to keep the cylinders supplied with steam. A whole generation of steam engineers had given up the task as hopeless. But the coming of the public railways now was giving new impetus to the search for a solution; and there were those in New York, a few, who believed that some day the iron horse would work and would take her place upon the railways. It stirred the minds of many men.

But these men were not New York; and New York, in her preoccupied, abstracted way, was not interested. New York was a waterways town; you must never forget that. It was her immense good fortune to lie at once beside the ocean and at the heart of a most extensive system of enclosed waterways—at the common junction of Long Island Sound, Raritan Bay, Newark Bay and the Hudson river. All these came together in New York Bay; and they linked up in a single network a thousand miles of navigable rivers.

This was the all-important fact about New York, and it stood to reason that, if full advantage could be taken of it, New York might easily become a greater city than either Baltimore or Boston. The problem was how, with limited resources, to make the most of her natural advantages; and for two generations now New York had been addressing herself to this problem with all her might. She had a great deal to show for it, too; she had her deep-sea shipping, and she had schooners—hundreds upon hundreds of schooners. Morning and afternoon they sailed for Hackensack, Newark, Passaic and Paterson, Elizabeth, Amboy, New Brunswick and Red Bank, as well as for all the shore and river towns of Connecticut and all the towns of the Hudson Valley for a hundred and fifty miles upstream. New York had the beginnings of a tremendous river trade; and in that arrogant, self-centered way of hers, New York knew that her fortune lay upon the water. Was England building railways? The question was remote, irrelevant. The supreme event in the commercial history of New York was the opening, in 1825, of the Erie Canal, connecting the Hudson river and the Great Lakes.

It was strange, for 1825 was also the year of the Stockton & Darlington, over in Eugland, the first steam railway in the world. One year later —a direct retort to the opening of the Erie Canal—ground was broken for the Baltimore & Ohio, an animal-traction railroad. And then, in 1829, the *Rocket* flew over the rails of the Liverpool & Manchester with a full train at twenty-nine miles an hour, and steam railroading was in with a burst.

The *Rocket*, built by Stephenson, had everything but steam brakes, and she acquired them quickly enough. Built in England, she was partly of American descent, for she had a multitubular boiler, and this, as Stephenson candidly declared, was the invention of Nathan Reed of Salem, Massachusetts. She also had a steam blast; that is to say, she was so equipped with pipes that the steam exhausted from her cylinders was sent "puffing" through her stack, thus creating a vacuum above the stack and pulling a fierce draught through her firebox. And it was this steam blast, in combination with her multitubular boiler, that solved the whole problem of steam locomotion; that made the *Rocket* a fast-steaming engine and one of the great victories of engineering science.

She was well named; for she burst upon a world determined not to see her with a glare that could not be overlooked. And among the few New Yorkers who believed in her the news of her achievement struck like a thunderbolt. It was only a matter of weeks, then, before the New York & Harlem Rail Road Company was being organized; and only a matter of months before it was chartered by Legislature.

At first the whole city was against it; a city, now, of 200,000 people. But the scheme had a most active and forceful promoter in a tall, dream-shot man with nervous lips and flashing eyes—an exiled Irish rebel called Thomas Emmet. He and a fellow Irishman, Benson MacGowan, got the ball arolling; formed a company of thirteen men. They overlooked no chances. They pursued everybody known to possess a little money. "I'm a steamboat man, but good luck to you," said the man who had just broken the back of the Fulton-Livingston steamboat monopoly—a big, bumptious, tobacco-chewing fellow called Captain Cornelius van der Bilt.

But they won over Campbell White, the city's Representative in Congress; and John Mason, the founder and president of the Chemical Bank. In a swift reshuffling, Mason, the financier, became the railroad's president. In the end, he became a symbol, too, for it was forty years, and the Civil War had come and gone, before the American people grew tired of calling a streetcar a "John Mason."

It was a hard fight all the way, but Mason knew finance, and Emmet was a beautiful fighter. He was the elder brother of Robert Emmet, the young Dublin aristocrat who was hanged as a rebel in his bright green uniform, trimmed with gold; and who remains to the present day the foremost hero of the long fight for Irish independence. A doctor as well as a barrister, a man accustomed all his life to impress on others his own way of thinking, Thomas Emmet was accounted the most brilliant lawyer at the New York bar. It happened that he was also the Attorney General of the State. The New York & Harlem Rail Road was chartered in the summer of 1831.

The charter was made subject to approval, however, by the Mayor and Common Council of the city, and it was nearly six months before the Mayor affixed his signature to it. The plain fact is that the company was begging for a right-of-way; and what they got in the end was a beggar's bargain. The city forbade the use of steam; and, though the locomotive fever had made victims of them all, the company agreed to operate by animal-traction. (And so they did, too. For forty years the trains were hauled, within the built-up sections of the city, by great teams of horses.) And when it came to the main question of a right-of-way, the city would make but one concession; they could lay their tracks from the fourteenth street to the Harlem river along the center-line of that still theoretical fourth avenue.

It was the worst route possible; but there was nothing to do, of course, but accept it. It meant the building of tunnels through sheer granite. And, in the end, it meant one tunnel in particular that was to govern the whole design of Grand Central Terminal and make of it the thing it is today.

The first track was laid in the Bowery, along the crown, or middle, of that street; and by the fourteenth of November, 1832, the railroad was able to begin operations from Prince street north to what presently acquired the simple and straightforward name of Fourteenth street. (It would be five years before the tracks reached Harlem, the upper end of Manhattan island.) To begin with, a single coach was placed in service, the *John Mason;* and that was how it happened that streetcars in general came to be known for a generation of American history as "John Masons." Within a fortnight or so, two more coaches were added to the company's roster. All three were then made up into a train, and this was kept shuttling back and forth upon a single track. Drawn by a team of horses, the train stopped anywhere to pick up or discharge a passenger. The fare was "six and a quarter cents," according to one authority; according to another, "an English sixpence." They were English coaches, each consisting of three compartments, carpeted and rather finely upholstered with quilted sides and ceilings.

The tracks were carried northward and southward at roughly the same time—northward by slow labor and toil, over and through the gigantic rock formations; southward by swift periodic advances. The company set up its first terminal at the corner of Centre street and

Chambers, just east of the City Hall, where the Municipal Building now stands; but it wasn't meant for a terminal, and before long the Harlem railroad was pushing southward again, extending its tracks across Chambers street and along the right-hand side of Park Row to Broadway at the lower tip of City Hall Park. The plan was, ultimately, to build a fine terminal at the corner of Broadway and Wall street, just across the street from Trinity Church. It never got there, however, for the new tracks in Park Row—it was Chatham street in those days—had just been completed when a new quarrel with the city, for some time growing hotter, abruptly boiled over.

It was steam that caused the fury. After the first year's operation, the company had ventured to place two locomotives in service. But they were poor things, not to be compared with the *Rocket*; in competition with the horses they did badly, and within a few months both of them blew up. In 1836 the experiment was renewed, and by 1841 the company had a roster of 140 horses and six locomotives. These were somewhat better locomotives, but they still blew up from time to time. Cautious souls were panic-stricken, and the cabmen, and the anti-railroad element in general, made the most of things. The protest was uproarious, and the Common Council took action. Locomotives were barred below Fourteenth street.

A new practice arose. At the steam terminal, at Fourth avenue and Fourteenth street, incoming trains were broken up and one by one the cars were drawn by horses the rest of the day down to the Chatham street terminal, at Broadway opposite Saint Paul's. And the horse-drawn cars, northbound, were made up into trains on reaching the steam terminal and thence were drawn by locomotives—though a few continued on to Harlem sandwiched in between steam trains.

The anti-locomotive law was the first of a series of decisive restrictions. In 1859 the deadline was pushed back to Twenty-sixth street where a once famous station was erected. And a few years after that the city fixed the location of the present-day Grand Central Terminal by adopting a bylaw that forbade the operation of steam locomotives on Fourth avenue below Forty-second street.

"And that," said Ichabod, "is how the thing worked out. The Harlem railroad received as a right-of-way—to be shared, however, with all other street traffic—the crown of Fourth avenue, because Fourth avenue was too rocky to be of any use to the city anyhow. (And present-day Park avenue is only upper Fourth avenue rechristened.) And then, years later, the city drew the line at Forty-second street. In each instance, the railroad had no choice but to accept. . . .

"That's one point. No one ever quite chose the site of Grand Central Station. It was never a case of foresight on anybody's part, it was just the result of a series of accidents—the accident of L'Enfant's putting an avenue where the city couldn't use it . . . of the beggar's bargain . . . of the company's long series of disputes with a city that didn't want a railroad in the first place. . . .

"But I haven't finished telling you about the granite," he added abruptly, "and how it played the devil with every plan to make Grand Central a really first-class terminal—every one, that is, but the last.

"'You can't appreciate Grand Central," said Ichabod, "until you see it, not merely as a building, but as the outcome of seventy years of struggle to operate trains in and out of New York; unless you see it, first and foremost, as a triumph of *railroad* engineering and a victory over great odds . . . and the greatest of the odds was the granite. It was bad enough at the beginning. When the first Grand Central was built, even then it prevented the building of an adequate number of terminal tracks—I'll tell you about that later. And when the third Grand Central was built, the present Grand Central, no less than two million cubic yards of granite alone had to be blasted and carried away to make room for the new tracks and the new terminal.

"I'm not counting gravel and clay—there was another million cubic yards of that. I'm just counting the granite, two million cubic yards of granite; and if you want to know how much granite that is, I'll tell you. It was enough to fill 260 railway dump cars every day, and to keep on doing it day after day, week after week, month after month—for ten years.

"It cost more to clear away the granite than ever it cost to build the terminal once the site was prepared; and that isn't the end of the story, either, for the site was still comparatively small, and 'back of' Grand Central today you have little more than half a mile in which the main-line tracks fan out to meet the terminal tracks. . . . For example, at Waterloo Station, London, the terminal fan has an altitude of three miles. The builders of Grand Central had to do their work in roughly a sixth of that distance. That's why they had to spread downward instead of horizontally; that's why you have a double-decked fan at Grand Central. And that's why trains cannot move in and out of Grand Central today as they move in and out of Waterloo—at high speed.

"It all goes back to the granite," said Ichabod. "All Grand Central is contained in a single gallery cut deep in the rock, and the remarkable thing is that so much has been crowded into so little space.

"Now," he announced abruptly, "I'll show you around. . . ."

It was 7:40 by the Golden Clock.

KISSING GALLERY

FOR MORE than three-quarters of an hour Ichabod had been standing in the West Balcony, orating before the most casual group of auditors, mostly strangers to himself. Now he was off in a tremendous hurry, dashing down the marble stairs to the floor of the Concourse; turning sharply to the left; pushing his way into the corridor below the balcony; then cutting off to the northwest, diagonally, across that broad gallery that underlies Vanderbilt avenue—followed all the way by half his little crowd, and looking taller and lankier than ever as he hurried along with his loose clothes bagging and fluttering about him.

When he had left the Concourse two or three hundred feet behind him, he led the way through glass doors to a chamber ninety feet square and forty feet high, all of polished marble. He crossed the floor. He examined the blackboard on the west wall. He spoke to the attendant. He swung about sharply.

"Everything is late," he said. "There's been more snow, and No. 66 hasn't reached Buffalo yet. No. 66 is the *Advance Commodore Vanderbilt*. She left Chicago at half-past one yesterday afternoon and was due at Buffalo at 11:45 last night; due here at half-past eight this morning. But she won't be in till evening now. . . . And that's the way it is with all of them. . . .

"Yesterday was one of the worst days in years, and, by the look of things today is going to be pretty bad too.

"Above and below Lake Erie," said Ichabod, "the New York Central follows two different routes between Buffalo and Chicago; and both cut through the heart of the Blizzard Belt. It's the worst place for snow on the North American continent. . . . Somewhere over the prairie provinces of Canada, hundreds of miles away, a cold wind awakes. Tearing and plunging, it sweeps along . . . It roars down Lake Huron. Lake Erie catches it broadside. The driven clouds pile up, the cold is bitter, and so the snow comes heavy and often. . . . There isn't a railroad in America," said Ichabod, "that gives the snow such a battle as the New York Central.

"Well, the blizzard was still blowing over Lake Erie yesterday, and at Grand Central today everything on the board is late. You'll see the effect of that. All day today Grand Central will be crowded with tired, cross people, who hurry here to meet their friends and relatives from out of town, only to find they'll have to sit around and wait for hours. . . . This is the way things are at Grand Central," said Ichabod, "each time the blizzard blows in across the lakes from Canada."

Then he remembered his lecture.

"This is the Arrival Station," he said simply; perhaps a little needlessly. "The five arrival tracks are downstairs, below the floor we stand on; and upstairs is the Hotel Biltmore, as I said before. Over there, at the northwest corner of the room, is an elevator that carries you directly to the foyer of the hotel. . . ."

Ichabod was interrupted by the voice of the train crier: "*Advance Forest City*—Train from Chicago, Elkhart, Toledo, Cleveland, Cincinnati, Dayton, Columbus, Buffalo, Toronto, Rochester, Syracuse, Utica, Montreal, Saranac. Track *Forty*-ONE!"

Ichabod whistled.

"She's been on the road since night before last! She's No. 90. She was due here early last night," said Ichabod, who now began a nervous fumbling in his pocket.

"He said this train is from Chicago and Cincinnati too—and also from Montreal."

"That's right," said Ichabod. "Look her up in *A Thousand and One*."

"What's that?"

"I have it here," he said triumphantly. "I knew I had it. *A Thousand and One* is the pet name of Form No. 1001, the principal New York Central timetable. Inquiry desk men and ticket agents all over the United States know it by that name. . . .

"It shows," he continued, "that No. 90 left Chicago at 11:30 the night before last. . . . At Cleveland the *Midnight Special*, No. 442 out of Cincinnati, was tied onto her tail; at Buffalo she picked up No. 372 out of Toronto; and at Utica she took on No. 2 out of Montreal.

So, as she pulls in here, she represents a consolidation of four different trains.

"That's a point to remember about the liners that arrive at Grand Central. A train from Chicago isn't merely that; in almost every instance, on the Central Railroad, she's a train compounded of many trains. Like a river fed from many sources, she drains into New York a region as big as Central Europe. . . ."

Quite casually, then, No. 90's people began pouring in through the doorway from Track 41, and passing on about their business with hardly a look to the left or right. People from Chicago, people from Ohio and Upstate New York, people from Canada—you could not have told one from another; for that matter, you could not have told but what every last one of these was a New Yorker home from his travels.

Except for a hurried handful, they came through the doorway with apparent unconcern; not with a rush, as children burst out of school, but in such an offhandish way that you were almost disappointed. It struck you that people, after coming such a long way, ought to be excited about arriving in New York. But none of these betrayed the least bit of excitement. They came through the door without apparent eagerness. They almost drifted through. A few of them were met by relatives or friends; but even their greetings were subdued. The bulk of them were not met. They simply came and went their many ways.

Some of them went off to the left, through the glass doorways and on through the corridors that lead to the Concourse. Others bore to the right, and, passing through doorways at either side of the blackboard, were out upon the sidewalk of a kind of underground street—a cavern below the pavement of Forty-third street, where taxicabs wait in line beside a ramp that leads to daylight. And still others of the incoming crowd went straight ahead (as the designers of Grand Central intended them to do) and up the marble staircase at the center of the south wall.

At the head of those stairs, of course, they were in a lobby, whence they could simply turn to the right, and they'd be in the foyer of the Biltmore; or continue forward, and they'd be out on the sidewalk on the north side of Forty-third street, west of Vanderbilt avenue. Built into the lower right-hand corner of the huge hotel, the Arrival Station lobby is a whole two blocks away from the main entrance to Grand Central at Forty-second street and Park avenue.

People from other trains were pouring in now, and the announcer was busily correcting the blackboard and "calling" still more trains—in a strong, clear and rather fine voice. There's a certain "Irish" quality in his voice, and he looks, curiously, very like the late John McCormack. He's a big man, with dark hair and rosy cheeks, with a smallish mouth and big eyes, and long, curling, black eyelashes; the sort of Irish good looks that some women rave over.

"His name," said Ichabod, simply enough, "is Keogh—Billy Keogh."

As there aren't any ticket offices here, Billy is the railroad's chief representative in the Arrival Station. His place is back of the high marble counter along the west wall. He's there to answer questions; he's in charge of the blackboard on the wall just back of him. He watches a telephone, a teletype and a telautograph.

The teletype, a sort of long-distance typewriter, is operated from Dispatcher's office; keeps Billy *au courant* with all the inbound trains as they come racing through the blocks, sometimes two or three abreast, from Chicago to Fifty-seventh street. The telautograph reproduces on a paper tape the handwriting of the signal-tower chief out amid the terminal switches this side of Fifty-seventh street; reproduces his order assigning each arriving train to a particular track. In that clear, melodious voice of his, Billy "cries" the arrival as soon as the telautograph gives him the track number; two minutes, as a rule, before the train is on the track and coming to a stop. At other moments, guided by the teletype, he keeps the blackboard "up to the minute," writing with lemon-colored chalk beside the designation of each incoming train: "On Time," or "5 Mins. Late," or "10 Hrs. Late," as the case may be. And in between times, he "talks to the customers"—answering questions in a genial, almost personal sort of way; or passing the time of day with anyone who has to wait long for an incoming train, and who had rather stand and talk than sit, lonely, on a bench.

Just verging on forty, Billy has been at Grand Central now for twenty years. "But that includes," he hurried on to say, "three years and seven months in the army. Railroad seniority ratings, you see, were not interrupted by war service; my seniority kept accumulating all the time I was in the army—I was a sergeant in the Medical Corps, down in Arizona. Excuse me."

Without stirring in his chair, Billy picked up his microphone, mounted on an old-fashioned telephone from which the receiver hook had been removed; and the telautograph had hardly stopped its jerky clicking when he was calling a new train. Then he stood up to enter the track number upon the board.

Ichabod conducted the cross-examination.

"I was born right over here at Forty-seventh street and Second avenue, Saint Agnes's parish; but I grew up in Harlem, Saint Paul's parish; attended Saint Paul's parochial school. . . . People come here occasionally, point to the board and say: 'That's parochial-school handwriting.' . . .

"In 1925 we moved over to Queens. . . . My father bought a two-family house. . . . Since then, we've lost our father and mother and one of our brothers, but the rest of us are still together in the same house. My two unmarried brothers and I live together upstairs; my married sister and her family live downstairs. We've always been very affectionate of one another. . . ."

It's one of the strange things about Grand Central that Billy Keogh is not classified as a train crier—for here there is no such classification. Instead, Billy is a doorman—that is to say, a gateman—and "doorman" is the word that appears in large black letters on the nickel-plated badge upon his cap. But the point is technical. The stationmaster is in charge of all three stations at Grand Central. In the Arrival Station from 7 A. M. to 3 P. M., Billy Keogh is his permanent deputy.

"It's a poor show today," said Ichabod, "so many of the trains are running late. In normal weather, when they keep to time, more or less, you really get your money's worth in the Arrival Station this time o' day. . . .

"Fact is that eleven New York Central liners arrive at Grand Central (according to the timetable) before the first liner pulls out each day at 9 A. M. First in is the *Easterner* from Chicago, and trailing her you have the *Seneca* from Rochester; the *New York Special* and the *Fifth Avenue Special*, both from Chicago; the *Detroiter*, the *Genesee* from Syracuse; the *Cleveland Limited*, the *Advance Commodore Vanderbilt* from Chicago; the *Wolverine* from Detroit, the *Pacemaker* from Chicago and the *Southwestern Limited* from Saint Louis. All these are in by nine o'clock in the morning, and—one minute after the last of them has rolled to a stop—the *Empire State Express* leaves the Concourse, the first liner of the day to pull out of Grand Central.

"You have a total of twenty-three New York Central liners arrive at Grand Central every day—twenty-three that really amount to anything. And of these, thirteen are scheduled to arrive by nine o'clock in the morning, three more get in by noon, and only seven arrive in the whole twelve hours from noon to midnight. . . . It isn't the railroad's doing, of course. The generality of people, when they come to New York, like to arrive here early in the morning, that's all; and the timetable is only a reflection of the public demand.

"Departures are just the other way about—light in the morning, heavy at night. The sleeping-car has a lot to do with it, of course. . . .

"Naturally, it works an effect upon Grand Central. You'll see it," said Ichabod, "in the changing character of the crowds . . . less excitement in the morning, more excitement in the late afternoon and early evening. . . .

"And now," the tall fellow said abruptly, "I've got to show you one thing more—about the Arrival Station, that is. I've told you about the Kissing Gallery, and all the fuss the newspapers made over it in the last few years before Grand Central was thrown open to the public. . . ."

Demolition of the old station was begun in June, 1910; and the plans for the new Grand Central were given to the newspapers for publication on Sunday, June 26. (The plans were subsequently altered out of all recognition, but that's another story.) It was a stunning announcement, from the railroad's point of view; and the publicity department poured into it a rich and fervid eloquence.

Perhaps it was his own idea, or perhaps he plucked it out of the two and a half pounds of railroad publicity matter thrown into his lap; in any case, the rewrite man over on the *New York Herald* put the matter thus: "From there [the train platform] passengers will pass out into the 'kissing gallery.' This is what railroad men call the place where persons wait to meet incoming travelers."

It was a striking phrase; inevitably other writers picked it up and, as the months flew by, it echoed back and forth across the country, from one newspaper to another. Willing pens were only too quick to describe the gallery, and presently a writer in *Munsey's Magazine* was able to assure his public: "Of the many innovations [at the new Grand Central] the 'kissing gallery' will be one of the most striking. This is a balcony in the incoming station, specially arranged for people who come to meet friends or relatives. There will be . . . sufficient elevation to get a perfect view of the doors through which the travelers arrive."

Other writers picked up the description from *Munsey's*, drew more deductions, glowingly presented the most elaborate details; and in the end, of course, the point was pretty well established among New Yorkers that the Kissing Gallery was to be a balcony, or at least an elevated platform.

But that was not the plan at all. In engineering parlance, a "gallery" can be any of half a dozen things, including (1) a subterranean chamber, like the galleries in a mine; or (2) any room that similarly has no windows and is lighted artificially or by skylights, like an art gallery. By gallery, the Grand Central engineers back in 1910 meant merely a room without windows. And when the *Herald* man spoke of the "incoming station" as a kissing gallery, he meant only to compare it, perhaps, with a "kissing platform." This was railroad slang. In the jargon of the operating crews, any arrival platform, crowded with people come to meet their friends and relatives from out of town, was a kissing platform. There would be no such platform at Grand Central, however; and so the term, it would seem, was by analogy applied to the gallery in which the meetings would occur.

"A lot of young people were sadly disappointed," said Ichabod. "When the new Grand Central was opened that Sunday morning, the second of February, 1913, without the sort of gallery they had been led to expect, they considered themselves cheated. But the fact is that they got all the railroad ever meant to promise them. . . . This Arrival Station, just as it stands today, is the Kissing Gallery."

The tall fellow again took out his watch. It was 8:05.

"You've now seen the Arrival Station," he announced briskly; "or most of it. The Railroad Museum is—"

A quiet, gray man—an exceedingly quiet, sober, industrious-looking man—had come in through the glass doors to the east and was standing, watch in hand, peering at the clock upon the west wall; and Ichabod, who is nothing if not abrupt, said we could forget about the Railroad Museum for a moment, because *there,* on his morning round, was Jake.

CLOCKMASTER

MOST OF the clocks at Grand Central have, as you may have noticed, no glass before their faces. That was Jake's idea. He thinks that without the glass they look better and are seen more easily. Of course, they gather dust. But that's all right too. When they get dusty, Jake has the pleasure of cleaning them. Jake—Jacob Bachtold—is the keeper of the clocks, a pale, slender man with a long face, tired blue eyes and thick eyeglasses; a master watchmaker from Schaffhausen, in the High Alps of Switzerland.

You can often see Jake on his daily rounds, comparing every clock with the watch he carries in his hand. And once in a while you can see him at work at the top of a high ladder, for some of his clocks are twenty feet high on the wall. Jake is never long on a ladder, though. After forty-odd years of service he knows the clocks too well. When something goes wrong he can usually tell you what the trouble is without looking. And so, as a rule, he's able to correct the fault in less than a minute. Or, if he cannot do that, he turns to his box, brings forth another movement, takes the ailing one back to his little shop in room 4834 on the fourth floor of the Terminal Office Building. Sometimes you can see Jake trundling a heavy mechanism across the marble floor of the Concourse on a hand-truck—slowly, carefully, with a patience that's enough to throw an eager-minded person into a cold sweat.

Once upon a time, years and years ago, Jake had a helper. It was thought the proper and fitting thing; it was thought that the keeper of a thousand clocks ought to have an assistant. But it went against the grain with Jake who was too long bred in the way of his lonely craft, and when the man left, Jake made it plain that he was through with helpers. The fact is that Jake has a belief; a belief he lives by. He tells it over and over again. In a slightly tremulous voice, but with German finality, he assures us: "When I do the work myself, I know it's done right."

So Jake is on his own today, in charge of all clocks at Grand Central, and of all clocks in all the signal towers and stations for seventy miles out on all three eastern divisions of the New York Central Railroad. They fall short of a thousand in actual service; but they exceed a thousand if you count those held in reserve and those that are "on the bench" in Jake's private shop—a shop that's littered with clocks; clocks going and clocks stopped, clocks on the wall and clocks on the workbench, clocks decently clothed in their cases and clocks naked, clocks and clock movements in every known stage of disintegration and repair.

Seventy-five clocks are visible to the public at Grand Central; and "behind the scenes" are hundreds more. One is an electric clock—a single, solitary one out of them all. Of the others, most are wound by electricity, and corrected every hour by electric impulse from a master-clock in the Train Dispatcher's office. The rest, of course, are wound by hand; among them, scores of clocks in the towers and way stations out along the line. Every so often Jake is out visiting these; and the story goes that he has an uncanny way of knowing where trouble is going to occur and of being there precisely when it happens. He shrugs. He tells us simply, in that strange High German accent of his: "Each clock is an individual." And then, in a burst of confidence, he adds: "In the end it all comes down to me and my watch." Jake has carried that watch now for thirty years.

He was born in 1877 at Schaffhausen; and in that village he served his long apprenticeship. He came to America, a master clockmaker, in 1900; and three years later became the Clockmaster at Grand Central. There were hardly seventy-five clocks to be cared for then. Perhaps fifty were out along the line. There were scarcely twenty-five at Grand Central.

Today, after forty-odd years of it, Jake still works from 8 A. M. to 5 P. M.—and he's on call for any hour of the day or night. He lives in Brooklyn—with a telephone at his elbow.

As he begins each day, sharply at eight o'clock in the morning, Jake is standing, watch in hand, before the master-clock in Dispatcher's office. From there he goes out to Forty-second street to check the Big Fellow. (That's Jake's name for the great Flamboyant French clock enshrined in concrete "sculpture" atop the main façade of Grand Central Station.) After that he goes to the Concourse to see the four-faced Golden Clock, just above the Information Desk. And so the daily tour continues, and the Clockmaster, never departing from the route he worked out for himself years ago, checks every clock in the station against his wonderful watch.

He works till five in the afternoon—except when the weather works the wrong way upon his clocks. Then his telephone in room 4834 never stops ringing. Clocks are misbehaving all over the place, and Jake is forever grabbing his tool kit and dashing off. On days like that he works till the job is done. He never complains, though; for time is everything to Jake and, therefore, time is nothing at all; devoting his life to it, he's heedless of it and, except professionally, he's never been caught watching the clock. On his days off, Jake plays an occasional game of solitaire, or—as a hobby—tinkers with old and curious clocks.

The Big Fellow is Jake's favorite; the Big Fellow out front, with its fourteen-foot dial of rose-colored glass and its tongues of fire radiating from the center. Let the critics say what they please about the art of the Flamboyant period; according to Jake, the Big Fellow is the most beautiful clock in the world. What's more, he assures us, it's one of New York's most accurate clocks. It's had its bad days, of course, but these have been so few in its thirty-odd years of service—possibly six or eight days in all—that Jake thinks it fair to say that the Big Fellow is "seldom" wrong.

Twice a week without fail he takes his tools and wiping-cloths and his cans of oil—a vegetable oil of a sort that does not freeze in our climate—and climbs a stairway high up in the attic above the Waiting Room at Grand Central and, beyond the stairhead, climbs a ladder to a platform back of the Big Fellow. There he cleans, polishes, oils, very delicately regulates. And once every year the day comes when Jake drops everything else and gives the Big Fellow his whole attention, replacing parts and going outside to tighten up all the screws in the great bronze hour and minute hands. Each Roman numeral on the face of the clock is mounted upon a door which opens inward, and through which Jake is able to reach outside. A great crowd is sure to gather in Forty-second street when he does this; and then, that one day a year, Jake is king.

The Golden Clock in the Concourse is the master's second favorite. But you'll never see him at work there, except to dust off the four dials and the four sets of hands; for the mechanism of this clock is in the machinery room two stories down below the Concourse. Its motion is delivered to the hands by a thirty-foot verticle shaft.

Third favorite is the master clock in the Train Dispatcher's office. This is an automatic wind with a double-weighted pendulum, a plain face and a plain wooden case—a most ordinary looking thing that every hour sends forth an electric impulse which corrects to the last fraction of a second some hundreds of other clocks at Grand Central. The master clock is always right; or as close to right, in all probability, as any clock in New York has ever been.

To keep it right is Jake's eternal passion; for changes in temperature and atmospheric pressure can cause it to gain or lose as much as two seconds in twenty-four hours, and Jake—who has the soul of a precisionist—says that that's intolerably bad. So it's part of his routine to keep in touch with the Weather Bureau; to keep a sharp eye on the barometer, and to know the temperature and the percentage of humidity hour by hour. Jake, in fact, is a top-flight weather expert. (And, as we shall see, he is not the only one at Grand Central either.) Each day, then, he works out the weather changes that are likely to occur within the ensuing twenty-four hours; and, assuming these, he estimates the effect they'll have upon the clock. And then each day precisely at noon—when the time signal comes in from the Naval Observatory at Washington—Jake delicately adjusts the pendulum to compensate in advance for the next twenty-four hours' weather effect. The story goes that every day at noon, ever since the Clockmaster first wound it up, the master-clock at Grand Central has been "dead on the second."

YANKEE RAILROAD

It was now 8:17.

"Before we leave the Kissing Gallery," said Ichabod, "you still may like to know about the Railroad Museum. . . . It's over there to the left of the board, in that tiny alcove at the southwest corner of the Arrival Station. . . .

"Railroad fans aren't greatly impressed by it. It amounts mainly to an exhibition of old photographs. Two or three are fairly interesting; they show the original Grand Central Depot, that was opened back in 1871. . . . Another shows the famous old 'ghost train' of the 1890s, the New Haven railroad's New York-and-Boston flyer that was painted all white and gold. . . . She terrified the country people who caught a first glimpse of her speeding through the night. . . . They took her for the *Heavenly Express*, which carries to Paradise the souls of all railroaders killed in wrecks.

"Anyhow," said Ichabod—but then he stopped; for Billy Keogh was calling another train, this time a train from Down East, the *State of Maine Express*, due from Portland at 7:23 but running late, also on account of snow.

"Seven twenty-three train from Portland," Billy added as a kind of final summary, "*State of Maine Express*, on Track 42." And Ichabod turned abruptly to this new subject.

"She's No. 125 on the New York, New Haven & Hartford Railroad," he said, "but here at Grand Central—and anywhere within the jointly operated terminal area—she's Y–125, to distinguish her from the New York Central's No. 125. The Y stands for Yankee. Among themselves," said Ichabod, "the railroad men about here seldom speak of a New Haven train; to them it's almost always a Yankee train. . . . And right here," the tall fellow went on to say, "we arrive at one of the two or three most important facts about Grand Central.

"Grand Central Terminal—it has a lordly sound. And if, in the back of your mind, you've always connected Grand Central with New York Central, I don't suppose anyone can blame you. Fact is, though, that the original Grand Central was built and owned by the New York & Harlem Railroad, and its name was intended to imply that it lay—where it certainly did *not* lie—at the center of New York.

"It was some time before the first New York Central train ever thrust its nose into Grand Central Depot. Folks don't seem to appreciate that," said Ichabod. "The New Haven came into New York, over New York & Harlem tracks before there ever was a New York Central Railroad; and the New Haven was operating in and out of the Harlem company's terminal when the New York Central, for the better part of twenty years, was wholly an Upstate railroad, following the prehistoric Mohawk Trail between Albany and Buffalo. . . .

"And that's a story, too," said Ichabod; "the story, I mean, of the New Haven's being here longer than the New York Central—and how the New Haven got here in the first place. . . ."

The Harlem, as we have seen, was organized in a town that didn't want a railroad; it was built against the wishes of a majority of the people; it was fought every inch of the way for fifteen years. A mob tore up its tracks in the Bowery, and mass meetings were held with a view to forcing Legislature or the Common Council—for it was not yet clear where the authority lay—to cancel its charter. But it pushed on anyhow. From Thirty-third street northward to the Harlem river, it fought its way against the granite, at times by as little as twelve inches a day. It crossed the Harlem on old Gouverneur Morris's toll bridge; and it reached White Plains, the county seat of Westchester, in 1844, and thereupon declared, what the steamboat men had all along suspected, that—its goal was Albany.

Roughly a hundred and fifty miles above New York city, Albany also lies upon the Hudson; but the Harlem was extremely careful to avoid the river, to avoid touching any of the towns already served by the steamboat lines. (Steamboating was already the richest, and at this moment was still the fastest-growing business in American history.) Leaving steamboat territory to the steamboats, the Harlem laid out a route through the all but uninhabited highlands far to the east of the river towns. Through a hundred miles of forest they cut and filled; they tunneled through rock, they threw their bridges across mountain gorges. It was costly. Above all, it was slow.

And then the Railway Mania struck; railroading at long last had captured the imagination of the American people, and there was no limit to what we were going to do. But when the tide turned, when unreasoning opposition abruptly gave way to equally unreasoning enthusiasm for the railroads, and the people at last were willing to pour their money into them, the Harlem was literally in the wilderness —battering its way through the mountains of Putnam, Dutchess, Columbia and Rensselaer counties—in the upward push that presently became a mad race for Albany.

The struggle began in 1846 when the Hudson river towns grew tired of being icebound for three months out of every year, and a company was organized in the river town of Poughkeepsie to build another railroad. This was to be the Hudson-River Rail-Road; and it was to run, in blazing defiance of the steamboat men, straight along the edge of the river and straight through all the east-bank towns from New York to Greenbush—directly opposite the west-bank city of Albany. There would have to be some tunneling, of course, where the cliffs came sheer to the water's edge. There would have to be built many miles of sea wall to protect the roadbed against the surf; for the Hudson is big enough to surge and break and pound when she's angry. There would be difficulties; but the new railroad would be at water-level all the way. The work was begun in the fall of 1847. Fighting with its head down, the Harlem pushed on through the mountains.

In 1848 the Harlem needed money, needed it badly; and it was fortunate that, just as the proper moment, the New York & New Haven Railroad, with tracks laid out to the Westchester County town of Woodlawn, came looking for trackage rights into the city. The bargain was struck, and the New York & New Haven—later on to become the New York, New Haven & Hartford—acquired the right to operate over Harlem tracks from Woodlawn to the Harlem terminal in New York city . . . forever! It was a compact of high importance. Eighty-four years later, in 1932, in a rate case before the United States Supreme Court, the New Haven placed a value of fifty-five million dollars on its right forever to operate in and out of the Harlem Railroad's New York terminal, which today, of course, is Grand Central Station. No physical assets were included in that figure; only that intangible right that can never be taken away from the New Haven. Inevitably, the New Haven lease of 1848 was one more factor in making Grand Central the station it is today; it became, indeed, at one point the most important factor of all, for the New Haven company's veto of a very different kind of station was what forced the building of the Grand Central that we know.

In 1848 the covenant enabled the Harlem to push on a little faster toward Albany; but it still took four years more to reach Chatham, which lay in the mountains between Albany and the Massachusetts border. From there the company acquired trackage rights to Greenbush, and the Albany ferry, over the line of the Western Rail Road of Massachusetts. They got their first train through from New York to Albany, thus, in 1852. They were a whole year too late.

Running out of a New York terminal at Chambers and Hudson streets, on the Lower West Side, the Hudson-River Rail-Road had begun service to Albany in 1851. It did poorly against the competition of the steamboats; freight rates were cut to unbelievable levels. But it made the run to Albany, at water-level, in five hours, whereas the Harlem trains, laboring over the mountains, took seven hours. And so the Hudson took the lion's share of that fast passenger business which the Harlem had counted on getting. (It was eighteen hours to Albany by steamboat.) And so all through the 1850s, while scores of other railroads were paying huge dividends, the Harlem only fell deeper and deeper into debt. In the early 60s came the Civil War—and, down in Wall street, Harlem was in a highly vulnerable position.

"But that," said Ichabod abruptly, "is another story. I only meant to tell you about the New Haven . . . how it's been coming in here for a hundred years; and how it came by its right to come in here. . . .

"Today the New Haven occupies pretty much the same position here as the New York Central. Both roads have equal rights to all terminal facilities; train dispatching, tower control, track assignment—all terminal operations, in fact—are in the hands of a neutral terminal authority, and the cost is apportioned between the two roads on the basis of the number of cars each brings into the terminal in the course of a year. . . .

"The ratio remains pretty steady nowadays—two Yankee cars for every three Central cars; 308,316 Yankee cars in 1945, for example, as compared with 566,184 Central cars. The total," said Ichabod, "is just about 2,400 cars a day, in; or 4,800 in and out."

Ichabod nodded. More crowds were coming up from the arrival platforms; and they were rather different crowds now. At least, they were more obviously excited on arriving at New York, and so many more of them were met by friends and relatives, all buzzing with excitement, that the whole station seemed to have taken on a more cheerful, human air.

The tall fellow studied the board for a moment. "This," he announced, "is a Yankee train too—No. Y–55 from Springfield, Massachusetts."

There was a stirring at the doorway. Two women stepped aside, politely. A man burst through ahead of them; a foreigner of some kind, carrying a boy against his shoulder; a Pole, you might have guessed, or a Slovak; probably from one of those Slavic settlements along the Connecticut. There was something about him. He was obviously tired out. And he was bewildered. He rushed forward. He stopped abruptly. He peered anxiously into the crowd. He swayed a bit; his big body sagged wearily. He held the boy against his shoulder as he might have held a ten-weeks-old baby. But the boy was no baby. He could not have been less than ten or eleven years old, and big for his age; a fine, strapping youngster—but limp. The boy, obviously, was very sick. The father, undecided, started forward again. A policeman approached. The father spoke. "Meester, please!" The words came brokenly. "Horspital! My boy, he seeck!"

"Through that door . . . and take a cab to Saint Vincent's. . . . Here! Follow me," said the copper, and the two of them disappeared through the doorway to the left of the blackboard.

Ichabod followed them with his eyes, then slowly shook his head.

"New York is an awfully important place to some folks," he said. "That fellow probably passed by a dozen hospitals on his way here—good hospitals, too; just as good as ours. But in a crisis . . . when he imagined, or when he was told, that the boy's life could be saved only if he were placed in a hospital . . . nothing would do but a New York hospital. You can just see the old fellow, arriving home after a hard day's work, maybe, and dashing off to New York with the boy in his arms. . . ."

A woman's voice rose melodious and clear above the bustling of the crowd: "Jessie! Jessie! Here we are!"

Across the floor came a second voice, as musical as the first: "Joan! Hello, there!"

"Mount Holyoke," Ichabod half muttered.

"How do you know?"

"Well, possibly Smith. . . ."

It was as though they would have rushed into each other's arms had they been able. Neither Jessie nor Joan was a day over thirty, and it was clear enough that they had not seen each other in several years. They made their way forward rather slowly, the one leading a two-year-old boy and the other a girl of about the same age. They said the usual things as they drew near. Joan exclaimed over Jessie's little girl, and Jessie exclaimed over Joan's little boy. They kissed. They asked about "everybody at home." They protested that it was "years and years" since they had seen South Hadley, Massachusetts.

"I told you they were a couple of Mount Holyoke girls," said Ichabod. "The old-line New England women's colleges . . . have an accent. You learn it after the first couple of—"

Ichabod stopped short. His lips, curling higher at one side of his face than at the other, slowly assumed a sort of tilted smile. And those strange eyes of his glittered greener than ever; and, make no mistake of it, they *are* green eyes.

"Fact is," he began—but paused.

Silently, unabashedly, and without any prompting, the little boy had walked straight up to the little girl and kissed her.

MORNING RUSH

It was 8:36 by the Lower Concourse clock, and the commuter trains were streaming in. Rather, they were *still* streaming in. Already there had been a falling off. Half an hour earlier, while Ichabod was expatiating upon arrival tracks and loop tracks, main-liners and deep snow in the Blizzard Belt, not to mention the depth of New York's archaeozoic granite—in short, while Ichabod was lecturing—the "morning rush" was at its peak. Now the crowds were thinning. But the difference was not great; for the morning rush, spread over two or three hours, gets under way slowly and slowly peters out. (It's the evening rush, concentrated in a single hour from five to six o'clock, that's abrupt and wild.) Anyhow, the commuter trains were still arriving; the crowds were still pouring in from the platforms. The show was still on.

It was a show all right. . . . Throngs of people . . . talking, laughing, eager-minded people . . . well-fed people . . . moving along smoothly in paths they've long been accustomed to . . . adhering to those paths with deep-rooted fidelity . . . and keeping up a noisy chatter and shuffling of feet that has the Lower Concourse ringing with sound. It isn't the usual chatter of New York. This is commuter talk:

"We stayed in the city last night and saw a show."

"American Air Lines is up a point."

"Life is slow in getting started again after the war."

"The Russians fought when we gave them what it took. We controlled the throttle-valve of supplies."

"The new seed catalogs are out."

"Good mawning! Good mawning! G*aw*geous *maw*ning!"

"What we need is more snow to leech the manure into the ground."

They're a peculiar race, these New York commuters; but it isn't true that they talk only of business. They embrace all classes and degrees of suburban society, from corporation lawyers, bankers and merchant nobility, at the top, to the Slavic immigrant, at the bottom, who cleans the office windows in Wall street and keeps a home and family on the outskirts of Yonkers or New Rochelle. But the vast majority are middle-class business men and office workers, comfortably well off and satisfied that life is good.

With the same unending chatter, the same ceaseless shuffling of feet upon the marble floor, they continued with each new train's arrival to stream across the Lower Concourse to the ramp that begins near the center of the south wall:

"We're having choir practice tonight."

"Don't ever use chemical fertilizer; it kills the earthworms."

"In the next five years there's going to be more business done in this country than the world ever saw before."

"Both my kids are down with chicken pox."

In a way, these commuters are one of New York's historic institutions. They trace back the better part of three hundred years in direct line of succession to one Jacques Courtelyou, land surveyor, who in 1660 drew for the Dutch West India Company the first map of Manhattan; who had a home on Long Island and an office in what was then the city of New Amsterdam; and who traveled back and forth between the two each working day. According to I. N. Phelps Stokes of the New-York Historical Society, Jacques was the city's first commuter. He was an ardent advocate of public economy, remembered in history for having denounced Peter Stuyvesant as "the most spendthrift" Governor ever inflicted upon the New Netherlands. And so he was not only the first, he was rather typical of today's commuters.

It would be pleasant and courteous, perhaps, to say that he was altogether typical; but on one or two points, unfortunately, the records aren't clear, and we can't be sure of the old boy. Could he, for instance, have lived long on a breakfast of half a cup of coffee and a wild dash for the train? Could he have wakened every morning at precisely the same minute, whether or no he had remembered to set the alarm clock the night before? Would he, indeed, have known an alarm clock if he had seen one?

The crowds kept pouring in:

"I had to thaw the ice with hot water before I could open the garage doors."

"The only newspaper colyumist I read is Sokolsky."

"In a few weeks more we'll have leaves of lettuce pushing their way right up through the snow."

"His wife had twins the other night."

"The robins hibernate under the leaves, all covered over by the snow, in the lee of the Palisades . . . and don't let anybody tell you otherwise. I *know*, because I *came* upon a flock of them once and *saw* them."

In tone and finish the Lower Concourse is much the same as the Arrival Station, resplendent with Botticino marble. It's immensely larger, though; it's 100 feet wide, 340 feet long.

The ceiling is comparatively low—as, after all, it would have to be, for the Lower Concourse lies directly below the main Concourse; two stories below street-level and therefore windowless. But you are not oppressed by that low ceiling. Indeed, the most remarkable thing about the Lower Concourse is the sense it gives you of space and air and headroom; and one reason for this is that the architects here succeeded in creating somewhat of an illusion—an illusion that the ceiling is higher than it really is.

The abundance of lighting helps, of course. It's only a dark ceiling that really oppresses you, but somehow an immensity of light overhead produces the effect of the out-of-doors. But here the trick was not turned so easily as that.

You'll notice, for example, the octagonal Information Booth at the center of the Lower Concourse floor. In particular, you'll notice the sleekness of its lines. That, too, was intended to give lift to the ceiling. Delicacy, rather than strength, was emphasized. You'll observe that delicate touch again in the fine carvings where the booth, like an eight-sided pillar, approaches the ceiling.

And then you have the gates—the row of eleven gates along the north wall; the doorways that open upon the train platforms. These too were quite obviously designed to give the place a look of airiness and headroom. Over each is a lintel, for the great steel beams that carry the upper-level tracks come down to within eight feet or so of the Lower Concourse floor. But over each lintel is a high round arch, and within the arch is a bas-relief trellis with oak leaves and branches, all worked in ceramics. Some think the ceramics are worth admiring in themselves;

in the dining room of the Architectural League, for example, they are rather well spoken. But their importance lies in the fact that they "reach" above the gates; their gloss catches the light and adds a touch of gaiety to things above the eye-level of the crowds; in short, they play a carefully calculated part in giving height to the Lower Concourse.

As a mere matter of measurement, the ceiling is sixteen feet high. The effect is of a beamed ceiling; and between the beams the long, narrow coffers are lighted brilliantly. The lights are strong, not numerous. Each one separately is set in a sort of inverted bowl, to the inside of which carved leaves and cherry branches cling in brilliant defiance of the laws of gravity.

The Information Booth, of course, is directly under the Golden Clock. The mechanism that runs that clock is housed in the Machinery Room, which is another story down below this Lower Concourse; and, as Jake made clear, the motion is delivered to the Golden Clock by a vertical shaft that passes up through the middle of the Lower Concourse Information Booth. To protect it, of course, the shaft is enclosed in a bronze tube—a kind of sleeve. And about this sleeve is wrapped a winding stairs for the use of the information clerks in passing back and forth between this booth and the Information Desk directly overhead and below the clock, at the center of the upper Concourse.

It was nearly ten minutes to nine but still the commuter crowds came pouring in from the train platforms:

"I'm late this morning, I ought to hurry along."

"It won't be long till spring now; my young hopeful wants me to bring him home a baseball glove tonight."

"Any snow out your way?"

"I'm a member of the vestry of our church."

"Business is moderately good."

"I've a touch of the grippe, but I won't give in to it."

"Business is rotten."

"I've got to stop in at the seed store."

TRAIN DEPARTURE

No. 51, the *Empire State Express*, was leaving at nine o'clock, and the tall thin fellow, back from his lonely breakfast, was on hand to see her off; which means, of course, that Ichabod was standing opposite Track 34 in the corridor below the West Balcony, just off the northwest corner of the Concourse—the corridor that leads to the Vanderbilt avenue gallery and, beyond that, the Arrival Station.

It was 8:50 by the Golden Clock.

In that strange, absorbed way of his, Ichabod was watching the people pass through the gate, one by one, each presenting a ticket to the gateman. He could not see the train. By straining, he could barely catch a glimpse of the switching locomotive which had hauled her in, tail foremost, from the make-up track at the Mott Haven yards; and which would lie trapped between the train and the bumper at the near end of Track 34 till the train pulled out of Grand Central. Ichabod could barely see that switching engine; he referred to her contemptuously as the "goat." Perhaps, too, he could see one of the two red lights that marked the rear of the train. But that was the limit; and, once the gates were closed, he would see not even that. Just the same, he was here to *see* the great train off.

In which case it may be asserted that millions of visitors to Grand Central never catch the remotest glimpse of a train; for there isn't much to be seen through the doors and only passengers may venture out upon the platforms. But scores of men like Ichabod, men who have never outgrown their boyhood love of the railroad, are still able, curiously, to capture some of the old thrill by simply observing the incidentals of a train's departure: the hurrying of people; the tenseness in the air; the farewells, all spoken here before the traveler passes through the gate; the warning cry of the gateman and the final, breathless charge of the stragglers; then the clangor of the iron doors closing upon them, the switching out of the lights that play upon the train-board, the gateman's unobtrusive touch upon the secret button—the more or less secret button—that signals to the train's conductor that the gate is closed, that the last passenger is out upon the platform; and, after that, the remarkable stillness that seems to hover about the gate and then to slowly dissipate. There's hardly the sound of a train pulling out. There are, at Grand Central, only these evidences, these second-hand indications, of the Limited's departure. But, to the initiates, they seem to be enough. And that's what Ichabod meant when he said that he was here to *see* No. 51 pull out.

"This is how it is at Grand Central," he said simply; "and the radio is all wrong—that radio program, I mean, called 'Grand Central Station.' The sound effects are wrong; or they were the last time I listened in. . . . You heard a steam locomotive full-working and whistling for a grade crossing. Next, by an impossible trick, she was coming to a stop—but on a fearful upgrade, presumably, because she continued steaming to the last half-turn of her drivers. And then, what's very wrong, her blower began working. . . ."

The tall fellow shrugged.

"The last steam locomotive ever seen in these parts pulled out of the old Grand Central at midnight, the thirty-first of December, 1906. That was six years," said Ichabod, "before the present-day Grand Central was completed. As early as that the whole terminal division had been electrified. . . .

"But you know why they do it, of course—the radio people, I mean. They select the most widely known of railway station sounds, and they call it 'Grand Central' because . . . well, obviously because of the glamour attaching to that name. It just goes to show what Grand Central means to the hundred million Americans who have never seen it. . . ."

He added slowly, reflectively: "It's one of the things Grand Central needs most."

"What is?"

"Just that," he said quickly; "the smell of steam, the fragrant tang of soft-coal smoke, the distant wail of a locomotive whistle. Folks miss all this at Grand Central. . . . The marble and the bronze don't quite make up for it."

It was 8:56. The Concourse was filled with sunshine. The crowds were tense. There were odd bursts of laughter. There was excited shouting, always the same: "Hurry, hurry, hurry!" And there was the firm cry of the gatemen, endlessly repeated: "All tickets, please! Have your tickets ready!" There was talk; there was an ocean of talk.

"Are we late?"

"Come on, we gotta go to Penn Station."

"I had twen'y-fi' dollars last night. Now I got about fi' dollars left."

"Do you know how to handle these timetables?"

"Want me to carry Baby? Here, give him to me."

"Usin' all them big words ain't gonna getcha nowhere."

"We got a swell organization up at our office. With us, insurance is a *profession.*"

It's different from commuter talk. This now is city talk; this is New York, abrupt and sharp and jerky, and with just a touch of that fatuous bombast that the Depression never quite beat out of us.

"I'll give y'a guarantee: the business ain't there."

"Will you *please* hurry? We gotta get that train."

"You're a liberal, ain't you?"

"I'm always stuffy with medicine."

Perhaps it doesn't truly represent these morning crowds, coming mainly from the loud and blatant ones. But even they are not easily heard, and the mature and quiet ones can hardly be heard at all. The curious fact is that the only ones who show up well in the Concourse are the red caps. Their Negro voices naturally ring, but the main thing is that they know the pitch that's called for. The Concourse is forever ringing with echoes and re-echoes (the acoustics are abominable), and talking against that ocean of sound is very like talking to a deaf person: if you know the pitch, you can make yourself heard without raising your voice. When the tumult is at its worst, a good Negro baritone can call to a gateman quietly and be heard from a hundred feet away.

The bad acoustic properties of the Concourse, by the bye, are one reason why there is no public-address system at Grand Central, and why you cannot ask the station authorities to page somebody in the crowd. It took months and months of experimenting with different instruments and various types of amplifier, placed in various positions, before the organ concerts were made possible.

Anyhow, conversation in the Concourse is face-to-face, and astonishingly private; and so, in general, it's only the raucous ones you overhear.

It was 8:58½. The gateman cried his train for the last time: "*Empire State Express!* Nine o'clock train for Albany, Schenectady, Utica, Syracuse, Rochester, Buffalo, Cleveland, Toledo and Detroit! All aboard!"

The groups of people near the gate broke up with a sudden burst of good-bys. The travelers picked up their bags, went quickly to the gate; the others for the most part stood their ground, waved after them.

It was 8:59. A soldier with olive skin and luminous brown eyes—a sergeant of infantry—calmly and nonchalantly kissed his relations good-by. He kissed his mother, kissed his father, kissed his first brother, kissed his second brother, kissed his third brother. He was standing at the center of a ring of five smiling adults; all obviously proud and happy, and quite unconscious of the eyes that were upon them. Turning on his heel, counter-clockwise, the sergeant went round the circuit a second time. Quickly, but not too quickly, he took his mother in his arms and kissed her. (There was no mistaking the relationship.) Likewise he embraced his father with the enormous gray moustache; and his first brother, and his second brother, and his third brother. He embraced his mother a third time. Then he charged the gate with a yell that might have curdled the blood of an enemy. His father heard that yell and cheered, as if it stirred him deeply. His mother smiled, his brothers laughed, gaily. For a fraction of a second the gateman wavered . . . held the door. The sergeant was the last man through.

"Them Eye-talians!" said the gateman, and was silent—as if he intended in some disapproving kind of way to be eloquently silent.

Overhearing him, a young man in a double-breasted gray suit chuckled complacently.

"It's an old Latin custom," said Joe Guardino, the stationmaster's clerk.

The gateman turned sharply.

"Us," he said, not without embarrassment, "we ain't that way. When my boy joined the Navy, he just shook hands and said: 'So long, Pop!' "

It was 9:01, and the *Empire State Express*, the first liner of the day to leave Grand Central, was beginning her fourteen hours' run to Detroit. Out on the Concourse, under the great blue ceiling, there was no sound or sign of her departure though. To prove it, there was only the clock—the clock and Ichabod's assurance that the operations timetable is always one minute later than the passengers' timetable; and that No. 51 begins to roll dead on the minute of 9:01 A. M.

Ichabod nodded toward the retreating figure of Joe Guardino. "Since you've already seen Joe," he said—

Again the tall fellow interrupted himself. Something else had caught his attention. That strange, tilted smile of his appeared again; and those remarkably green eyes rolled upward as if he had just now discovered Helleu's great star-studded ceiling overhead.

A few yards away a good-looking boy of twenty-two and a good-looking girl of twenty were being introduced to each other by their respective mothers. The most romantic-minded observer must have noticed that the two mothers were the more genuinely elated, but—the young people were obviously pleased with each other too. . . .

"Fact is," the tall fellow began—

"Well, what?"

"Oh, nothing."

WAITING ROOM

IN ALMOST any other station in the world the waiting room would be the main thing. Here the main thing is the Concourse, and the Waiting Room is decidedly second best. But it's big just the same; it's 50 feet high, 65 feet wide, 205 feet long. . . . In towns and cities all over America there are churches and five-story buildings that would not fill this room. . . .

It lies between the Concourse and Forty-second street; more precisely, it lies between the Concourse and the stores that face on Forty-second street. It lies back of those stores; so it's well back from the street. Along the south wall of the Waiting Room you have a series of doors, of which three are rear entrances to the stores.

On the vertical scale also the Waiting Room lies between the Concourse and Forty-second street; well above the level of the one, well below the level of the other. At the center of the south wall, a ramp leads upward to the street. At the center of the north wall, a ramp leads downward to the Concourse. The path from Forty-second street to the Concourse cuts straight across the center of the Waiting Room. . . . It forms the short axis of the room, sixty-five feet long.

A similar passageway, parallel to Forty-second street, divides the room lengthwise . . . and leads eastward to the women's room, westward to the men's room. There's a barber shop at one corner of the men's room—and a stairway leading down to the white-tiled spaces . . . where private dressing rooms are available and commuters can change into evening clothes before attending the theater. The tiles are, strictly speaking, not tiles at all, but great sheets of opaque, white glass. So it's probably the worst place in the world for collectors of graffiti.

An important feature of the Waiting Room is the ceiling. We have here the same buff-colored walls that set the tone of the Concourse; but the ceiling is Flamboyant. Beams divide it crosswise into five great coffers, rich with elaborate cornice-work and moldings, and five great chandeliers hang from rosettes, one at the center of each coffer.

The seating capacity is a great deal less than you'd suppose. The benches accommodate 250 average adults, or 270 persons including an average number of children. The benches are widely spaced, however, and it would not be difficult, perhaps, to double their number. But the fact is that New Yorkers seldom make use of the Waiting Room. They make a point, rather, of arriving at Grand Central just a few minutes ahead of train time. In any case, they show a decided preference for the Concourse—which is a great deal sunnier—and had rather stand and wait there than sit down in the Waiting Room.

Waiting for a train at Grand Central you can, of course, while away the hours in the Waiting Room, as you might do at any other station in the world; or you can spend your time idling in the Concourse; or you can attend the newsreel theater under the East Balcony. It's said that no other railway station contains a theater. This one serves two purposes: it enables the commuter, with a minimum loss to time, to keep abreast of the newsreels, and it takes the boredom out of waiting. (An illuminated clock up front keeps you informed of the time.) And for the privilege of serving these purposes it pays the railroad a handsome rental.

Upstairs, directly over the Waiting Room, is the great television studio of the Columbia Broadcasting System. This occupies a single vast room across the front of the station—a room virtually as large as the Waiting Room. Today it was in process of partitionment into a series of lesser studios and galleries to which the public would soon be admitted.

And above the television studio is the Grand Central Art Gallery, open to the public each weekday, admission-free, from nine to five. "In the world of art, the Grand Central gallery is looked upon as an annex to the National Academy"—and whether that's high praise or cruel blame is for the Academic and the anti-Academic forces to quarrel about. We simply note the fact of the gallery's eminent position. And John Kieran doesn't know, he says, "of any other gallery which has sold a million dollars' worth of paintings by a single living artist." Over a period of twenty years the Grand Central Art Gallery collected just a little more than that sum for the works of Frederick Waugh. It gives us some idea, perhaps, how much there is to see while waiting for a train at Grand Central.

The Grand Central School of Art is closed up now, a victim of the late war; but once it was famous, and in the last year before Pearl Harbor it was attended daily by more than a thousand students. They came from every state in the Union, from Canada, from Latin America, and even from England; and below the glass roof of the Office Building (north of the Concourse) they worked under famous painters, sculptors and water-colorists. Perhaps it would have been fair to look upon the school too as an annex to the Academy, for the faculty was composed almost entirely of Academicians. It was founded in 1924 and remained open for seventeen years. It was one of the surprising things about Grand Central Station.

Still more surprising is the office of John W. Campbell. You may have heard of Campbell; he was chairman of the board of the Credit Clearing House for many years prior to 1941, when he retired and his company's work was taken over by Dun & Bradstreet's. CBS moved into Grand Central because it found here "the biggest single room in New York"; and twenty years earlier Campbell moved into Grand Central because he also had found here what he wanted—the biggest ground-floor room in New York.

It still remains his private office. It lies just off the West Balcony, at the southwest corner of the building; and it's the most remarkable office, probably, that New York has ever seen. When he rented it, back in 1923, it was a bare barracks of a room, thirty feet wide by sixty feet long, and with a ceiling twenty-five feet high. He transformed it into the galleried hall of a thirteenth-century Florentine palace; it was said at the time that the decorators lay on their backs for months painting and mellowing and aging the newly timbered ceiling. And when the place was finished, Campbell furnished it with chairs and tables that came, in fact, out of Italy and out of Italy's magnificent thirteenth century.

He installed in it a fine pipe organ and a finer piano. He covered the whole floor with a single Persian rug, and other rugs he flung over chairs and tables or hung upon the walls. They are said to compose one of the world's best collections; they are said to have cost three hundred thousand dollars.

And they are not the only treasures. There are flowered vases, too, and fine statuary, and collections of rare books, petrified woods and uncut precious stones. And there, under the gallery at the far end of the room, is the massive Florentine desk at which Campbell for many years conducted the affairs of a very lucrative business; at which today he writes his letters, signs his checks, and keeps in touch with the world.

It was always more than a business office, though. From the first it was also a museum of beautiful and precious things, and by night it became a reception hall where Mr. and Mrs. Campbell together entertained their friends. Fifty or sixty guests might come here of a single evening to hear famous musicians play the pipe organ, or the concert grand piano, or both of them together. The Campbells live well out in the suburbs—good, sensible people that they are. But they love crowds of company, and by leasing that great barn of a room at Grand Central Station they solved their social problem.

THE OLD MAN

"A girl of nineteen or twenty—a particularly pretty girl, they say—woke up the clerk at the Golden Clock . . ." Ichabod halted, looked thoughtful for a moment, and then began again. "It was 4:17 A. M. The clerk noticed that; so did the gateman and the red cap. And it's worth our noticing, too, for the story is told precisely, and with candor and a great wealth of detail. I won't bother you with detail," said Ichabod.

"The girl was lost, and bewildered; obviously too, embarrassed. Quite simply, she asked her way home, and gave an address that was just off Lexington avenue, in the upper Forties. The red cap suggested a cab, but the gateman said it wasn't worth it; it was only up the street, and he was quitting work anyhow, and he was going that way, and he'd escort her home. The clerk grinned, and under his breath gave a brief, subdued howl—the call of the wolf, you know.

"As they walked up Lexington avenue, the girl talked a great deal at first. She seemed to be in a state of nerves . . . and she was worried. She talked about the aunt she lived with, and what her aunt would think of her being out so late. She said she had never before been out alone after eight o'clock at night—and she said it in such a simple, matter of fact way that the gateman found himself believing her. . . .

"As they cut across the avenue, the girl fell silent. For the next block or so she uttered not a word. . . . And when he had turned the corner and walked a few yards eastward, the gateman discovered that she was no longer at his side; so he doubled back to the avenue, thinking that perhaps she had paused for a moment to look in one of the show windows. But she was nowhere in sight. . . . And that," said Ichabod, "might have been the end of the story; she had given him the slip.

"But the gateman didn't see it that way; he couldn't get it out of his head that the girl was lost, and so he began looking for her—looking up and down the avenue, poking his head into every doorway, trying every door. She had made a strange impression on him, and the more he thought things over the more agitated he became. . . .

"At last, when he could search no further, he went to the address the girl had given him, and—though it was still the dead of night—rang the bell. A terrified old woman came to the door. He told her everything. And she replied: 'It happens this way every year. She was my niece. She was in the gas explosion when Grand Central was being built. She was taken to the hospital, and a few hours later—thirty-eight years ago tonight—she died.'

"Well," said Ichabod, "that's the story of the Grand Central ghost. . . . It crops up, in pretty much the same form, every six or seven years, and today . . . it's going the rounds again.

"Folks," he added, with a very serious nod, "like to know the kind of stories that cling to a place like Grand Central.

"Fact is," he then declared, "Grand Central *has* a ghost. . . . But that's a different story—because every word of it is true. . . ."

The Civil War had begun in April, 1861. By the fall of 1862, New York—already a great munitions town—was prospering as she had never prospered before; but even in the bosom of prosperity the New York & Harlem Railroad was doing poorly. Its route to Albany, as we have seen, lay through the wilderness far to the east of the Hudson; and this, slowly but inevitably, was proving a fateful, if not a fatal, defect. But then suddenly, in the fall of 1862, something happened to the Harlem Railroad.

It's to be noticed that Harlem had outstanding a total of 110,000 shares of stock. Nominally these were worth a hundred dollars each. Actually you could have bought as many as you pleased at nine dollars each. They weren't paying much if anything in the way of dividends. But there was always the wild chance, of course, that some day the road would prosper; and at nine dollars there were plenty of men willing to take that chance. On the Big Board in Wall street, Harlem had for a long time been rather steady at nine.

And what happened in the late fall of 1862 was this: On the Big Board in Wall street, Harlem started going up . . . to ten, twelve, fifteen, eighteen. Wall street rubbed its eyes; looked about for an explanation. There had been talk, lately, of extending the Harlem tracks from Chatham street into Broadway, and down Broadway to the Battery. Perhaps the rally was to be attributed to these rumors; the experts rather believed it was. And the experts knew, of course, that nothing would ever come of those rumors; for the Harlem would first have to get a franchise to extend its line, and a railroad with so little money back of it was not going to get a franchise. That settled, the experts decided to realize a profit; rushed in to sell Harlem at eighteen. That wave of selling, of course, should have broken the market, causing Harlem to fall again to its proper value of eight or nine. Harlem wavered —but "only fractionally," as they say in Wall street. It steadied again at eighteen, and within the week it was over twenty. And then, of course, it was obvious that somebody was buying Harlem.

All aflutter, Wall street studied every possibility; decided it was Old Man van der Bilt—who had some years earlier become Van Derbilt. (That was Double-Dutch, and eminently stylish in a city that was beginning to take pride in its Knickerbocker origin.) And Wall street was right about the old fellow. In the seventieth year of his life the old steamboat captain—big, strutting Cornelius Van Derbilt—was going into the railroad business; an untutored genius, explosively profane over little things, and tremendously cold and clear-thinking in the most frightful emergencies. He had made millions—and acquired the nickname of Commodore—as the owner of fleets of ocean-going vessels as well as river craft. And why was he turning, now, to railroads? "Waal," he said, "ten per cent talks louder than five." In which case it may be added that the Confederates had pretty well driven his boats off the high seas, anyhow; whereupon he had sold the lot of them to the Navy —at three times their value, it was maliciously reported to Congress.

Wall street decided that the old man, in his dotage, had set his heart on losing in railroading all the millions he had made in shipping. Wall street squared off to reap a profit when the crash came. Harlem rose from thirty to forty; it was building for a beautiful crash. Van Derbilt bought all the shares he could lay hands on, then posted them as collateral for loans with which to buy more. That was a dangerous tactic; it made him vulnerable. Wall street was atiptoe with excitement. Forty was a crazy figure, brought about by nothing but one man's mad desire to possess the Harlem. Wall street said there had to be a crash. Harlem rose to fifty. And Wall street decided that Old Man Van Derbilt had something up his sleeve.

By the April of 1863, Van Derbilt had cornered somewhat more than 55,000 shares of its stock, and was the master of the New York & Harlem Railroad. He went before the Common Council and told them what he wanted; frankly and straightforwardly he paid them, cash on the barrel head. The aldermen knew something he did not know, but they took his money anyhow, and delivered the franchise, authorizing the Harlem Railroad to continue its tracks from Chatham street and Broadway down the center of Broadway to the Battery. On the Big Board in Wall street, Harlem shot up to seventy-five—and, under the coaching of Daniel Drew, the bribed aldermen swarmed into Wall street and began selling Harlem at seventy-five. They had no Harlem shares, as a matter of fact; but they sold for future delivery, intending to buy shares cheaply after the crash and before delivery fell due. In brief, they were "selling short."

The Commodore heard about this within the hour and concluded, rightly, that the franchise was illegal. That was bad news; for if the price of Harlem broke seriously—if Harlem fell sufficiently to impair the value of his collateral at the banks—he plainly stood to lose every dollar he possessed. On the advice of his broker, a remarkable man called Leonard Jerome, he bought and bought as the aldermen sold and sold. And between them all, the aldermen sold in very brief order a great deal more than 110,000 shares, which was all the shares there were in existence. They had not thought about that; they had thought only of the crash that was bound to occur. Then came in swift succession two moves they had counted on from the beginning. The State Legislature granted the Broadway franchise to another company, and the other company obtained a writ of injunction forbidding the Harlem to lay tracks in Broadway. Whereupon the aldermen, who had previously been warned that all city franchises were illegal, solemnly "repealed" the Harlem franchise and sat back to watch Harlem take a tumble in Wall street.

But the crash didn't quite come off. From seventy-five, Harlem fell but three points to seventy-two. And already it was time for the aldermen to make delivery—to Van Derbilt—of all the shares they had sold short; all the shares he had strained his resources to buy up. Under the impact of their mass buying, the price skyrocketed; and in the end they had to go to Van Derbilt himself and buy of him, at 179, the very shares they were under contract to deliver to him at seventy-five. The aldermen were ruined. The tough old Commodore came out of the scrimmage with a clear profit of more than five million dollars. And it was rather apparent that the New York & Harlem Railroad, which had done so poorly, was now at last in strong hands.

"And that," said Ichabod, "was the opening chapter of the greatest railroad story in American history."

The second chapter, which began at once, was like it.

•

Commodore Van Derbilt had great plans for the Harlem; but they were plans that also looked well beyond the Harlem. The technical aspects of railroading he was not too much interested in, though he knew, as an old ship's captain, that everything would have to be shipshape or his money would be lost. He called in the Harlem engineering staff and told them, roughly, that he was paying the bills, and that their job, within the limits of a proper economy, was to make the Harlem—track, car and locomotive—a first-class railroad. Then he dismissed them and turned his attention to the best built and best equipped railroad in the United States: the Hudson-River Rail-Road.

This, as we have seen, ran out of a New York terminal at Chambers and Hudson streets; it was a splendid road physically, but highly vulnerable to steamboat competition. For the first twelve or thirteen years of its existence, deficit had been piled upon deficit; and its shares were going cheaply in Wall street. Van Derbilt got hold of it in 1864, just one year after he had taken hold of the Harlem. He announced that he was going to combine the two roads as the New York, Harlem & Hudson-River Rail-Road, and—again the signal for a raid—Harlem went up sharply in Wall street.

It's hardly believable, but the records are not to be denied. Van Derbilt required an act of Legislature to enable him to consolidate his two railroads; and Van Derbilt—forthright fellow that he was—walked straight in, told the legislators what he wanted. . . . Perhaps he should have known better, after last year's experience with the New York aldermen; but for that matter, perhaps, the legislators should have known better too. Anyhow, they took his money. Harlem was well over par. They introduced a consolidation bill and spoke on it favorably. Harlem shot to 150, and the Commodore began selling—to reduce his excessive holdings, to redeem his bank loans and, of course, to realize a maximum profit on the shares he was parting with. And then the legislators swooped into Wall street, selling short. Harlem began to waver; whereupon Legislature politely voted down the consolidation bill and Harlem plummeted to ninety.

Van Derbilt was in a serious predicament. At ninety his collateral was still sufficient to cover his bank loans; but, if things got worse, he would be brought face to face with bankruptcy. And if, on the other hand, the legislators now bought at ninety, and made delivery of the shares they had sold at 150 only a day or two earlier, they would have realized a fortune. But their raid, of course, was a carefully organized attack—organized by no other than Daniel Drew—and none of the legislators broke front. Instead of realizing a profit of sixty dollars a share, they launched another wave of selling to force the price down to fifty. They sold thousands upon thousands of shares for delivery at various dates throughout the summer; Drew assured them that before the campaign was over they could buy and deliver at nine or even eight. And, under the influence of their continued selling, Harlem sagged further and further.

Van Derbilt now was in desperate straits. But a few friends stuck to him. An aged deck hand off one of his old boats came in with a million dollars that the Commodore had made for him in Wall street years earlier; he still had the million, and in his benefactor's extremity he offered to give it all back. And there was, of course, his broker, Leonard Jerome. Jerome again helped him organize his defenses. For weeks the going was frightful; more than once it was touch and go.

But the Commodore, as well as a trapped man could, kept buying. And the hour came when he was able to lay down his pencil and whisper across the table to Jerome: "We've won." He had been using the pencil to add up his purchases. He has bought 137,000 shares of Harlem stock; which was 27,000 more than there were in existence. Tucked away neatly in his own safe, he had every last share of Harlem stock in Wall street. And it was the hour when the legislators would have to begin delivery of the shares they had sold.

When these fellows came into the market to buy, of course, they were paralyzed. To find a single share there was nowhere to go but to Van Derbilt himself, whom they had treated with what passed for treachery even in those roaring days of public and business immorality. Van Derbilt was merciless. He smiled. He assured them he would sell them all the shares they needed to make delivery. The price was one thousand dollars a share.

But that, of course, was impossible. Leonard Jerome took a hand in the bargaining; appealed for mercy, not indeed that they deserved mercy but that "every house in Wall street would be wrecked" unless Van Derbilt made concessions. And Leonard Jerome, who had stood by him through two gigantic battles, won the concessions he demanded. A brilliant strategist, and a man of quite exceptional charm, Jerome was the father of Lady Randolph Churchill, and the grandfather of Mr. Winston Churchill, the wartime Prime Minister of England.

The Commodore compromised at 285, clearing a profit that would have exceeded twenty-five million dollars had not some of the legislators gone into bankruptcy. He destroyed that Legislature. It goes without saying, of course, that his own hands were not clean; but just the same he broke the back of a corrupt political gang. And he came out of these two battles—famous in the history of Wall street as the Great Harlem Corners—with a reputation for marvelous adroitness and skill no less than for sheer fighting capacity.

"And that," said Ichabod, "was the second chapter. . . . The moral was that fate—more accurately, Wall street—was furnishing Old Man Van Derbilt with enormous sums of money and that that money was enabling him to build a railroad system such as America might not otherwise have seen for a hundred years after his time. In the third chapter, the old rascal saw to it that the process would continue. . . ."

From the close of the Civil War in 1865 to the late fall of 1869, Van Derbilt went on building up the physical assets of the Harlem and improving the already peerless Hudson-River Rail-Road. He had wanted to consolidate his two companies, but, unable to do so for want of a mere act of Legislature, he went on operating them separately. Naturally, he gave most of his attention to the Hudson-River road, which ran such an easy, water-level route to Albany, and stopped at so many fine towns along the way. He set out to make it earn a profit—which is another way of saying that the old man was going to war.

As everybody had known it would, the Hudson-River Rail-Road had paid a fearful penalty for going into competition with a waterway; and to make anything out of it now was a tremendous undertaking. It involved war with the steamboat lines. So it also involved that incorrigible raider, Daniel Drew. And before it was ended it was to bring the Commodore in violent collision with an Upstate railroad called the New-York Central. Baffled and beaten twice as a result of the Harlem Corners, Uncle Dan decided—while nursing the bruises, perhaps—that Van Derbilt's first move now would be to establish touch with the Central, and rig up a treaty for the interchange of freight and passenger traffic between the Central and the Hudson-River roads. It took no special wit on Daniel's part to arrive at this conclusion, though. The New-York Central ran from the great river port of Albany to the Great Lakes port of Buffalo. It was a prosperous railroad. Against the competition of the shallow Erie Canal—which had failed to meet the strains of Civil War traffic—it poured into Albany every day a rich commerce in things from the Mohawk and the Genesee valleys as well as Buffalo and the West; and it stood to reason that if the Hudson-River Rail-Road could capture the down-river part of this trade, it would drive the steamboats out of business. Van Derbilt knew that as well as Daniel Drew. But Drew—who was a steamboat owner as well as a Wall street raider—got there first.

The truth would seem to be that the New-York Central was afraid of Van Derbilt, who was both tough and diabolically clever. In any case, the Central entered an alliance with Drew, as head of the People's Steamboat Line. And when Van Derbilt came looking for a treaty—they made a deal with him too. They agreed on terms, and they authorized each other to sell through passenger tickets and to accept freight for shipment from any point on the one railroad to any point on the other. That was not to say, of course, that the Central *would* sell any through tickets, or *would* hand over any through freight; it was merely to set up a method of handling whatever interchange there might be. In short, it was a bargain for cunning old Dan Drew to cackle over. But it was the best agreement the Commodore could get. And he proceeded to make the most of it.

He fed traffic to the Central. He waited patiently for the Central to return the favor. He ran his trains across the new bridge into the Central's own terminal in Albany, thus avoiding the transshipment of passengers and freight across the river by ferry, across the ice by sledges in the wintertime. He advertised his treaty all through the Central's territory as well as his own; and that, in the end, was vital, for it led shippers to stipulate for carriage "all the way by rail." He protested against the Central's continuing to give all, or nearly all, of its down-river traffic to the People's Line. He threw into the Central's freight houses a force of spies, and got all the evidence he needed to show that the Central was really accepting freight to go "all the way by rail," and was diverting it to the steamboats. He horrified the Central managers by calling this to their attention. But there was little that he could do about it, for New-York Central shares were virtually not to be had in Wall street.

Then the unexpected death of their president threw the Central managers into a panic. They began to sell shares; they were hedging. The winter came on, and Van Derbilt tempted them. It was to be a prosperous year; he urged them to accept all the freight they could get for New York, and—they rose to the bait. The river was already frozen. The freight trains poured into Albany. The freight piled up in the terminal—and so did the company's liabilities. On an hour's notice, Van Derbilt abrogated his agreement with the Central, refused to accept any of its freight, stopped his own trains at Greenbush, threw the passengers out of the sleeping-cars at two o'clock of a bitterly cold morning, and let them carry their own luggage across the ice.

Faced with appalling liabilities, and conscious that no court would hear their case—they had been too many times caught cheating the Commodore—the Central managers ran to Legislature screaming for help. And on the Big Board in Wall street, New-York Central fell to panic prices.

After a stoppage of only twenty-four hours, the traffic agreement was reinstated, and Hudson-River trains were moving the freight out of

Albany. In those twenty-four hours, of course, the New-York Central had acquired a new owner.

Van Derbilt paid a fortune for the Central, and now he spent two million dollars more upon it, improving its roadbed and rolling stock. And to help finance his great new enterprise, or perhaps merely to take the greatest possible advantage of his new position, he nonchalantly sauntered into Wall street and turned the stock market into a vast source of revenue. He brought the Central to a new level of prosperity; and then, of course, Wall street clamored for shares. Van Derbilt held off, whereupon the price rose furiously. Next, without warning, he unloaded heavily, forcing the price down—and bought back at the lower figure all the shares he had just sold at the higher. This gave him a huge profit of ready cash and left his position unchanged.

He whispered it abroad that, to compensate for profits plowed back into the railroad, he intended to issue to all stockholders additional shares equal to 80 per cent of their current holdings. And, with such a plum in the offing, Wall street could not restrain its impulse to buy Central. The price rose. The Commodore dumped, and after the crash bought everything back at a further profit. He kept on doing this; and all the while kept talking about the 80 per cent stock dividend, the actual declaration of which, however, he always, for one reason or another, kept putting off. "He milked Wall street dry, and in the end nobody in the street had any money left." Then he declared the wonderful dividend—on a day when he himself happened to be the only person in the world who owned any worth-while amount of New-York Central stock. The distributed shares had a market value of twenty-three million dollars.

Then he got control of the Erie, and settled an old score by ruining its president—Daniel Drew. Drew came to him the next day in tears, got down on his knees, the story goes; appealed to him as one old man to another; and Van Derbilt restored him to the presidency of the Erie but under orders to do as he was told. Drew brought in Jay Gould and Jim Fisk to help him. At a critical moment they "planted" in Wall street a hundred thousand fraudulent shares of Erie stock, and Old Man Van Derbilt—still in the market for all he could lay hands on—had bought up seven million dollars' worth of these before he discovered their treachery. Then, in a passionate burst of profanity, he he swore out warrants for their arrest, but ten minutes earlier they had escaped across the river to New Jersey, with some odd millions of dollars in suitcases and six millions more done up in bales and carried in a hackney coach. A few days later Gould was in Albany bribing Legislature to pass an ex post facto law to legalize the stock issue. Van Derbilt raced up to Albany, but the Senators voted for Gould whose money, naturally, was free and easy. The law was passed. Van Derbilt retorted by having Supreme Court Justice Bernard rule that while the statute had the effect of legitimatizing the shares, the original fraud remained. Under a compromise agreement then, Van Derbilt withdrew the charge of fraud and recovered five of the seven millions they had robbed him of. After that he quit the Erie, which was now too crippled, financially, to compete with his railroads.

And after that again the old man laid plans to insulate himself and his companies against the jeopardy of Wall street raids and booms; and presently we find him conducting his financial affairs in terms of both dollars and pounds. It was at first, perhaps, a tentative, experimental move. In the end, the effect was incalculable. It divided all Van Derbilt railroad shares between the New York Stock Exchange and the Royal Exchange, London. It gave them stability. It opened up vast new resources of money against the demands of an oncoming titanic struggle for railroad supremacy.

Meanwhile, however, Legislature gave consent and on the first of November, 1869, Van Derbilt consolidated his two principal companies, forming a new railroad under a new name—the New-York Central & Hudson-River Rail-Road. At the age of seventy-six years, the old boy had pieced together what was up to that moment the most extensive and probably the most efficiently operated, and what was presently to become the most profitable railroad in the world.

To celebrate his triumph, in the next two weeks, he broke ground for the first Grand Central station at Fourth avenue and Forty-second street, and he solemnly attended the dedication of his own memorial—a great bronze statue of his own burly, swaggering self, atop the new freight terminal at Saint John's Park, on the Lower West Side of Manhattan.

"End of the third chapter," Ichabod announced abruptly.

"Briefly, then," he continued, striking the forefinger of his left with the forefinger of his right hand; "briefly, we've glanced over the first seven years of a career which had not begun till the hero of it was already in the seventieth year of his life. . . . We've seen the piecing together of the New-York Central & Hudson-River Rail-Road, which in 1914 became the present-day New York Central Railroad. We've seen the beginning of a disengaging operation that would virtually take the Van Derbilt railroads out of Wall street (for a time) and make the Central-Hudson—as the Commodore called it—to a large extent an English-owned railroad; and that explains a great deal about the present-day Grand Central. . . .

"We've seen the breaking of ground for his great new passenger terminal. At Forty-second street, this was far out from the city. As the newspapers remarked at the time, it was 'out in the woods,' it was 'at the end of the world,' and it would take a business man in Wall street a whole hour to reach it. . . . But the Commodore was proud of his new station. After hard searching he found a name that would do it justice. The newspapers jeered. They had a name of their own for it. They called it the End-of-the-World Station. The Commodore let them jeer. It was his station and he alone had the right to christen it. He called it proudly the Grand Central Depot.

"We've seen all this—and we've seen the old gentleman solemnly dedicating his own memorial. . . ."

That was a vast and complicated thing, in which the old boy stood forth, erect and grand, before a background of ships and trains and all kinds of cowering "classical" figures intended to symbolize his power and place in the world of transportation. The allegory was lost upon the city, for the monument stood so high upon the freight house that only the dominating central figure could be seen from the street. But it was there just the same, and the city at least was able to read the glowing details. Admiring newspapers rhapsodized upon it, called it "a biography in bronze." For sixty years atop the freight house it braved the sea air of New York and the smoke and soot of ten thousand locomotives.

And then it was taken down—in 1929, just as the big crash in Wall street was about to change the whole character of American life. It was taken down and, quite irreverently, junked; all, that is, but the heroic figure of the Commodore himself. And this was carted over to Grand Central and placed upon a pedestal where you see it today, at the center of the main façade, facing the viaduct over Forty-second street.

It is a plain pedestal, quite devoid of symbolism. But the unveiling ceremonies—intended to mark the sixtieth anniversary of the absurd and ridiculed End-of-the-World Station—were held amid the crashing of an economic system; and there were those present who knew, some of them, that they were witnessing the end of that world of which the Commodore himself is our most imposing symbol.

"You can't ever forget the Commodore," said Ichabod. "His gigantic statue is out front. The street to the west is named after him—Vanderbilt avenue. And, flanking Grand Central Station, are those two enormous railroad-owned hotels—the Commodore and the Biltmore—both named for him. Biltmore? That's a form of Dutch. It means Bilt Manor, or the manor house of Bilt—which was the town in Holland whence the Commodore's ancestor, Jan Aertsen van der Bilt, came to New Amsterdam back in the seventeenth century. . . .

"Again, the Grand Central system today is pretty much the same as when the Commodore worked it out. There's the gatemen, for example; and narrow platforms, and therefore the greatest possible number of tracks to the acre. It was the Commodore who planned it this way; and so it is in our day that a soldier's mother cannot see him safely aboard his train, but has to say good-by to him in the Concourse. And so it is, too, that the Concourse is so big; the railroad has to provide for that kind of thing, and the space saved on the platforms was, of necessity, added to the Concourse. . . . It all grew out of the Commodore's way of doing things, and I should say," said Ichabod, "that we see the old man's hand in the very largeness of the Concourse. . . .

"And you recall his broker down in Wall street. He was Leonard Jerome. A few years later, you remember, his daughter Jennie was going to marry Lord Randolph Churchill and become the mother of Mr. Winston Churchill. . . . Jerome stood by the Commodore's side battling old Daniel Drew; and the two men stood together to the end, and their families stood together, and the day came when a Vanderbilt married a Churchill too and became the Duchess of Marlborough. And it was that Duchess of Marlborough whose portrait was drawn by the Frenchman, Paul Helleu. . . . It resulted in Helleu's designing the great blue ceiling at Grand Central, with all the stars and constellations in reverse . . . with stars that rise in the West and set in the East.

"You see what I mean," said Ichabod, "when I say that the Commodore's decisions and the Commodore's history are built into the very fabric of present-day Grand Central . . . that the spirit of the Commodore, if not his wraith, clings tenaciously to Grand Central. . . ."

Ichabod hardly ended his lecture. He simply fell silent. He had been chattering merrily all this time. A schoolteacher by calling, he knows a lot, and—in the words of an unpleasant faculty colleague—he "likes to spill it." But now he was silent for a moment or so; then he began again.

"You must have heard," he said, "of Metzman—Gustav Metzman. Since the summer of 1944, he's been the president of the New York Central Railroad. . . ."

But Metzman, after all, doesn't quite belong to Grand Central. His offices are in the New York Central Building, a many-times taller structure that straddles Park avenue from Forty-sixty to Forty-seventh streets.

They're large and spacious offices, with high ceilings and paneled walls; and the portraits of eleven earlier presidents look down upon them. In particular, one masterful man, old Commodore Van Derbilt, peers from his massive gilded frame, and seems to follow with his sharp eyes all who enter and speak and transact business there. The paneling, it's to be noted, is from the Sherwood Forest, Nottinghamshire, England.

The story goes that some mordant wit among the architects, recalling the Commodore's financial wizardry, decided upon the paneling.

"But they all agreed to it," said Ichabod, "including the present-day Vanderbilts—who still retain the real power in New York Central affairs. They decided that the Commodore's spirit would be happier in an office haunted, as it were, by memories of Robin Hood."

SEATS IN THE GALLERY

IT WAS 10:02 by the Golden Clock. A midmorning calm had settled upon the Concourse, and the North Balcony was quiet as a church. After Ichabod's forty-seven minute lecture we had gone there—for no better reason, perhaps, than Tommy Atkins had for joining the army:

For to admire an' for to see,
For to be'old this world so wide . . .

The North Balcony is never crowded, and so is almost wholly uncommercial. At the east end it has today a telephone station with two or three attendant operators, but that is all. No Union News Company stand is there to ornament or disfigure it; and, seen from either end, it looks not unlike the broad aisle of a cathedral. Along the north side, a wall of marble, glass and steel is pierced by doorways leading out to a taxi-stand upon a weirdly lighted plaza; an indoors plaza, built on bridgework above the tracks and below the Grand Central Office Building. And along the south side, from column to column, are the marble balustrades—and the benches—from which the professors of mass observation gaze (mainly in disapproval) upon their fellow mortals in the Concourse below.

Today the benches were almost empty. In fact, it's hard nowadays to find even one or two of the professors on duty. But time was when they were numerous. During the Depression they sat and smoked and observed the crowds for hours and hours, and sometimes—not often—consulted with one another in a profound sort of way, as became professors. With so few of them left, the North Balcony isn't what it used to be; but there are those who still insist on calling it the Philosophers' Gallery.

Day after day, week after week, for years at a stretch (back in the

930s), the professors sat and smoked and watched the crowds in that uriously detached way of theirs, and occasionally—not often—exhanged a few penetrating observations, mainly to the effect that people re a squirming, stepped-on mass of maggots, and that life is an evil oke. But after Pearl Harbor, it would seem, they got jobs again; or else ne war overcame their sickness. (The maggot theory died at Dunkirk.) nyhow, they disappeared from the North Balcony; or most of them id. And so today it can be said of the Philosophers' Gallery (and with nmensely more of truth) what the Londoners have long said of *Punch,* nat it "isn't what it used to be—and never was."

But still it's a comfortable spot, and on a bright day it's a pleasant one. nd it is, of course, the best possible vantage point from which to see ne goings on in the Concourse.

From where we sat we could see the crowds come down the ramp rom Forty-second street and Park avenue, directly opposite; see them own the first ramp, then across the center of the Waiting-Room floor, nd finally down the second ramp to the floor of the Concourse. The tory goes that a pair of opera glasses comes in handy here—and that if alzac, instead of eavesdropping in Paris, had only sat here and read the ps of the people coming down those ramps, *La Comédie Humaine* night have been the better for it.

Grand Central was the first building in America in which it was proosed to use ramps instead of stairways. It wasn't the first to contain amps; for Grand Central was long abuilding and a score of other ructures, designed later, were completed earlier—and they all had amps. But the idea began here, and if you go by the blueprints, Grand Central was the first of all.

The idea was that of an architect from Saint Paul, Minnesota—a nan who had a theory about the management of crowds. He believed, he story goes, that a man is one thing, but a crowd is something else gain. He wasn't certain about the man, for men are wilful, unpreictable; but he was sure he could trust the crowd to follow, unquesioningly, the law of gravity. And so he laid out the ramps for Grand Central Terminal in such a way that, if you were to roll a barrel in rom Forty-second street, through any door at all, the barrel—drawn y gravity alone—would roll down a ramp, and by the curved and super-elevated ramp would be steered and guided into the Concourse where it would come to a stop on level ground, directly in front of a ticket window.

That's the story, anyhow. As they were built, of course, the ramps are straight. So the barrel trick would hardly work today. But the idea remains; and the most bewildered stranger has never entered Grand Central from Forty-second street without feeling, somehow, that the ramp had led him precisely where he had wanted to go.

And that notion of crowd management has been carried straight through the design of Grand Central. The Concourse, as we have seen, is the main-line departure station. True, arrivals occur there nowadays: lots of them; and the Concourse is no longer *exclusively* a departure station, as it was designed to be. But it still remains *essentially* a departure station, and it is, of course, the only station from which mainliners depart.

It may be necessary, in this connection, to think of the Concourse as a somewhat larger entity, embracing the Concourse proper and three minor extensions of the Concourse—the northeast corridor, the northwest corridor, and the Vanderbilt avenue gallery that lies, as we have seen, between the northwest corridor and the Arrival Station. (We'll get the hang of it before this day is over.) In single array, the departure tracks extend from about the middle of the northeast corridor to the northwest corner of the Vanderbilt avenue gallery. But all this is detail; the important point is that the Concourse is your departure station, and that the main body of travelers who leave New York for other cities all cross the floor of the Concourse.

That's one thing; and equally important is the fact that their movement is a one-way movement all the way through. As they enter the station, and before they can find breath to ask a question, they find themselves at the ticket windows, then the baggage counter below the East Balcony, and then—the train gate. Everything is laid out that way, and there isn't any doubling back, but all movement is forward from the curb in Forty-second street to the outgoing train. And that one-way movement of travelers through the departure station is rarely fluttered by a rush of incoming travelers moving the opposite way; Grand Central is so organized that, for the most part, the crowds never collide.

Except for its echoes, and the seemingly quite distant surge and bustle of the Concourse, the North Balcony was unusually quiet today; and then, abruptly, three young British naval officers burst through the doorway back of us and caught their first glimpse of the sunlit interior of Grand Central:

"Will you look at *this?*"

"Oh, I say!"

"Isn't it a knockout? My hat, but this is spiffing!"

"Doesn't it seem strange after London? People wearing new clothes. . . . Women wearing colors. . . ."

"Is this the booking-hall? I wonder if it is!"

"Of course. Don't you see the wickets?"

"Concourse? It's called the Concourse? But the concourse is the people, isn't it? To me a concourse means a throng of people. Does it also mean a place?"

"I say, Jonesie! Next time we come here, fetch over Euston Station like a good fellow, will you? And—ah, let me see now! Oh, just stow it away for a bit in that far corner of the Concourse!"

They had been there for hardly two minutes when a fourth young officer hailed them from the door; whereupon the first three turned upon us jauntily, saluted, and dashed away as abruptly as they had come.

They were not the only visitors, but they were the only ones who spoke much above a whisper. In twenty minutes sixty or seventy persons passed along the entire length of the balcony. But, strangely, you paid little attention to them.

It's the Concourse that fascinates you here; the Concourse and its people. The crowds were still passing through, but lazily now; without the hurry that was noticeable an hour ago. They came in by the southeast corridor, and cut across the center of the floor to the northwest corridor, as if they had come out of the East Side subway and were on their way to work somewhere in the region of Madison avenue and Forty-fifth street; or they went just the opposite way. They came in by the southwest corridor and followed a path diagonally across the marble floor to the northeast corridor, as if they were on their way from the Times Square shuttle to the region of Forty-fifth street and Lexington avenue; or they went the opposite way here too. They came from every corner, they came down the stairs from the West Balcony and down the ramps from Forty-second street, and they went by every possible way across and about and around and through the Concourse, and with never a pause they continued straight on out again about their business. Or the bulk of them did. The rest—obviously railroad passengers and their relatives and friends—gathered together in little groups that were now rather evenly distributed over the whole floor. The Concourse rang with chatter and the shuffling of feet upon the marble pavement.

Military Policemen and naval Shore Patrolmen passed through all the crowds, stopping the men in uniform, demanding to see their papers Other policemen, blue-coated members of the Grand Central Termina Police force, moved unobtrusively about, each man upon his beat. Rec caps went among the people, soliciting bags to carry, sometimes getting them.

Within the crowds there was a casual drifting now, a sort of aimlessness. And mixed with it, every so often, was a nervous darting this way or that way in search of a lost child, or a train. There was a cry of "Al aboard!" and there was the answering charge upon some closing gate There was a call to the gateman, clear and very calm. After all, a gateman will heed the call of a heavily burdened red cap, rules or no rules.

A newcomer stood beside us at the balustrade. He turned out to be a newspaper man, who had dropped in, as it were, on a professiona visit. A financial writer, he called the Concourse his "business barometer." When the crowds are thick in the Concourse, he said, business i still on the upgrade, and when the crowds grow thin, it's time to watch your step; for as the human tides go at Grand Central, so the busines tides in Wall street go. That was the gist of what he said.

"So it's a good tip to play the stock market from a bench in the Philosophers' Gallery?"

"I'm a newspaper man," he retorted. "I just know the facts day by day. If I could be sure of what the facts *mean* I'd be rich."

It was not infallible, now and again it might even prove misleading but twenty-five years' experience had satisfied him, he said, of the usefulness of his method. "For a quick estimate on your way to work each day . . . it's a way of spotting a new trend. It's my way, anyhow."

Unconscious of the tribute paid them, the crowds in the Concourse went steadily on with their own serious affairs; and a never-ending stream of people continued pouring in and pouring out, rushing for the train gates and idly sauntering across the floor . . . whispering; chattering in voices high and low; sometimes calling aloud to one another.

It was 10:19 now, and Grand Central was as nearly quiet as it ever is by day; quiet, but not silent; for the Concourse is never silent. The fact is—and you can't sit long in the Philosophers' Gallery without having it borne in upon you—that the Concourse has a voice; and the voice of the Concourse, born of a thousand human lips and the shuffling of a thousand human feet upon marble, is never still. Never a buzzing sound, not even a roar, it's a wide-open, spacious sound like the autumn wind in a forest, or the sea breaking on rocks; and through it runs—unnoticed by the tone-deaf and the unobservant—a rich variety of overtones, a kind of accidental music that forever achieves little patterns and loses them again; a wild, fugitive music, like the tune fragments that race through the ringing of the rails and the clicking of wheels over the points.

It's hard to catch those overtones; they trace a fortuitous course against a background of mere noise. In the case of Grand Central, it's especially hard to catch them, the acoustics of the Concourse are so unfavorable. But the music is there just the same.

"Don't forget Arthur Honegger and *Pacific 231.*"

Quite so. What Honegger did there was to discern the play of overtones amid the noise and rhythm of a working locomotive, and to strip the noise away, thus, as it were, liberating the music.

"Now if somebody could do the same thing for Grand Central—"

"Who? *Me?*"

This last was from a young man who had lately posted himself beside us, planting his elbows upon the balustrade with great deliberation and then pitching his weight suddenly upon them. You would have said he was the type. He had dark, liquid eyes, black fingernails, and a flowing black silk tie; by all the rules, he should have been a musician—perhaps even a composer. But he turned out to be only an aspiring novelist (temporarily a shipping clerk) from Greenwich Village. In which case it may be stated that a young intellectual from Greenwich Village—which any true New Yorker would have called the Old Ninth Ward—came this day to the Philosophers' Gallery for inspiration.

DISPATCHER

HE'S A QUIET, modest man. He's one of the happiest men in all New York. And for almost thirty years, calmly and with quite exceptional ease, he has held the most tremendous job at Grand Central. You'll find his name on the roster of railroad officials: Andrew F. Durkin, Chief Dispatcher. But everybody calls him Andy, and he has the grace that suffers a man to be called by his first name without loss of dignity.

He's in room 1836. That's on the second floor of the Terminal Office Building. But the second floor at Grand Central is called the first floor, English-fashion; and Room 1836—as the first two digits indicate—is on Floor 1, Corridor 8. Anyone you meet in Corridor 8 will tell you where Andy's to be found.

He was sitting at his desk to the left of the doorway as we walked in upon him; facing the wonderful master clock that Jake, the clockmaster, told us about. Andy rose and put forth his hand—a tall, slender man who looks at you with steady brown eyes and a quiet smile. You notice that smile; and try to fathom it. You think about it when you should be listening to what he says. And Andy says a great deal. He talks with great fluency and ease, as becomes a man whose parents came from Ireland. He talks with pride about Mathilda and their four children. He answers the telephone half a dozen times in half an hour—three different telephones are on his desk. He talks across the room to his two assistants. He never lifts his voice above the quietest of conversational tones.

There are moments when the smile disappears; as when he tells of the tragic death of a brilliant younger brother. But it quickly reasserts itself; and it isn't long before the notion strikes you that here is a most unusual man—a man profoundly at peace with himself and all the world.

He rose and put forth his hand. Then he turned, with a kind of old-
ashioned courtesy, to introduce the men on duty back of him.

"Here," said Andy, "are two fine old veterans; two of the best dis-
atchers on the New York Central—Harold Stegman and Solomon
chultz."

He presented each man separately. But each was talking to the tower-
nen out along the tracks, and each was keeping a "sheet." In the cus-
omary way of Dispatcher's office, each raised a hand in recognition;
ach gave us a quick smile to confirm the signal, and the sheets con-
inued spinning back and forth across their desks.

"Sol has District A, and Harold has District B," said Andy. "District
and District B together form the New York division. District A—
hat belongs to Sol—embraces all tracks from Grand Central Terminal
o White Plains North. District B begins at Mott Haven Junction, and
xtends from there to Croton-on-Hudson. . . .

"District A," said Andy, "is the trunk of the old New York & Harlem
ailroad; it's still the main stem out of Grand Central. District B em-
races tracks of the old Hudson-River Rail-Road, following the water's
dge . . . and cutting into the Harlem's trackage at Mott Haven. His-
ory laid them out that way, and that way they still remain. . . .

"Sol moves every train in and out of Grand Central; moves everything
n Harlem company trackage this side of the tower at White Plains
North—even the crack trains for the West. The *Century*, for example
. . Sol takes her out as far as Mott Haven. There he swings her over to
Harold; and Harold takes her from there on out to Croton-on-Hudson,
here he swings her over to the Hudson Division dispatcher at Al-
any. . . ."

You catch the astonishing implications of all this if you keep in
nind a very simple distinction drawn, upon the railroad, between two
reat classes of track. First, you have the *line*, over which trains run
om terminal to terminal. This is the *iron turnpike* of the early railroad
uilders, spoken of today as *high iron*, or the *big pike*, or simply the *pike*.
Only a civil engineer would call it *line* track.) And, second, you have
ard track, or *low iron*. Yard and pike, low iron and high iron, the dif-
erence between these two is sacred. And the law of the railroad is this:
ow iron is free; but no train, no engine, not even a hand-car, may ven-

ture upon high iron except on orders from Dispatcher; and, once out upon the pike, Conductor must take his train to her destination as expeditiously as possible and, upon arrival, must get her as promptly as possible off the pike—out of the channel of traffic, into the refuge of low iron and free trackage; off the turnpike, into the yard.

A yard, according to the engineering book, is a sidetrack or a group of sidetracks. But railroad law defines it simply as trackage on which wheels may turn without orders. So it's *off* the big pike; it's outside Dispatcher's jurisdiction. It's free trackage; all kinds of operations can be carried on there, and wheels may turn to suit the convenience of the men who are doing the work.

But the enormously important fact is that, on high iron, no wheel may turn without orders; no movement can be attempted until Dispatcher has found a place for it in a carefully integrated program of operations, and has authorized it. The timetable is only a compilation of Dispatcher's general orders; special orders must issue for every single movement not covered by the timetable. Dispatcher decides each case and his local deputy, the towerman out along the line, issues the order in writing. Dispatcher also has control over the signal system; employ it as a vast instrument for the conveyance of orders to moving trains.

He's a huge figure on the railroad, though the public never sees his work and hardly knows of his existence. The engineman—whom the public calls an engineer—operates one train, and all the enginemen together can do no more than run trains. But Dispatcher runs the railroad which is something else again. He calls every move; orders and controls and interlaces all the concurrent train movements within a whole division. A dozen different trains may be racing forward all at the same instant. That's because Dispatcher has opened up routes in front of them—routes clear of other trains—and is calling them on with green lights or the upturned blades of semaphores. What's actually happening is this: A hundred different trains are taking part in a vast symphony of motion. And Dispatcher is the conductor of that symphony—and, as we have seen, he's the principal composer of it, too.

"Sol," said Andy, "takes her out as far as Mott Haven. There he swings her over to Harold; and Harold takes her from there on out t

Croton-on-Hudson, where he swings her over to the Hudson Division dispatcher at Albany. They never lose sight of her a minute . . . faithful men.

"Harold has four tracks to work with. . . . His district covers wenty-eight point four four miles; not a very extensive line, but one f the heaviest traveled in the world. It includes the station at Harnon, where the liners change locomotives, from electric to steam oing west, from steam to electric coming east. It embraces the whole commuting area on the Hudson river side of Westchester County.

"All the rest of the New York commuting area," said Andy, "belongs o District A—that's Sol's district. And just as the Hudson trains cut in rom the west, the New Haven trains cut in on Sol from the east.

"In the next room here I have two more dispatchers, doing singleack work—a very fine art. One of them works the Putnam Division, ie other works the Harlem Division from White Plains North to Chatham. I'll take you in there later; I want you to meet a grand old eteran, Andy O'Connor.

"Andy travels on a golden pass today; good anywhere on the New ork Central System. That's for fifty years' service, but Andy's had it ow for five or six years. He's an Upstate man, from Boston Corners. In ie Blizzard of 1888, on Sunday the eleventh of March, he walked seven iiles to Mass. . . . Andy is a faithful man.

"But all these dispatchers are faithful men." Andy Durkin threw out is arm in a kind of all-embracing gesture. "They wouldn't *let* me make mistake."

Andy paused for a moment. Solomon Schultz and Harold Stegman, if we had never entered the room, were still at work; lonely, inomitable figures gravely shepherding the trains through the blocks; lling the orders that caused the blade of a semaphore to tumble to the orizontal, or a switch to open, or a train to be swung out of her place in ne to a more favorable track. They were deaf, apparently, to all that ndy had been saying. You could hear their low voices as they almost hispered into the mouthpieces; you could hear faintly the voices of e towermen coming in through the receiving horns. You could hear e crinkle of the paper as the two dispatchers continued spinning

their sheets to the left or right in order to find the proper column fo
each entry.

"These boys," said Andy, "would no more let me make a mistake—
why, I tell you. . . . If either one ever caught me in a false order—he
might be doing something else, he might seem to be miles away in hi
thought, but he'd hear me all right, and he'd be out of his chair in a
flash and he'd be . . ."

The greatest of railroad tragedies are traceable to Dispatcher's errors
Andy did not mention this, but the subject fills a dreadful chapter in
the history of railroading. Well known is the story of the dispatche
who, in a momentary lapse, sent two trains into the same track from
opposite ends of the block. He realized his error just too late; he en
dured the agony of knowing that the wreck would not occur for anothe
ten minutes and that, meanwhile, he could do nothing to prevent it.

The story goes that with calm precision, he called out the wrecker an
sidetracked everything to let the wrecker through; and when he ha
called out the local doctors and ambulances, he knew that the train
would crash head-on in another six minutes—and after that they too
him to the madhouse, where he spent the rest of his days counting th
minutes, up to six.

Lightly, and by way of illustration, Andy touched the desk of Solo
mon Schultz. From this desk, he said, an "open wire" telephone—als
called an "automatic" telephone—runs the entire length of the lin
from Grand Central to White Plains North. The open wire passe
through every tower along the line, and when Sol speaks here at Gran
Central, his voice is heard over loud-speakers in all the towers at once.

"He's addressing a single towerman," said Andy, "but *all* the towe
men hear him, and every towerman hears what every other towerma
says to Sol—for it's a two-way conversation, with loud-speakers instea
of telephone receivers, and microphones instead of telephone tran
mitters. . . . They're all engaged in the one job of ushering the train
through the blocks, and every man is listening in on every other man—
to be aware of the minute-by-minute situation, but also to catch th
first man who makes a mistake. . . .

"But with a good, faithful dispatcher in the chair—" Andy put u his hand in a grave sort of way and slowly shook his head. He did not finish the sentence, but that tranquil gesture was all that was needed to convey his meaning.

Each towerman keeps a record sheet, and it's part of his job to identify every train that passes, Andy told us, and to enter upon the sheet the precise time of her passing. When he's done that, the train is "on the sheet." Steeped in the idiom of the old Morse operators, railroaders call it "*O S*"—then turn the expression into a verb and speak of this part of a towerman's job as *O S*'ing trains. But the job doesn't stop at the tower sheet, and the train is not completely *O S*'ed until the towerman so notifies Dispatcher; whereupon Dispatcher enters upon his own sheet the precise minute at which that particular train passed that particular tower. So Dispatcher's sheet is really a composite of all the tower sheets, and shows at every minute of the day the position of every train on every track within the whole district.

It shows up a gathering traffic jam before the thing can actually eventuate; and signs of a gathering traffic jam are what bring Dispatcher to his feet in a frightful hurry. When things go really wrong, that's when Dispatcher shows his mettle; and on those occasions you can see him, pale with anxiety, barking orders to the towermen, tossing the timetable to the winds and improvising a whole new set of maneuvers; sidetracking the main-liners, getting the commuter trains in motion and speeding them up till they are all back on their proper schedules, then slowly "bleeding" the liners—and after them the freight trains—into the re-established fabric of mutually integrated movements.

A voice awoke in the horn beside Harold Stegman's ear: "Calling Dispatcher—Croton."

"All right, Croton."

"*O S* at Croton, C-r-o-t-o-n, No. 168, o-n-e, s-i-x, e-i-g-h-t, at 10:42, o-n-e, n-a-u-g-h-t, f-o-u-r, t-w-o."

"No. 168 at Croton," Stegman repeated back, "at 10:42. Train number o-n-e, s-i-x, e-i-g-h-t. . . ."

With a flick of his hand, Stegman sent his own sheet spinning across the desk. It's a long sheet; possibly ten feet long. And the bulk of it is always hanging over one or both sides of his desk and curling up at the ends, as if it had recently been rolled in a tube and had not since had the curl taken out of it. Once started, it continued running across the desk of its own momentum, like a broad white ribbon slipping under Stegman's fingers; till Stegman put his hand down and stopped it abruptly, just at the proper column, and entered "10:42" where the vertical column for Train No. 168 crosses the horizontal column for Croton. Then Stegman for the first time lifted his voice.

"Andy," he called, "No. 168 was seventeen minutes late at Croton."

Andy nodded thoughtfully, as if he intended to keep the fact in mind.

The telephone rang and Andy was across the room in two or three long strides.

"As I was saying," he resumed a few minutes later, "these dispatchers are in instant touch with all the towermen; and every minute each knows the whereabouts of every train within his district. He has it on the sheet, of course. But he doesn't have to refer to the sheet. He remembers it; he keeps it up forward in his brain, always ready.

"It isn't as if we had to improvise a new schedule every day. After years of experience, a dispatcher knows the timetable thoroughly, and he only has to look at the clock to tell you—within a few yards—where every train should be. On any given day, then, he notices which trains are running late—and how late. There was No. 168, for example, seventeen minutes late at Croton. Harold won't forget that. . . . He'll have to order the towerman at Spuyten Duyvil to clear through the junction, in advance of No. 168, trains that should normally trail her through. . . ."

"She made up one minute's time getting away from Harmon," Stegman volunteered.

"You see what I mean!" said Andy.

"I was born," said Andy Durkin, "in the Upstate village of Tilly Foster, on the Putnam Division, fifty-six point five four miles north of Grand Central. Tilly Foster had an iron mine when I was a boy; one of those many eastern mines that were put out of business by the opening of the Mesabi Range, in Minnesota. But I read in the *National Geographic* lately that ours in Tilly Foster produced the highest grade ore in the world. . . .

"My father was from the County Sligo, on the west coast of Ireland, my mother from the adjoining County Mayo. It was a love match . . .

they ran away to America. My father found work in Tilly Foster; and my earliest recollections are of playing, as a child, around the railroad station there. Strangely, I can't remember a time when I did not know Morse. From infancy I had heard the chatter of the telegraph in the stationmaster's office, and as a very little boy I could tell by the character of the clicking what it was saying. I believe that this was before I learned to spell. . . .

"I tried hard to get an education. When I was twelve, my elder brother got a job as stationmaster at Carmel, New York; and I went to live with him, because there was a high school at Carmel. I attended high school for less than two years. Then I had to go to work . . . as a messenger boy for Western Union.

"The wages weren't much, but they were needed, little as they were, to let my sister go to Normal School, and let my younger brother stay in grammar school. . . . My sister became a teacher. And William, my younger brother, turned out to be a brilliant scholar. He took his degree at Columbia University, and when he died, in 1938, at the age of forty-nine, he was chairman of the history department at Theodore Roosevelt High School in the Bronx. . . . He slipped in the bathtub in the home he made for Mother. . . . Mother died a short time later.

"I wasn't a messenger long; I quickly became a telegrapher. Then I followed in my elder brother's footsteps and became a stationmaster. You may have heard of my elder brother, Martin Durkin. In the First World War he was a captain in the Army Intelligence Corps, and when the war ended, instead of coming back to the railroad, he became a newspaper man. He died in 1931. He was then the managing editor of the New Orleans *Times-Picayune*. . . .

"I was a stationmaster on the Putnam Division till one day H. E. Brown, the assistant superintendent, dropped in at my station and talked about a great many things. When he was leaving, he said: 'Andy, don't stay on the Putnam; transfer to the main line.' So I applied right away and was made a towerman on the Hudson Division. Four months later I was called in to Grand Central and became a dispatcher. . . .

"I worked hard—it isn't easy, dispatching trains. And then, on the third of June, 1916, I became Chief Dispatcher. . . ."

"Andy!" Solomon Schultz was calling, and there was that in his voice that brought Andy out of his chair with a spring. "Melrose says that Y–71 is stopping at his place!"

"What's she stopping there for?" Andy demanded with an energy we had not previously caught sight of. "Have that conductor call me up instantly!" Fairly blazing with alertness, Andy pounced upon his telephone.

"Train hasn't stopped yet," Schultz continued; and then, through his horn, you heard the voice of Melrose: "Two trainmen are on the ground. . . . Conductor just hit the ground. Engineman says he stopped on air whistle . . . doesn't know what the trouble is. He's already whistled a flagman back to protect his rear. . . . Trainmen are climbing under the third car. . . . Conductor now coming forward. . . . Dispatcher! Conductor of Y–71 reports he stopped his train because he smelled smoke from the rear truck of car No. NH 7958. Investigation showed the generator belt was burning. Belt was removed and conductor is now taking his train to New York."

"Well," said Andy, "that's that. I'm glad it wasn't anything more serious. What's the *O S*?"

Schultz repeated the question: "*O S*?"

"Not yet," said Melrose. "Engineman's whistled in the flagman, but —there! He's just now got the air whistle, and he's starting. . . ."

"*O S*?"

"Not yet. . . . All right, now! No. Y–71, Y-for-Yankee, s-e-v-e-n, o-n-e. . . ."

"Her name," said Andy, "was Mathilda Weber, and she joined the New York Central as a clerk-stenographer in the fall of 1918. She was sent to the freight house in West Thirty-third street, but six months later Superintendent's office here at Grand Central sent out an *S O S* for the most efficient stenographer in the New York terminal division, and right away Trainmaster said: 'I've got her!' And he meant Mathilda . . . and that's how Mathilda came to Grand Central, and that's how I met her—in the spring of 1919. . . . We were married in 1920, and Mathilda was the only bride I ever saw who could hardly have used a coach to take her to the church. She walked straight out the front door of her father's home, straight across the street, and straight down the middle aisle of the Catholic Church of Saint John the Evangelist, over in Bergenfield, New Jersey. . . .

"Today I'm a trustee of that church. . . . We've lived there in Bergenfield ever since our marriage. . . .

"And that's about all—"

"Andy!" This time it was a girl stenographer from one of the near-by offices. She had come in the door with a burst and called his name without realizing that, as it were, he had company. She became confused, embarrassed; but Andy was smiling, and she went to him as a girl would go to her father.

"Andy," she said, "I need your knife again."

Before she could say another word, Andy had whipped the knife out of his pocket, had opened the blade and was giving it to her.

"Thanks, Andy," she said, and was out the door again.

"It's somebody's birthday," Andy explained. "Every time anybody has a birthday around here, the girls find out about it. Then they all chip in and one of them goes out and buys a cake; and that little girl comes in here and borrows my knife to cut the cake. . . .

"It doesn't matter whose birthday it is. You know," he said tolerantly, "it's only an excuse for those young people to stop work for a few minutes and have a party. . . . Come to think of it," he added happily, "this is the second party in two days!"

RED-CAP CHIEF

In the thick of things, out on the Concourse, Jimmy stood like a bronze statue, heavy and solid. There was a movement of his eyes perhaps, for he was there to watch his men, and he has the reputation of one who sees everything. But for the rest he was immobile, impassive. For two minutes by the Golden Clock he never stirred a limb or twitched a feature. He was like an old-time sergeant-major on parade, his body motionless, the corners of his mouth drawn tightly down, his face as unrevealing as the Sphinx. And the effect was striking; suggestive, somehow, of his having simply been left there amid the ceaseless flow of people.

Jimmy—James H. Williams—Chief Williams—is in charge of the red cap force at Grand Central. He has a private office, just beside the gateway to Track 39; but most of the time you'll find him in the Concourse. He is not a tall man, but he gives the impression of having been a powerful man when he was younger; and he carries well the gifts that time has brought him—the iron-gray hair, the heavy fatigue of his brown cheeks, the well-tailored uniform, the cap with its proud legend, "Chief Attendant."

He hardly stirred when we addressed him. He didn't even nod, as any reasonable person would understand a nod. To say he gave half a nod would be an exaggeration. He gave a small fraction of a nod, accompanied by the slightest imaginable change in the placid expression of his face. And when he spoke—very softly, and after the lapse of a second or so—he fixed his eyes upon some object at the far side of the Concourse and pronounced the words as immovably as if they were not his. In anybody else it might have seemed a churlish thing; but Jimmy, in some strange way, made it seem extraordinarily polite.

"I was the first colored man ever employed at Grand Central as a red cap," he said, with a curious detachment. "I came here in April,

1903. . . . Mr. Walsh, the information chief, was a porter then; he was transferred to the clerical force, and I got his job. . . .

"All the other colored men have come here after me. I've seen them come and go, and I've seen some of them 'graduate.' . . . Boys that used to work for me, as red caps here at Grand Central, are professional men today—doctors, lawyers, ministers, architects, college professors. No, they weren't just college boys working as red caps for the summer vacation. They were regular, full-time men, with eight or ten years' service to their names. One was here for fifteen years while to went to night school; he's a certified public accountant today with a good job in Wall street. . . . They're what I call the graduates of the red-cap force at Grand Central."

Jimmy said all this in that strangely reserved way of his; then he heightened the effect of detachment by slowly raising his hands and clasping them together upon his stomach.

"Not every red cap is a colored man," he said. "One is a white man. He's been here longer than I have. He came here in 1900, when the porters all were white. He's the last of them—last of the white porters at Grand Central. . . . You can't see him now; he works nights. Come around tonight; he's on from 4 P. M. to midnight. Ask for No. 148, that's him. His name is Newman—Milton Newman. He's the only Jewish red cap I ever heard of."

Without removing his hands from his stomach, Jimmy slowly unclasped the fingers and clasped them again the other way round.

"I have four children living, two grandchildren and two great-grandchildren," he said. "One of my great-grandchildren—my deceased boy's grandson—is fifteen years old now. My father was still alive when this little fellow was born, and they knew each other for seven or eight years, got along together fine. There were five generations of us then, all living. . . .

"I had six children in all. Now I have two sons and two daughters left. One daughter keeps house for her husband. The other's a trained nurse. My young boy—he's the youngest of the family—is an electrician by trade. My big boy has the highest fire department job ever held by a colored man in American history. He's a battalion chief, commander of the Fifteenth Battalion, New York Fire Department."

Jimmy lowered his eyes as he said this. His soft voice became even softer. His hands fell to his sides. Those were the only outward signs; but by their means, or else by means impossible of detection, Jimmy conveyed very effectively the feeling of immense pride. Then, after a few seconds, he turned to us and bowed a restrained and gravely tranquil bow. It was the high climax of the story of his life, and he was ending the story there. His son is a battalion chief of the New York Fire Department.

"Thanks, Jimmy."

Jimmy bowed again; then for the first time smiled. It was a broad, quiet smile. But it was sudden and, in a way, disconcerting. Jimmy, apparently, had been having a bout with the dentist lately—for the smile was toothless.

They number about three hundred, the Negro red caps at Grand Central; and, if you care about such matters, they do *not* speak the minstrel-show dialect imputed to them by some of our sophisticated magazines. Their grammar is not too bad; for New York, it's better than average. Their diction is good, sound, working-class diction. And years of residence in New York have not robbed them of their deeply melodious voices. All in all, their speech is not unbeautiful; and that's more than can be said for New York as a whole.

Before Pearl Harbor they were young, middle-aged, comparatively old; they ranged from twenty to sixty-seven years of age; they averaged thirty-five. Then the fighting forces drew off all the young men, or nearly all; and some of these aren't back yet, and some won't ever come back. And so today the outside men, recalled from their retirement and still assigned to meet incoming taxicabs, are in three or four instances well over seventy years of age. But they bear their years well; and, as a class, the Grand Central porters are a striking lot of men in their gray whipcord uniforms and red caps.

"Red Cap" is their official designation; not a nickname, it's the term used at Grand Central instead of porter. True, the word "attendant" appears upon their caps, but "red cap" is the expression used in the wage agreements, and on the pay roll, and on the assignment board, and wherever else these men are referred to. Their locker hall, where they change in and out of uniform, and sit or lie down in their rest periods, is the Red Cap Room. (It opens off the northeast corner of the Lower Concourse.) Jimmy Williams, as we have seen, is Chief of the Red Caps. (Two assistant chiefs and sixteen captains serve under him.) And, in fact, a very clear distinction is made between "red-cap work" and the all-embracing duties of an old-time station porter.

There are, of course, the usual number of novices at Grand Central, and among the novices you'll probably find the usual percentage of misfits. Jimmy says it takes two years to whip a red cap into shape, ten years to make a really seasoned man of him. You can pick out these fellows for yourself and, if you're strictly fair, you'll more than probably arrive at some such conclusion as this: that the red cap is a trained manager who takes you in charge as well as your luggage; who steers you the right way, by every possible short cut, and gets you through the gate before the gateman slams it shut; who talks as well as any gentleman's gentleman should; who cheers you with a flashing smile, bows like a nobleman, and—pays you the tribute of overestimating your importance.

THE MERCHANTRY

IT WAS AN Irishman, the brother of an Irish hero, who got things going in the first place. As Ichabod's researches have made abundantly clear, it was Emmet, ably supported by MacGowan, who set in motion that long train of events that culminated in the building of Grand Central Station—just *where* it is, just *as* it is. "And the Irish have had a finger in the pie ever since!" Have it so. Among all the people employed at Grand Central today, Irish names, Irish faces, are unusually numerous.

It isn't to be wondered at, of course, that a very substantial percentage of the railroad employees are of Irish decent; for railroading has been a favorite occupation of the Irish in this country for not less than a hundred years. It was "Paddy on the Railroad" as early as 1850; and by 1900 it was no accident that

Superintindint wuz Flannigan;
Boss av the siction wuz Finnigin . . .

What is at first glance astonishing, however, is that the Irish are just as strong in the non-railroad jobs. It would seem fair to say that "business" at Grand Central Station is to an unusual extent in Irish hands. It may even be said that the Irish have set the business tone at Grand Central.

Let's look at all the stores and shops that make Grand Central a revenue-producing terminal—they face alike on Forty-second street and Vanderbilt avenue; they line the corridors to the east and west of the Concourse; some even face upon the ramps and the Lower Concourse; they represent a total of eighty-four leaseholds. Well, let's look at them.

The first and most lasting impression you receive is that the Irish-American James P. Carey made a huge success of things at Grand

Central. Over the doors of both barber shops appears the legend: J. P. Carey & Co. Over the doors of the haberdashery you read: J. P. Carey & Co. On the windows of the men's clothing shop is painted: Florsheim Shoes—Worsted-tex Suits—J. P. Carey & Co. Presently you discover that the parcel rooms at Grand Central are all operated by the J. P. Carey interests. The large fleet of chauffeur-driven Cadillac cars for rent by the day or mile represents another Carey enterprise; and the Careys also operate the "drive-it-yourself" car-renting agency. What with one thing and another, they conduct twelve different business enterprises at Grand Central; they have (apart from the restaurants) the biggest and the most prominent stores, the cream of the lot; and the impression it makes upon you—such is the sheer power of repetition—is that the J. P. Carey interests are even more widespread than they really are.

The story is told in certain real estate offices—and we ought to take notice of it because it is one of the living legends of Grand Central—that the Careys have a ninety-nine years' lease on all the business space in the terminal, and that all who do business here subrent from the Careys. But the story is not true. All space at Grand Central is rented by the railroad directly to the occupier, and the J. P. Carey concern stands on the same footing as any other tenant. It's the holder of twelve out of eighty-four leases. It isn't the largest tenant at Grand Central. It isn't the oldest.

Actually, the Union News Company stands at the head of the list. Union News is the holder of thirty-six leases. It operates one cigar stand, two soda fountains, nine bootblack stands, twenty-one newsstands. It operates the Gateway Restaurant, at the south end of the last corridor west of the Concourse. It also operates the Grand Central Terminal Restaurant & Oyster Bar.

"And isn't it true that only Christian firms may rent space at Grand Central?"

That's the *whispered* story about Grand Central Station. It is not true. Five or six of the present-day tenants are Jewish. The percentage, it has to be admitted, is unusually low for New York; but the reason for that is not the reason suggested by the whisperers.

The reason is twofold. It relates to the railroad's not unfair practice of allowing its own tenants to bid first for the space that becomes available when expiring leases are not renewed—a practice that makes the way of the newcomer hard no matter who or what he is. And it relates also to the past failure of Jewish families to cling to their holdings at Grand Central. Time was when Jewish merchants here were numerous and well-to-do. The fact is, however, that with hardly one exception, there has never been a second generation of Jewish merchants at Grand Central. Prospering, the Jews almost invariably made accountants, bankers, lawyers and doctors out of their sons, and each business disappeared as the founder of it died. The Mendel family tried to carry on; but their real interests were elsewhere, and after a year or two they gave it up. "Mendel's Restaurant, in the Grand Central Terminal, serves an oyster stew that is famous throughout the country," said *Valentine's Manual* for 1920. But as soon as the lease expired after Abe Mendel's death, his sons pulled up their stakes and got out; withdrew to fairer fields.

The space they vacated was auctioned off among the remaining tenants, the railroad having previously fixed an upset price—a minimum below which no bid would be entertained. If that minimum had not been met, of course, the space would have been advertised, and an outsider might thus have found his way into Grand Central. But the minimum was met and exceeded. Union News was the high bidder, and where Mendel's used to be, the Gateway Restaurant is today.

And it's that time-honored method of auctioning off station space—the established practice of nearly all American railroads, encouraged if not compelled by the anti-discrimination rules of the Interstate Commerce Commission—it's that method of renting, together with the Jewish people's habit of reaching to the professions for happiness, that accounts for the situation at Grand Central today. It's a curious situation. It's a phenomenon that ought to be of more than passing interest to students of social behavior. But it is not a result of discrimination for or against anybody.

Between them, as we have seen, the Careys and the Union News Company hold forty-eight of the eighty-four leases at Grand Central. The remaining thirty-six are divided among twenty-two different tenants—small tenants, mostly—of whom one is particularly interesting. This is the John S. Nicholas Company, florists and fruiterers; and, second only to the Union News Company, the oldest tenants of them all.

As a young man recently arrived from his native Greece, Nicholas opened a fruit stand in the original Grand Central Depot; and his company, now in the hands of his sons, carries us back, as it were, to the golden age of the American railroads. When he began business, the Commodore was still vividly remembered, and the Commodore's great depot was just as he had left it.

It was advertised as the biggest railway station in the world. But it wasn't. It was built when Barnum was in his heyday, and it bore the brand of Humbug.

The New York & Harlem Railroad was still stabling horses and locomotives in the same shed when Commodore Van Derbilt strode upon the scene in 1863. "Mixed operation," by animal and steam traction, was still the order of the day. The terminal—but simply the end of the line—was at the lower tip of City Hall Park; and the steam terminal, the city's first important railway station, was at Fourth avenue and Twenty-sixth street.

This was Harlem Depot, large and handsome, bigger than the City Hall. It was only a few months old that night in February, 1860, when the Connecticut Abolitionists came trooping through on their way to Cooper Union to hear the Senator from Illinois, a man called Lincoln, deliver a speech. Then the troops from Massachusetts passed through on their way to the Potomac—and Harlem Depot, to the end of the Civil War, as the Irishman said, was "like a circus with horses." A rich and handsome young man called Henry Bergh worried about the horses, decided they were poorly treated, organized meetings of protest; and out of those meetings came the American Society for the Prevention of Cruelty to Animals.

Harlem Depot was still the big station when the war was ended and the Down East regiments passed through again on their way home. By then, however, the city had moved back to Thirty-fourth street the deadline decreed against the locomotive; and great teams of sixteen horses each hauled the trains along the first half-mile of the way to New England. Four years later, in 1869, the city rubbed out the line at Thirty-fourth street and drew a new one at Forty-second—and the Commodore retorted by building the new terminal in Forty-second street.

He took all the horses and all the company's line below Forty-second street—including the Murray Hill Tunnel—and transferred them to a subsidiary corporation called the Fourth Avenue Rail-Road; and as easily as that the intermingled forms were divorced, the Fourth Avenue became a streetcar line and the Harlem became exclusively a steam railroad. And Harlem Depot was abandoned. But that was not the end of it. It was handsome and well built, it was the largest thing of its kind in the city. It was turned into a boxing arena. It took a new name and made that name famous—Madison Square Garden.

A great number of iron foundries had sprung up in New York during the Civil War. They were among the town's principal war industries. They specialized, many of them, in casting cannon balls and cannon for the Union armies; and, as profitable contracts were easy to get, they multiplied and expanded, building bigger and better furnaces by the hour, till suddenly the war ended and the bottom fell out of the iron trade. Then, in a desperate fix, the iron masters cast about for something else to keep their furnaces going. And, by a great stroke of luck, they hit upon cast-iron "architectural forms."

These came in a great variety of sizes and shapes, which were, however, always "classic," always "beautiful." They were, in simple fact, columns, arches and pediments, doorways, cornices and window casements—everything, in short, that man had ever dreamed of in the way of stone masonry, all made available now in "handsome," "modern" cast iron. They were a kind of veneer to be applied to the faces of plain brick structures; they were immensely cheaper than cut stone but, properly painted, gave the same general effect—and a New York which had grown tremendously during the war years, and was making a desperate effort to catch up in its building operations, bought them up as fast as the foundries could turn them out.

You can still see these iron fronts, street after street of them, in the older parts of the city; notably in the region west of Broadway between Canal street and Barclay. Even the thousands of people who work back of them today—in the Cotton district, for example—assume that they're of good old solid stone. They're simply hollow iron, anchored to brickwork and covered by now with a half-inch crust of paint. In their day they gave New York a characteristic look; gave her, perhaps, the only aspect she ever wore that was definitely, distinctively, unmistakably New York. And the old Commodore's Forty-second street terminal was that sort of thing—a three-story structure of red brick embellished with tons and tons of cast-iron "trim"—and the trim was painted white to look like marble.

Essentially, the terminal consisted of a train-shed closed in on two sides—south and west—by a comparatively shallow, L-shaped station. We can overlook the train-shed, for the moment; in its own day it was generally overlooked, though it was, in fact, the terminal's one redeeming feature. But it would be ungracious of us to overlook the station, the architect so obviously laid himself out to attract attention. It was, then, a three-storied affair with five towers, and the style was a rather clumsy Renaissance—if so graceful a spirit *can* be clumsy and still be Renaissance. And over it was clapped, willy-nilly, an unusually awkward mansard roof. But it was forceful enough, and against the rather bright red of the bricks the white trim produced, we are told, an "exceedingly gay" effect.

Also, it was big; it was frightfully big. Along the south front, facing Forty-second street, it was 249 feet wide. Along the west front, facing a new street that had no name as yet, it was 630 feet long. And as the palace of the Russian czars reared above the open tundra, so this loomed even bigger than it was above a surrounding wide-open country. To the front of it lay a Forty-second street which up to then had never been paved, and which boasted but a handful of poor dwellings and a few flimsy, one-story clapboard saloons. Cow pastures lay to the west of it, and back of it were the rocks, one of which, within its very shadow, rose a sheer forty feet above the general level. It lay, in fact, so far outside the city that "explorers" armed with yardsticks professed to have found it several inches closer to Albany; and the newspapers agreed, as we have seen, that it was at "the end of the world." But the Commodore, who loved bigness, loved his big new station and gave it that resounding name of Grand Central Depot.

It was to be opened with great celebration on the ninth of October, 1871; and for weeks before that "signal event" in the history of New York the newspapers tried valiantly to find out some of the details. But they tried in vain. The company was silent; it was attempting, perhaps for the first time, a careful considered play for publicity. It was holding back news, reserving everything for a final, heaven-rending burst.

And then the great day came. The city was called upon to rejoice. The flags were out, the drums were beating, the crowds came pouring in. The politicians beamed approval, and the station rang with the eulogies of the orators.

But not one newspaper rose to greet the miracle. The newspapers dismissed it in a single paragraph, or passed over it entirely. The newspapers that day were interested in something else, and so, for that matter, was all New York; for the night before had gone down in history as the night of Mrs. O'Leary's cow, and the ninth of October, 1871, was the day of the Great Chicago Fire.

Grand Central Depot! It was built as a locomotive terminal, but when the Commodore saw what a magnificent thing the train-shed was, he changed his mind . . . and for years to come no locomotive was ever known to enter Grand Central.

Strictly, of course, it was the property of the Harlem Railroad; and for some time, in fact, the Harlem was the only road to make use of it. The more important New-York Central & Hudson-River Rail-Road was prevented from coming in, because the connecting line to Spuyten Duyvil Junction had not been completed. And the New Haven Railroad ran *through* it, and for months to come continued running through it and straight on down Fourth avenue to the old terminal at Twenty-sixth street.

With a no doubt maddening look of embattled righteousness, the New Haven was standing on a point of principle. It had a contract, a perpetual right. And it resented the assault on that right. Grimly suspicious of the Commodore, and perhaps wondering whether in a few years more the Harlem might not abandon even Grand Central and begin using the Central-Hudson terminal over on Tenth avenue—leaving the New Haven high and dry at Woodlawn—the New Haven laid it down firmly and clearly, there and then, that the Harlem had no right to change its terminal, at any time, for any reason, except with the full accord and consent of the New Haven. That was the principle at issue, and while the Commodore fumed and raged, the New Haven put on a great show of stiff-necked Yankee pride and imperturbability, and the great teams of shiny-coated Percherons continued to haul its trains to and from Twenty-sixth street, through a "temporary" opening in the gorgeous new station's Forty-second street façade.

In the closing weeks of 1871, however, the Central-Hudson transferred its passenger services—largely, but not wholly—out of its Tenth avenue terminal and into Grand Central; and in the end, of course, the Commodore had to buy the New Haven's consent to the new arrangement. (Almost immediately, then, the New York & New Haven consolidated with the Hartford & New Haven, becoming thus, in 1872, the New York, New Haven & Hartford.) Part of the price the Commodore paid, presumably, was in giving up the choice position at Grand Central Depot, the entire front of which, facing on Forty-second street, was turned over to the New Haven for its exclusive use.

So there were now three different railroads using it, and the Commodore's beautiful big depot was carved up into three separate stations that lay like dominoes along the south end and the west side of a single train-shed—the New Haven Station, facing Forty-second street; the Harlem Station around the corner from that, facing a newly cut street that presently became known as Van-Derbilt Avenue; and the Central-Hudson Station at the far end of the Van-Derbilt Avenue side, up in the neighborhood of Forty-fourth street. They were all contained in that single L-shaped building the Commodore was so proud of; and they all opened into the train-shed that all three railroads used in common. But they were separate stations, each with its own offices and waiting rooms; and they were not only separate but they were mutually isolated—so that to pass from one to another, a person had to go out into the street.

And that's the kind of station Grand Central was when the elder Nicholas began business here. They've come a long way since then. Perhaps you know their place; it's directly at your right as you come in the main entrance at Forty-second street and Park avenue, a combination fruit and flower shop with a combination ice-cream and luncheon counter along the east wall.

Florists and fruiterers, and restaurateurs besides, the Nicholas Company are also the contractors who put up the Christmas decorations in the Concourse—or have been in the past—and we have their word for it, by the bye, that the great Christmas wreath above the ramp that leads to the Waiting Room is twenty-five feet in diameter and weighs somewhat more than a ton. It's composed of a freight-car load of evergreens and holly, and the bow is made up of a hundred yards of thirty-six-inch wide red ribbon. It used to be built upon the floor, then swung seventy feet in air to its place between the two pillars. In recent years, however, the station has been too crowded for that, and Nicholas has had to build it in mid-air; relays of three men each, at work upon a steel scaffold, complete the job in three days and three nights.

And though it's the biggest, the wreath is only one of the Christmas decorations; but, for all that, the Nicholas firm is known at Grand Central today as the merchants who did business at the Commodore's Grand Central.

The case of the Union News Company is different. Union News, after all, is a corporation; it isn't the same as a small family concern. And Union News never began at the Commodore's Grand Central, anyhow; it began at the old Harlem Depot, down at Fourth avenue and Twenty-sixth street.

The Union News Company! You might suppose from its name that it grew out of a consolidation of newspaper distributing companies; but that isn't so. The Union News Company, the story goes, was named in a spirit of ardent patriotism at about the time of the Battle of Gettysburg; and it was named in honor of that Union that the Federal armies were fighting to preserve. The founder of it called upon Commodore Van Derbilt, who had just then emerged as the owner of the Harlem Railroad. He asked authority to sell newspapers, periodicals and tobacco aboard the Harlem trains, arguing that the passengers' comfort would be served thereby. "Yes, sir," said the Commodore, "but where do I come in?" The poor man was unable to pay cash for the privilege he sought; it was all he could do to risk his daily stock of newspapers. Intentionally or not, the Commodore taught him a lesson; instead of a privilege, he would have a *right*, if he paid for it. And pay for it he did. He agreed to pass through the train first with a bucket of water and a dipper, and to give a drink to each passenger who desired one; and in consideration of that service to the railroad, Van Derbilt sold him the right to hawk his newspapers, magazines and tobacco through each train. He thus became the founder of a pioneer enterprise; he became America's first "train butcher." And his Union News Company, now become a kind of protégé of the Commodore's, has had the "news butchering" contract with the Vanderbilt railroads ever since.

INFORMATION SERVICE

THEY'RE MEMBERS of the Brotherhood of Railway Clerks, and they live in a blaze of questions.

"What time is the next train to Carthage?" "How do you get to Times Square from here?" "Can I get straight-through Pullman accommodations from Indianapolis to Asheville, North Carolina?" "Where can I get a subway to Brooklyn?" "Where can I get the bus to LaGuardia Field?" "Where can I get a shot of whisky and still have time to catch that train for Syracuse?"

"What time is the next train for Greenwich?" "Did I just miss a train for Brewster?" "What time is the next train to Boston?" "Say, Buddy, don't look now, but where do I go to get a marriage license in this burg?"

"Can I go out on the platform to meet a child who's traveling alone?"

"Yes—if the Stationmaster will give you a pass."

"What's the next train for Tonawanda?" "Where can I get my pants pressed around here in a hurry?" "Will the train from Springfield be on time?"

"When does the train leave?"

"What train do you mean?"

"I don't know—the boss is in a rage and he didn't tell me."

"Then, where is he going?"

"He didn't tell me that, either. Must I go back and ask him?"

"Can I buy a ticket straight through to Louisville, Kentucky?" Do you still have a special car for women on the *Pacemaker?*" "What's the fare to Framingham, Massachusetts?"

"Is my niece's train in yet?"

"Where is your niece coming from, Madam?"

"From college. I'm sure I've missed her. Do you think she'll know the way? She's never been in New York before."

"What college does she go to, Madam?"

"Would that make a difference? Vassar, of course."

"Your niece's train has not yet arrived, Madam. Train from Poughkeepsie is coming in now on Track Thirty-seven."

"Oh, thank *you! . . . You said Track Twenty-seven, didn't you?"*

"Thirty-seven, Madam. Track THIRTY-seven."

"Yes, that's what I said. TWENTY-seven. Thank you so much."

"What's the next train out for Yonkers?" "Could I get a Santa Fe timetable here?" "Which is the sunny side of the train?" "Say, where the devil's that young daughter of mine traveling all alone from Vassar College? It ought not be allowed! When did she get in, and where is she now?"

"What time can I get a train for Amsterdam?" "Is there a train from Westport due in about this time?" "How late do you expect that Utica train to be?"

"Where can I get a wheelchair for an invalid arriving on the six o'clock train from Chicago?"

"See any red cap a few minutes before the train arrives. . . . He'll have a wheelchair out on the platform and take it right aboard the train."

"And what's the charge?"

"No charge—whatever you wish to give the red cap as a tip."

"Do you have a Rutland Railroad timetable?" "How do I get to New Jersey from here?" "What's the next train to New Haven?" "Is the *Knickerbocker* in yet?" "What kind of medicine should I bring in case my little boy gets sick on the train?"

"Are dogs allowed on trains going to Canada?" "How far is Saint Patrick's Cathedral from here?" "When is the next train to Rhinecliff?" "Would you please tell a stranger what's the best show to see on Broadway tonight?"

"Can I get a train for Pittsfield, Massachusetts, after seven o'clock tonight?" "Where's a good restaurant around here?" "If I take the *Century* from here tomorrow night, how soon can I be in San Francisco?"

"How much is a Pullman?"

"Where are you going, Madam?"

"That's my business, ain't it?"

"In that case, Madam, the answer to your question is fifty-two thousand dollars. Next."

They live in a blaze of questions, these railway clerks who man the Information Desk below the Golden Clock.

The desk is open twenty-four hours a day; and during the busy hours fourteen clerks are on duty here, each in his own compartment separated from the others by panels of glass. Directly below them, two more clerks are on duty at the Lower Concourse desk; and upstairs, grouped about long tables, as many as thirty clerks may be on duty all at once answering the questions that come in by telephone. In all, day men and night men, desk men and telephone men, clerks and supervisors, they number seventy-two, and their own best guess is that each man answers an average of seventy questions an hour eight hours a day. During the slack period, toward the middle of the afternoon, the questions hardly ever fall to thirty-five an hour. When the pressure is high, they exceed a hundred; and on "peak traffic" occasions—the day before the Fourth of July, for example—many a clerk will answer a thousand questions in a single day. Since 1940 the men themselves estimate, the average clerk has been answering roughly 167,440 questions a year.

To do so, he is required to know—as a matter of duty—the salient facts about all the principal New York churches, hotels, theaters and museums, and all the city's public buildings and notable skyscrapers; in short, he must know all that the stranger may ask about New York. In addition, he must be familiar with the street directories of a dozen other cities, must be well versed in the mysteries of steamship, bus and airline schedules for the whole United States and Canada, and must have a decidedly thorough knowledge of no fewer than sixteen hundred railroad timetables.

And does he? He's always exposed, of course, to any test that may occur to you. Mention Smithers, for example, and see whether the clerk doesn't hand you a Chesapeake & Ohio timetable; or mention Contoocock and see whether he doesn't flip down a Boston & Maine timetable.

If the question is out of the ordinary, he'll call the telephone bureau upstairs where his fellow clerks have access to all sorts of filing cabinets and reference books. Their exploits have the flavor of legend. By lifting up his telephone, back in 1942, one clerk at the Golden Clock was able to report in thirty-three seconds that the *Empire State Express* on the night of June the twenty-fifth, 1927, arrived on Track 39 at 9:57 o'clock. In seventeen seconds another clerk found out the date of Martha Washington's death. (The rule is that no question is silly, and that every question must receive the correct answer if it's within the power of the bureau to supply it.) And in twenty-nine seconds a third clerk turned up the name of Tut-ankh-amen's first wife.

Any questions?

"It takes two years under the Clock to train a self-assured, competent information clerk." "Most of the men have worked previously in railway information booths all over the country." "Some are ex-gatemen." "What's needed is a good memory, a tractable temper, a pleasing voice, and the ability to talk well." "The first rule is that every question is serious. It may sound frivolous, or even crazy, but to the man who's asking it, it's serious. We have to assume that." "With some people, a foolish question seems to be a necessary prelude to sensible speech. It breaks the ice, and gradually then, with a little cross-examination on our part, they get round to what they mean." "Sometimes I lose my temper; not often, though. Did you hear me tell that woman a Pullman car costs fifty-two thousand dollars? Well, it does—plus haulage from Pullman, Illinois."

Year in and year out, the clerks agree, the women take the cake for asking foolish questions. The men give them a good run for their money, though; and the margin isn't anything for the men to crow over. On the other hand, when the question is sensible and the answer is long and complicated, the women seem to be "quicker on the uptake" than the men; and, among foreigners, the Chinese of all people in the world appear to be the quickest. The clerks explain this by observing that the average man knows a great deal to begin with, but allows his knowledge to stand in the way of his learning something new; whereas the average woman begins by assuming that she is about to hear the final authority on the subject, and the Chinese begins, as it were, with a clean slate, having no formidable background of information with which every new fact has to be reconciled. In short, the women are given less, and the Chinese are given least of all, to "fighting" new information.

Any further questions?

"No, the work is not tedious, but—once you've mastered it—very interesting. After all, you're setting people straight, and that's a worthwhile job, isn't it?" "Information is one of the most important services of any railroad." "The manager is William P. Walsh. He came to Grand Central back in 1900, when he got his first job as a porter. There were only twelve porters here in those days, and all of them were white men."

"Hard nuts to crack? Plenty. There was the man who telephoned all the way from Rochester, asked us to look around the station for his son, who was a sailor, and tell him to come to the phone. As the place was full of sailors, we had to beg off. . . ."

"There was the woman who came up, all out of breath, and laid down a nursing bottle. . . . She asked us could she have it delivered to her baby aboard a train that left here half an hour earlier."

"There was the woman who forgot something and asked us to hold her baby while she dashed back to Macy's to get it. She left the baby on the counter and was gone before we could call a cop. We had to get a nurse down from the Medical Department to take charge."

"There was that fellow who spika da English no good. He had two clerks tied up for ten minutes trying to make out what he was trying to say. It was broken English of the Italian variety, so we sent for the night supervisor, Eugene Peduzzi, who spoke to him in Italian. The fellow stared for a minute, then grinned and said he was just an actor practising for a part on the stage. He had to play the part of an Italian immigrant . . . so he tried it out on us."

"There was the call for a surgeon who was needed to perform an emergency operation at once. He was aboard a train that pulled out a full two minutes before the call came in. . . . We got him off that train at 125th street."

They're members in good standing of the Brotherhood of Railway Clerks. They talk well. They remember everything. They're the best men in all New York to spin a tale and weave a story. And every hour of their working lives they live in a blaze of questions.

"What's the next train for Port Chester?" "Is there a train from Yonkers pretty soon?" "How do I get to the New York City Hall?" "How much is the fare from here to Harrisburg by the Pennsylvania Railroad?" "Say, bud, did you see a woman around here in a green hat?"

To take him at his face value, Bill Walsh is one of the mildest, gentlest men in all New York; and it would be a tenable opinion that he was placed at the Information Desk, as a young man, precisely for his face value. His face is round and full, his smile is frequent, childlike and soft; and any small boy would know instinctively that he's the sort of man would listen to a small boy's troubles and answer his questions.

He has a private office today. Room 2804 of the Terminal Office Building is called the telephone room; there the most recent changes in railway timetables, hospital visiting hours and Canadian quarantine laws are chalked upon blackboards, along with a host of other "useful" facts; there the "upstairs" clerks answer the questions that come by telephone; and there, at one end of the room fenced off from the rest by glass partitions, Bill has his private office and his private secretary. He stands up as you walk in upon him, and—as you see him for the first time, wreathed in smiles, at the far side of a huge flat desk—it strikes you rather forcibly that you've seen him before—or someone very like him.

You remember that round, cheerful face. You remember the spectacles, and the tired eyes that beam through them at the world, benign and friendly. You remember the whole figure of the man; not big, but agreeably large, comfortably bulky. And then it occurs to you, and you *do* remember; it occurs to you that if it were not for his pallor, if he only had a complexion, Bill Walsh would be the living image of Mr. Pickwick.

Appearances, of course, can be deceptive, and it would be foolish—as in the case of Winston Churchill, for example—to presume upon a childlike smile. Bill Walsh has the reputation of a good executive, and he keeps a tight control over his seventy-two clerks. He has a means of listening in upon their telephones, and Heaven help the clerk who fails in courtesy! For all his gentle demeanor, Bill has a touch of iron in him, too.

But that is not to say that the manner belies the man. The immortal Pickwick himself blew up on occasion: "In the frenzy of his rage, he hurled the inkstand madly forward, and followed it up himself." And Bill Walsh can be indignant too; but, essentially, Bill is just as mild as he looks, and the more you see of him the more certain you become that he asks little of his clerks, really, except that they share his own gentle enthusiasm for meeting people and solving their problems. It may not be true that Bill looks upon these people as "the meek and humble of the earth, needing protection in a rough world"; but it certainly is true that what stirs his wrath, what "gets his Irish up," is the slightest sign of arrogance toward them.

It puts him in a strange light; for a cynical world is not easily convinced of the genuineness of a spirit so naïve and so abounding in good will. But there is about Bill a simplicity of mind that baffles the cynic; and when he tells you, as he often does, that "the public is my friend, and I wouldn't like to hurt the feelings of my friend," you may be astonished, but you find yourself believing him just the same.

Employed by the terminal authorities—that is to say, by the two railroads jointly—Bill takes the view that his whole duty is toward the public. And he runs his office on that principle, passionately. All of which accords very well with railroad policy, of course; and if we grant Bill's deep sincerity, we can also admit that he never arrived at his present job, as Chief of Information Service, by accident.

Fresh out of Saint Patrick's parochial school over in Newark, New Jersey, he began work at the old Grand Central Station as a porter. That was back in 1900, three years before the first Negro porter appeared upon the scene.

"There were twelve porters then," said Bill; "but as half of us worked nights and none worked more than six days a week, there was seldom more than four or five on duty at the same time. . . .

"The work was different from that of the red caps today. About the only red-cap work we did was to load bicycles on the trains. For the rest, we were simply station workers assigned to various tasks. One, for example, was an interpreter. He was a good linguist; spoke eight languages. And those days, you know, the immigrant ships were bringing in hundreds of thousands of people every year. . . . Millions, in all, passed through Grand Central. Special immigrant trains took them to the Middle West. . . .

"Other porters specialized in train information. These fellows were posted one in each of three different stations. Every fifteen minutes they received by messenger boy from Dispatcher's office a sheaf of 'flimsies'—thin tissue-paper carbon copies of the towermen's reports that came in over the open-wire telegraph. . . . And when that original Grand Central was rebuilt for the first time, these information porters were brought together at a single desk. Half the desk was inside the new Waiting Room that faced Forty-second street, and the other half was out facing the concourse, under the Big Shed. That's how the Information Service began as a separate department.

"But I," said Bill, "was not one of those information porters, so I was not one of those first men to be classified as information clerks. I was still only a boy, newly arrived on the job. . . . When the first colored porter came here in 1903—that's Jimmy Williams, you know—I was made a messenger-clerk in the superintendent's office for a few months, and a clerk in the terminal manager's office for a few months more. And then, about a year after it was organized, I was assigned to the Information Desk.

"Edward J. Bradley was the chief in those days. I followed him up the ladder. I was with him when he had only two or three clerks, and I was his assistant chief when he had sixty."

Bill Walsh turned in his chair; pointed to a large framed photograph on the wall behind him.

"That's Ed Bradley," he said, "and a better man never lived."

In the telephone room, outside Bill Walsh's private office, you caught the clatter of a dozen different voices; uncommonly clear and melodious voices; carefully selected voices.

"We have an unusual machine here," said Bill. "It's an automatic switchboard . . . operates by relays. All the incoming calls pass through it. It distributes the calls automatically to all these various extensions. Up to a point, it distributes them in regular order—the first call to No. 1 extension, the second call to No. 2 extension, and so on. But if any given extension is busy when its turn comes, the automatic distributor passes it over. . . . And when all the extensions are busy at once, when we have 'a full house,' which is often enough, the automatic switchboard continues to receive every call that comes along. It stores them up, and distributes them in the order in which they came as fast as extensions become available. . . ."

With a kind of strange harmony, the clatter of voices went on. "Information!" ". . . the *Century* won't be in till very late this afternoon, Madam. We don't know. . . ." "Information!" ". . . leaves at four o'clock from Track . . ." "Information!" ". . . have to call the Reservation Bureau, Sir. We don't . . ." "Information!" " . . . Yes, Madam, this *is* the Information Bureau."

Bill Walsh smiled tolerantly.

"People haven't got use to our system yet," he said. "When they call us up, they expect a switchboard operator to answer them first, and so they go on asking to be switched over to the Information Bureau . . ."

"Information!" ". . . No, Madam, dogs may not enter the State of Vermont unless accompanied by a State or Federal certificate of health . . ." "Information!" ". . . Painted Post is on the Erie Railroad, Sir . . ." "Information!" ". . . you were properly advised, Sir. The fare from New York to Texas may be as much as three dollars more than the fare from the same point in Texas to New York. It's strange but true . . ." "Information!" ". . . tell the conductor you wish to stop over at Syracuse, and he'll . . ." "Information!"

"The one rule," said Bill Walsh, "is courtesy. I'm fanatical on that! As I said before, the public is my friend, and my boys here treat the public that way . . ."

"Information!" . . . "Information!" . . . "Information!"

RED-CAP PREACHER

IT WAS 12:06 by the Golden Clock, and deep in the northeast corridor seven men were gathered about the gate that leads to Track 13—an architect, a lawyer, a Canadian army chaplain, an office man, a company director, a Negro in the uniform of an elevator operator, a tall, thin, ascetic-looking sea captain in the gold braid of the Merchant Service. They were huddled all together, close to the gate. But no train was leaving from Track 13; the board was blank, not lighted. The men stood laughing and talking and shaking hands with one another. They were obviously glad and happy men; the mark of elation was in their eyes and in their talk. It was apparent that, however different in other ways, they were all alike men of enthusiasm; and, undoubtedly, men of the same enthusiasm; men who shared a common preoccupation that lifted them above the fretfulness and worry of the world. In short, they were men who had "found" themselves.

A red cap hurried to them, full of apologies for being late; and there was a new round of enthusiastic greetings and shaking of hands. The red cap—a light brown man of forty-five or so, slender and perhaps a shade below middle height—drew forth a bunch of keys at the end of a long brass chain. He opened the gate. The little group passed through; and we, of course, went with them. The red cap closed and locked the gate again. You may have heard about this man—Red Cap No. 42, Ralston Crosbie Young.

He smiled quickly.

"Just call me Ralston," he said; "it makes me feel I know you better."

Ralston led the way to a train that was lying idle on Track 13; "spotted" there, made up and ready for the evening race home to the suburbs. The cars were unlighted; and the car we entered remained unlighted, except by the rays of a platform light just outside the windows. The backs of two seats were flipped forward; and, with the usual squeezing and turning and bumping of knees, the seven men sat down in two groups directly across the aisle from each other. Ralston continued talking all the while.

"We come here three times a week," he said; "every Monday, Wednesday and Friday at noon. . . ."

Then he sat down and, for a moment, all was quiet.

"Jim," said Ralston finally, addressing the elevator man, "you begin"; and Jim began, leaning close to the window to catch as much light as he could upon the page of his Testament:—

Know ye not that so many of us as were baptized into Jesus Christ were baptized unto His death? Therefore we are buried with Him by baptism into death: that, like as Christ was raised up from the dead by the glory of the Father, even so we also should walk in newness of life.

Ralston seized upon the closing words.

"Newness of life!" he exclaimed. "That very thing God has given me!" And he went on from there, telling of many things, but telling in particular of the wretchedness, the sense of desolation and defeat, he endured for the better part of twenty years in a job—the red-cap job—that was hateful to him. But now— The words, of course, were not those of a theologian; they were those of a sincere and simple man who has made the great discovery that the spirit of man is free, and that, from the all-important point of view, it matters little what we do for a living, it matters tremendously how well we do it.

"No, sir," said Ralston with emphasis, "I wouldn't change this job now for the biggest pulpit in the city. I mean exactly that. . . . Grand Central Station is a parish—a big one, too; and a mighty good one."

Others broke in upon him, eager to give similar testimony out of their own lives; and when they had all had their say, and quiet had once more fallen upon that strange meeting of six white men and two Negroes, Ralston again assumed the leadership. He recalled that he had been the subject, some time earlier, of an article in the *Reader's Digest*. As a result of the appearance of that article, he had received a great volume of fan mail. Now he had still another letter. He reached into his pocket, drew the letter forth. He leaned toward the window for light. In a rich, clear voice, he read the letter through. It was a long letter:

Just this minute I finished reading . . . 'The Most Unforgettable Character I've Met' . . . In looking through my scrapbook I've found a baggage-check on which I'd written 'Red Cap 42!' I put it here to remind me of an unforgettable meeting—one of many during the day for you, but a God-sent few minutes for me.

I had just arrived from overseas . . . my nerves were pretty raw . . . I made the station just in time . . . It was right then, when my patience was at the breaking-point, that you appeared and said in quick succession, not giving me time to answer at all: 'Red cap, sir? . . . Which train? . . . Follow me, please.'

Well, we hurried along . . . neither of us said anything. I was trying to quell my hate of people, when you suddenly said, 'Captain, you gotta forgive some of these people. They haven't ever seen a Jap or lost a buddy.' It wasn't so much what you said, although it explained every bit of my feelings . . . it was the way you said it—and some hidden power behind the way you said those words that drove them in deep.

When you had deposited me on the train, and before you left, you spoke again, 'Thank you, sir, for what you've done. Please—don't thank me.' And you hurried away. I hadn't said a word . . . because I couldn't—and the tip was still in my hands! Your words, and the way you said them, were more valuable to me than any other thing . . . God bless you.

Ralston paused after reading the letter. Then: "I must say this makes me happy—very happy. But here's the real point, fellows: You know I expect to see that man again. I've written him and told him of our fellowship meetings here three times every week, and if he's ever in New York again I'm sure he'll drop in—yes, sir, I'm sure he will."

"We should all pray for him," somebody suggested.

"And pray now," said Ralston.

The eight men bowed their heads, and in the quiet of the empty day-coach, Ralston raised his voice again. "In Our Lord's words," he began, "may we be so bold as to say: 'Our Father, Who art in Heaven . . .' "

The prayer ended. The meeting broke up. The others hurried off to their luncheons. It was 12:18.

Ralston stayed behind a moment—to turn the seats back to their proper positions, to draw the shades again, to search the car carefully so as to make sure that his "parishioners" had left not even the tiniest scrap of paper for the trainmen to pick up after them. Then, when he was satisfied that the car was just as he had found it, Ralston left.

"We try to have the meeting over in ten minutes," he said, and then, in a kind of ecstasy demanded: "Isn't it wonderful, isn't it glorious, our coming together to talk of Christ in Grand Central Station? . . .

"We just talk," he hurried on to say; "talk and pray together . . . a group of men meeting with one accord to find a solution of our problems through Christ. That's the crux of the thing. It's missionary work. . . . One thing I want to emphasize, it's bringing men to Christ. I had to pray very hard before I began this work. I didn't know how the other red caps would take it . . . and even yet I've only succeeded in getting one red cap to join us occasionally. . . . The others, mostly, are passengers whose bags I've carried. . . .

"Now . . . the pet in my heart is to have a regular chapel in Grand Central Station, where people of all faiths can find peace and quiet and pray together. One chapel, not three! . . . The world must have Christ. They can't get along without Christ. . . ."

We were through the gate now, and Ralston, still speaking, turned to lock it.

"And how," he demanded, "are we going to bring them all to Christ if we have three different chapels?"

There was a sharp, querulous cry of "Porter!" There was a cheerful, almost joyous, cry of "Yes, sir!" And Red Cap No. 42 was back again at his work of carrying other people's bags—and, be sure of it, sharing their burdens.

It was not that the organ concert had begun at noon; what struck you with astonishing force was that the station, at this particular juncture, was ringing with the triumphant "Hallelujah Chorus" from Handel's *Messiah.*

STATION MUSICIAN

SHE'S A woman's woman, somewhat statuesque and with a flair for flowered hats; with a laughing smile, pink cheeks and bright blue eyes. It's unimportant, perhaps, that she's a member of the American Federation of Musicians, and that she's paid union wages for playing the organ at Grand Central. What's very important is that she believes her work to have a missionary value. She calls herself quite frankly a missionary of the Baptist Church. She's here to celebrate, and help spread the celebration of, the two great festivals of Christmas and Easter. Womanly, she tops her printed program with a staff on which a scroll-letter *R* appears as a different kind of clef-sign, followed by three notes—*E*, *A* and *D*. Her name, you see, is Read.

Her married name is Read; but her maiden name also was Read. Her father was a Confederate soldier who named her in honor of his general, Mary Lee. She married a Canadian who was also a distant cousin, and also a musician. Today, though you'd hardly guess it, she's a grandmother.

And she is, as we have seen, the only organist in the city forbidden to play "The Star-Spangled Banner." She played it once, some years ago. Amid the evening rush on the day after Pearl Harbor, she pulled out all the stops and played it *con fuoco*—and played the devil with the crowds. She brought the whole Concourse to "attention." She halted the flow of people; she caused a major traffic jam. She made commuters stop dead in their tracks and miss their trains—and among commuters it's considered just a bit disgraceful to miss a train. Within five minutes the railroad authorities had stepped in, and the national anthem was henceforth reserved for more appropriate places.

A harpist and pianist as well as an organist, Mrs. Read took a master's degree in music at Stephen's College, Missouri; and, back in 1921, she played at Denver, Colorado, what is believed to have been America's first railway-station concert. She came to Grand Central in 1928 with an electric organ borrowed from one of the city's big stores; and almost at once other stores came forward, demanding that they too be allowed to lend organs in return for the little line of type on the printed concert program that told where the organ came from. Among the terminal authorities there had been a great deal of disputing, the story goes, over the propriety of spending money for music in the Concourse; but the flood of letters that presently poured in from the public in praise of the idea settled the question for the moment. And when the letters showed no sign of falling off, but seemed even to gain in volume as the years went by, the authorities went further and purchased an organ of their own—an electric organ of Mrs. Read's own choice—so that they no longer would have to borrow one.

The "Hallelujah Chorus" had ended when we arrived at the east end of the Philosophers' Gallery, and Mrs. Read was busy showing off the console to a crowd of people who had gathered round. It's a two-manual console, with the usual pedals running two octaves below the "great" keyboard. The whole contrivance is mounted on runners, and thus is moved across the marble floor to the storage room where it remains between concerts.

With the power turned off, Mrs. Read ran her fingers lightly over the keys as she told the reasons for the two manuals, and went on then to explain the stops and the swell and the pedals, and why music is God's universal language and how she had dedicated herself to music at Grand Central.

"I bowed my head in prayer," she said, telling of that first day she had ever seen Grand Central, back in 1928, "and I asked God if I might be allowed to put music here, and that, if it were His Will, I would devote my life to that work. . . ."

Her next piece was "The Angels' Song" by Stickels; and after that she told of the four or five hundred letters she wrote every month to service men and women overseas all through the late war.

"Thousands of lads and lassies in uniform from all over the world," she said, "gathered round the organ here, when they had a few minutes' time while passing through Grand Central. They asked me to play their favorite hymns and love songs, and I wish you could hear them sing! Thousands of them wrote to me afterward, and I answered every letter within twenty-four hours. . . .

"There's a side to those boys in uniform that New York never seemed to realize. Soldiers, sailors and marines, only one in ten asked for anything jazzy. Six out of every seven, from the very beginning of the war to the end, wanted hymns—old-fashioned hymns, the kind you hear in country churches. . . .

"Most of them," said Mrs. Read, "wrote their names and addresses in this old hymnbook. I told each one I'd pray for him. Mostly their eyes filled up. . . ."

It was time for the next number now, and Mrs. Read began a piece of her own composition, "To the Navy." It was a spirited thing, and as she played it with obvious enjoyment, she turned to look down upon the Concourse. There was a rollicking passage that was rising to a good climax—but the climax never came. She was modulating; she was getting out of it, fast. She was improvising for a moment; covering up. And then, looking somewhat relieved, she was safely into Handel's "Largo." She played it through to the end.

She switched off the power again when she had finished. She sighed; then, turning full upon us, demanded: "Did you see that?" Of course, we had not seen that; and so she told us that just as she was reaching the high point of her own piece, she had caught sight of a funeral procession crossing the Concourse for one of the train gates.

"An awful lot of funerals pass through Grand Central," she said. "An awful lot of sorrow mixes in with all the doings in the Concourse. . . ."

It was 12:37 by the Golden Clock—time passes rapidly when you're listening to music. It was nearly time for us to meet the Stationmaster. But before we left, Mrs. Read had one thing to ask of us.

"I have some Testaments here," she said. "Would you like to have one?"

STATIONMASTER

STATIONMASTER'S OFFICE lies opposite the gateway to Track 34, just about halfway between the Concourse and the Arrival Station. It faces eastward upon the first corridor west of the Concourse; it lies at the corner of that corridor and the northwest passageway that links the Concourse and the Vanderbilt avenue gallery; and so it lies, too, at the southeast corner of that broad gallery.

As you come in from the east—from the general direction of the Concourse—you're confronted by a counter, back of which either of two clerks may be on duty. And beyond the counter you see the spiral staircase that leads to the men's locker room below; a few chairs and desks, a few telephones and typewriters; the usual flimsy files that railway clerks work with the whole world over. Telautograph and teletype machines are there too. They keep the staff abreast of train information; but their main purpose is to notify the Head Doorman—that's Fred Springsteel at this time of day—what gate his men must open at the very moment of each train's arrival.

Anne Hall was at the counter as we walked in; tall, brown-eyed, rosy-cheeked. At Mount Saint Ursula's Academy in the Bronx, a few years back, she was Anne O'Connor. She afterward took up dramatics and, by her ability and fine voice, won the attention of her teacher, who had been at the Moscow Art Theater. But when she married a pilot in the Army Transport Corps, she calmly turned her back upon the stage and all it seemed to promise her. She took a "wartime" job with the railroad. It's lasted long after the war, because Lieutenant Hall, one of the last officers to be sent overseas, is not yet home. And when he comes home, says Anne, she'll turn her back upon the railroad, too; and, if that calls for any explanation, it's because her father and mother both were born in the County Cork, and it's an old Irish tradition, and she comes of a big family herself, and—

"When Lieutenant Hall comes home," said Anne, "the first thing we're going to do is have a big family of children—an ideal married life. . . .

"Wait now," she abruptly added; "I'll see whether Mr. Connors is in."

Joe McAvoy walked over from his desk at the far side of the room; he's the chief clerk of this office, a brown-eyed, smiling Fordham Prep man with ten years' service on the railroad. But he had hardly begun to speak when Joe Guardino strode swiftly into the room on his way back from luncheon; with a flick of his arms threw off his overcoat and, just as lightly, threw off a "Good afternoon" to Mr. McAvoy, his immediate superior, and another one, accompanied by a broad, good-natured smile, to us. Once or twice earlier today, we had seen something of Joe Guardino. In the complex world of railway classifications, he occupies the position of stenographer-clerk, the same as Mrs. Hall; but he spends less time at the typewriter than at the counter meeting people, or out in the Concourse conveying messages to one or another of the assistant stationmasters. He's well suited to the job of meeting people—a cheerful young man with a good-natured face, good teeth, an abundance of wavy black hair, and a flair for jaunty clothes.

Serious, conservative, hard-working Joe McAvoy excused himself to call the other Joe's attention to some note or other upon his desk; then turned round to us again and began to say what, presumably, he had intended to say before he was interrupted.

"Stationmaster at Grand Central," he said, "is one of the neutral terminal officials, serving equally the interests of the Central and the New Haven railroads. . . . At the top is the terminal manager, and directly below him are Chief Dispatcher, Tower Director, Stationmaster. . . .

"Stationmaster has four principal departments under his supervision and control: the Red Cap force, the gatemen, the Information Service and the assistant stationmasters. There are seven assistant stationmasters, so that two are always on duty. . . . Their main job is to supervise the loading of the trains, to see that every passenger gets aboard safely, and the train steps off on time. . . ."

Anne Hall was back now, and Stationmaster was with her—Stationmaster Edward J. Connors, a short, broad-shouldered man with a hard face and a soft smile; a slow, thoughtful smile, bespeaking a certain gentle-mindedness. He spoke in soft and gentle tones; and his diction was that of a man who reads a great deal, and discriminates between words.

In the end, though, he didn't say very much—about himself, that is. He spoke about his clerks, what excellent persons they were. But what he said about himself boils down to two or three statistics: Railroad service record, fifty-three years; assistant stationmaster, thirty-five years; Stationmaster, since April of 1941.

And now he would have to go back to his private den; he bade us good-by, and that expressive mouth of his curled upward at the corners in the gentlest sort of smile.

"Good-by now," said Mrs. Hall—she always adds the "now," Irish-wise, lest anyone think she means forever.

"Good-by," said Joe McAvoy, thoughtfully.

Joe Guardino waved from his desk on the far side of the room. "I'll see you some more," he said brightly.

LUNCHEON FOR 10,000

It was 12:46 by the Golden Clock. The Concourse was livelier now. The luncheon crowds were coming in; and coming in with a rush. A certain gaiety came in with them. There was laughter and a kind of nervous shouting:

"Susie! Susie!"

"Good-by, Miss Williams." "Good-by, Allan! Good-by, girls!"

"Isn't it a glorious day? This kind of weather ought to be encouraged!"

"You must meet her! She's lovely!"

"Aren't they pretty? Smell them!"

There was laughter, and there was song, as a group of elated youngsters went trooping through the Concourse (New York Central property), chanting saucily the praises of "the Atchison, Topeka and the Santa Fe."

There were questions put to us:

"Friends, where could I find a barber shop in this estimable joint?"

"Which way out to Saint Agnes's Church?"

"Not a restaurant to be seen! But there is one hidden away someplace in Grand Central, isn't there?"

There were questions galore, there was laughter and song. There was the loud, carefree whistling of some bright spirit on his way to a good luncheon. And, as if insisting on the railroad's right to some attention, there was the incessant cry of the gatemen: "All tickets, please! Have your tickets ready!" The Concourse was flooded with sunshine. True, there was an undertone of tension still, but you could almost forget it. The crowd was in a jaunty mood.

It was the usual luncheon crowd, pouring in from all the surrounding skyscrapers; the same crowd that's been coming in at this hour every day for years and years, and will continue to do so, the chances are, for years and years to come. Some of them are ageless—the little cashier, who bounces as she walks in her ultra-high-heeled shoes; the white-haired office messenger, who talks about energy and grit, and about the book he read, called *Maxims of Napoleon;* the man who wears the black derby and the black suit and the high white collar that was fashionable back in 1916; the girl who wears the blue cape to conceal her withered left arm; the woman who wears the long skirts to hide her clubfoot. Every day they cross the Concourse on their way to luncheon; and so do the thousands of others—the stout and puffing fellows who in loud voices announce their preference for the Oyster Bar (where the dollar check is king); the pallid little fellows who patronize the sandwich counters (where coffee is still five cents a cup); and the in-between fellows who take their luncheon at the Gateway (where the check runs to sixty or seventy cents). And, mixing in with all of these, is the vast battalion of office girls. Dot and Carrie are a huge part of Grand Central. Some are saleswomen. A few have jobs in advertising agencies. The great majority are telephone girls, bookkeepers and stenographers—plain stenographers, who (curiously) are the prettiest; stenographers of a higher order, who call themselves secre-terries; and stenographers of the highest order, who call themselves secre-trees. Girls and women, men and boys, the employer and the employed, the mature and maturing and those who will never mature no matter how long they live—they all come trooping in together, mingling together. And the Concourse rings with their chatter:

"O. K., we're all together now. Let's go!"

"We can handle twenty carloads a week without embarrassment. Beyond that we begin to feel the pinch."

"Who wants an easy job? I had an easy job once—developed ingrown brains."

"But he ain't got the charm Al Smith had."

"Where do we eat?"

You know that the Waiting Room lies between the Concourse and Forty-second street, somewhat above the level of the one, somewhat below the level of the other; so that if you come in by the main door from Forty-second street and Park avenue, you walk down one ramp to he Waiting Room and down a second ramp to the Concourse. That's ne of the first things you observe about Grand Central.

But if you enter from the corner of Forty-second street and Vanderilt avenue—that's where the greatest crowds of all come in—you ollow a single ramp that brings you (northward) to the first corridor est of the Concourse; and from there you can walk obliquely (northastward) into the Concourse; or, turning to the right, you can follow nother ramp that takes you (eastward) down to a sort of landing stage here three ramps come together in full view of the Lower Concourse. nd this landing stage, a full story down, lies plumb below the ramp hat links the Concourse and the Waiting Room.

It's a vital point in the whole system of things at Grand Central. o reach it, you have just walked down the first ramp. By continuing traight ahead (eastward) you could now walk up the second ramp to a orridor east of the Concourse; by turning left, you could walk down he third ramp (northward) to the Lower Concourse; or, by turning ight, you could—as we did—step through a doorway (southward) into he foyer of the Grand Central Terminal Restaurant & Oyster Bar. Nothing elegant, it's a plain and hearty place; it has the longest name f any well-known restaurant in New York; and it smells simply grand.)

The dining room, over which the celebrated Gil presides, is to the ft as you come in; and the oyster bar is to the right—the oyster bar self plus the quick-service counters and the tap room. The dining oom is quiet, almost serene. But the oyster bar, at luncheon time, hrobs with a life that's loud and cheerful. Oyster bar and dining room –under a round-arch vaulted ceiling, they lie at either side of the oyer, one story down below the Waiting Room. And, by a stairway, n fact, you can pass directly back and forth between the foyer and the Vaiting Room.

Celebrities are not rare in the dining room, and Gil, the head-waiter –Anthony Gil, a laughing, blue-eyed Spaniard, small and stout—has great list of autographs of famous persons who have dined here. Ieading the list are two Chief Justices of the United States, Hughes nd Taft. Taft, says Gil, was an especially frequent guest, for he loved eñor Gil's fruit-and-vegetable salads, piled mountain-high with baked pples.

At the other side of the foyer Nick, successor to the mighty Viktor, presides in full canonicals over the oyster bar—which is likewise something of an institution, said to be the busiest oyster bar in the world.

Nick tells you, confidently, that no other bar even approaches his; and, if you want figures, he has them ready for you, too. Nick says he serves 1,500 customers on a dull day, 2,000 on a busy day; and—on the average—his customers consume 25,000 oysters a day all winter long. Thirty-six oyster-men work under him; and of these, twenty-six have been here for a quarter of a century. There is no word for them but "artist," according to Nick; and they're forever turning down offers to take charge of oyster bars all over the country.

It was Viktor who made the bar famous—Viktor Yesensky, a blond, blue-eyed Slav, born on a mountain farm in land-locked Slovakia; Viktor Yesensky, who was full-grown before he ever saw an oyster.

After an apprenticeship in Paris, he came to this country in 1905, and found work in the kitchen of the famous old Hotel Reisenweber. His rise was swift. Within two or three years he was a chef, and one or two years later he took charge of the oyster bar at the Hotel Knickerbocker (now become the Newsweek Building) at the southeast corner of Broadway and Forty-second street. He was again remarkably successful; almost overnight he made the Knickerbocker famous for the "best oyster stew on Broadway," and—as he worked on a commission basis—he had reason to rejoice.

Then, in the autumn of 1912, two things happened. The new Grand Central Station was so near completion that the railroad was able to show it off to its prospective tenants. Abe Mendel, who had had the great restaurant in the old Grand Central, would in the normal course of events have taken over the principal restaurant in the new. But Abe, when he saw where the restaurant was to be, tucked away back of the ramps, completely out of sight of both the Concourse and the Waiting Room, and with hardly any window space—when he saw this, Abe shook his head. And when the space was auctioned off, Abe selected the corner room, now occupied by the Gateway Restaurant. Shrewd business men agreed that he had done the wise thing.

The main restaurant, then, was knocked down to the Union News Company; and, as Mendel's had always been famous for its oyster bar —and would continue to be, as a matter of fact, for another ten years—

Union News looked about for the best oyster chef that love or money could buy. Union News went to Viktor, and Viktor agreed, as he used to say, on a moderate salary but a high commission.

He opened up the new oyster bar on the day the new Grand Central Station was opened to the public, Sunday morning, the second of February, 1913. And Viktor was here for more than a generation; till he grew old, in fact, and retired on a very comfortable pension in 1946.

But when he left, he left Nick in charge; and Nick—Nick Rossetos—knows and reverences oysters. Like all the other helpers Viktor gathered round himself, Nick is a Greek. Through the years he mastered the mysteries of Viktor's subtle art; and his own native shrewdness seems to have taken care of the rest.

Nick always does his own ordering, of course; in his business, he assures us, that is the secret of success. He has a head for figures and shows it in his talk. The most casual thing he says about his work is loaded with statistics . . . thirty thousand oysters today . . . tomorrow, twenty-six thousand will be right . . . twelve hundred bowls of stew yesterday . . . today, a slight tapering off . . . eight tons of lobster last month. . . . Nick has the figures always before him, always ready.

But all these figures have a certain steadiness about them; even their fluctuations are calm and smooth. The tricky business comes in the summer months, when oysters are out of season and clams are king. It's a strange thing, which he has never been able to figure out, Nick says, but a rainy day in summer brings to his oyster bar the year's greatest rush of business. Day after day, so long as the weather is fine, things may be slow; but then, suddenly, a rainstorm blows in, and all New York seems to come trooping to Grand Central in quest of clams—clam stew, clam broth, clam chowder, clams on the half-shell. Yesterday he might have got along on five thousand clams; but today it's raining, and for no better reason than that, Nick says, his boys are called upon to open forty-five thousand clams. (They have never yet opened so many oysters in a single day.) And Nick has to anticipate that demand—for the clams must be fresh out of the sea to be served at his counter.

So Nick falls back on the wisdom of his ancestors on the Ægean. He keeps in close touch with the Weather Bureau, of course; but all summer long Nick is also out on the sidewalk in Forty-second street several times each day—watching the skies, and recalling the old knowledge his father passed on to him when he was a boy in Greece. Nick is passionately certain that the old knowledge, folk-knowledge tried and tested over centuries, is right; and, according to the best authorities at Grand Central, Nick knows what tomorrow's weather will be as accurately as he knows what yesterday's receipts were.

As presiding genius of the oyster bar, Nick is responsible to Michael Scandalios, who for the moment is acting manager of this entire establishment—the oyster bar, the quick-service luncheon counter and the tap room and, on the opposite side of the foyer, Señor Gil's dining room. But the public hardly catches a glimpse of Scandalios, who is only a passing figure at Grand Central, anyhow; who is, indeed, the supervisor of an entire network of Union News Company restaurants. And for the greater part of each day, Scandalios is represented here by the acting assistant manager, George Jacques.

A tall, solid, dark-eyed man with somewhat of a presence, George is another "great catch" of the sort Union News seems to specialize in. He's rather new at Grand Central; he's been here for a little under three years. Before that he was the maître d'hôtel at a very famous place —the Algonquin. There he became the friend of many notable persons and just before the great man died, Hendrik Van Loon came to Grand Central in search of him, George tells us, and gave him an autographed copy of his last book. Even then Van Loon was dying, for he got only as far as the Concourse when he had to stop; whereupon he sent for him and apologized, says George, that he had not been able to walk further.

At present George carries on in that temporary post of acting assistant manager.

At present, too, he is the eagle-eye. He's the fellow, that is to say, who every minute sees all that's going on—and sees that nobody slips out without paying his check. It's a tribute to his watchfulness perhaps, that those who do escape average, from one year's end to the other, two each day; and two a day, out of the immense number of customers served, is considered an irreducible minimum.

Even so, that isn't the end of the story; for George has a reputation for uncanny skill in recognizing the cheaters when they come back. . . . There was a flashing smile. There was an ever so slight display of hands. There was a quick, subtle shrug. And in the accents of a diplomat George, who now stood before us, conceded: "Well, I have a trick memory."

But it's more than a memory; it's a good memory plus a quite astonishing ability to visualize a face from somebody else's description of it. At the close of each day's business, a post-mortem reveals what checks are missing. Their duplicates, retained in the cash registers, are then referred to; and these, taken separately, show (1) the amount the customer should have paid; (2) the waiter who served the customer; and (3) the time the check was issued, right down to the fraction of a minute. Then the waiter is called in. He's told the amount of the check and the time he issued it; and, almost invariably, he's able, for George's benefit, to describe the customer in very close detail.

This is because the great bulk of customers are old-timers; people who come here every day and occupy the same seats in the same order. The waiters prize these regular customers, and lay themselves out to attract as many as possible; and their sitting down and getting up imparts to the day's work a kind of rhythm—which is broken each time a stranger sits down. So the stranger makes a greater impression upon the waiter than he quite realizes; and the waiter—perhaps thinking of the "regular" whom the stranger displaces—notices more about that stranger than the average person would think possible. The fact is that strangers are not the usual thing at the Grand Central Terminal Restaurant & Oyster Bar which, as you may have noticed, is not at all a typical railway station restaurant. Anyhow, the waiter is able to give a thoroughly good description of the stranger, or to say at once—as occasionally happens—that the gentleman who walked out without paying his check was Mr. So-and-so. "Just forgot. He'll find the check in his pocket. Pay it tomorrow."

The absent-minded regular is not a man to be watched, however; and Old Eagle-Eye Jacques concentrates on the deliberate cheats—chiefly the fellow who eats at different counters a light meal and a large meal, and who tries to get out, and sometimes does get out, by paying the smaller check. In the usual, routine way, Eagle-Eye gets the waiter's description of that fellow; and, having succeeded once, the fellow almost invariably comes back, though it may be as much as two years later. But even after two years, Eagle-Eye remembers him, the story goes; and this time watches him closely, and catches him red-handed, and reaches into his little box and fishes out that other check now two years overdue. . . . It's astonishing. But that at least is the reputation George Jacques has in a very few years built up for himself.

It was 1:07 by the Golden Clock, and the luncheon crowds, who had come in with such a rush, were hurrying out again. But, coming or going, the crowds were there; and, as a sheer spectacle, the Concourse was still at its best—except for the injured men.

Strictly, perhaps, these weren't many. Certainly they were not what London or Rome or even Paris would have thought many; and Moscow might conceivably have thought them astonishingly few. But they were many for New York. They were soldiers from the Halloran Hospital on Staten Island, mostly. And so, perhaps, they were a portent; for some years to come the Concourse will see many of them.

There were five or six on crutches; they hopped about briskly, though, and looked exceedingly cheerful. There were others who walked with canes, slowly, laboriously. And there was a blind soldier; a tall, handsome fellow with dark glasses. He seemed cheerful, too, though his face was already acquiring that impassive look that is the usual mark of the blind.

He had a cane but wasn't using it. He was led by a girl of twenty or twenty-two; perhaps his wife. They passed by rapidly, going one way; then they passed us again, going just as rapidly the other way; and finally they passed us a third time, going the way they had gone originally. They were not lost, however; no couple on the floor looked quite so serene and confident as they, and it was obvious that, if they walked rapidly, it was because they liked to. Scores of people stepped aside as they approached, then closed in after them, followed them with their eyes.

Near the Golden Clock a boy was playing with a pair of green goggles, idly swinging them; and, tilted, they caught the light and sent forth a flash of green that played for an instant upon the marble floor. A shout went up; and out of the Commodore Hotel entrance—near the southeast corner of the Concourse—a young couple came rushing for the train gate, followed by a red cap who had their bags; and pursued by fifteen or twenty elaborately dressed young men and women who pelted them with rice and called upon all present to know that they had only this morning been married. The pursuers pointed accusing fingers at the bride and bridegroom. "Just married!" they kept repeating in the usual half-triumphant, half-malicious way. They varied the cry with shouts of "Niagara Falls! They're off to Niagara Falls!"

"Hey, Hank!" one of them called in a high piping voice. "Don't forget to send us a picture of the falls by moonlight!"

"Niagara Falls!" another shouted. "Niagara Falls at *this* time o' year! Can y'imagine that?"

An assistant stationmaster was at the gate awaiting them. The crowd fell back, and—without showing their tickets—the young couple passed through the gate and disappeared.

Joe Guardino was mixed up in this—quite understandably; for he is, after all, the Stationmaster's clerk. And we have Joe's word for it that, when the bride and bridegroom passed through the doorway as if to board the *Knickerbocker Express* for Buffalo (and Niagara Falls), they were adroitly spirited to one side, and then guided along the narrow outer concourse to a different platform, where they boarded a Yankee train for Boston.

In that complacent way of his, Joe shrugged it off as something of a lark.

"Last week," he said, "it was the baby's milk. . . .

"A woman called at the counter," he continued, with a toss of his head toward the counter in the Stationmaster's office. "She said her baby had to have a special kind of milk, on doctor's orders, and she wanted to know if our dining cars carried that kind of milk. I knew the answer to that. I said No, the dining cars carry a different company's milk. But she wasn't taking any chances; the doctor said one kind of milk and that was what it had to be.

"So I asked her where she was going, and when. She showed me her tickets . . . She was leaving for Syracuse the following Friday on No. 5. I took down her ticket numbers. Then I did some telephoning. It took me ten minutes, but I fixed it up. I told her: 'Madam, when the *Mohawk* leaves from Track 36 at 9:15 A. M. next Friday, her dining car will carry one quart of milk of the kind your doctor specifies."

We were walking westward in the Concourse. Joe was sauntering back to his post in the Stationmaster's office, and we were simply tagging along to hear the story out. We had escaped from Ichabod; for three hours now we had seen no sign of him, and Joe was telling us that we needn't worry, we'd see the tall fellow again all right, all right, when—suddenly—there was a scream of "Murder!"

POLICE CAPTAIN

It was a scream of terror—like the hardly human cry that escapes the lips of men who fall or throw themselves from tall buildings. The crowds froze in their places, and, for the slightest fraction of a second, unearthly stillness fell upon the Concourse. Then a half-involuntary gasp went up and a great surge of people swept in upon the spot from which the outcry came. With long strides, quietly, never running, the police closed in. And then, hardly half a minute later, a group of four people moved out of the crowd and over to the elevators (tucked away between the train-gates at the northwest corner of the Concourse).

The crowd wondered for a moment; then shrugged and shuffled off. They had their own affairs to attend to. They put the matter out of their heads, and with marvelous ease the Concourse settled back to its accustomed way. But backstage, at police headquarters in room 1629 of the Terminal Office Building, a new case was entered on the blotter of the Grand Central Terminal Police.

It was a woman, a psychopathic patient, traveling in the custody of a matron from a Middle Western to a New York institution. The desk lieutenant heard her with a great show of deference. She was confused, above all embarrassed; she was one minute voluble, the next minute overcome by shame. The lieutenant gave her all the time she needed, and gradually the simple fact became clear. As she had come in from the dark train platform and caught her first glimpse of the sun-filled Concourse, the recollection of her old freedom crowded back upon her, and that anguished cry, the cry of a prisoner, escaped her.

The lieutenant left his desk, came through the gate in the massive oaken bar. He showed the woman about. Having talked, she was now quiet again, and rational. He took her to the window, he showed her the speeding motor cars that passed within a few feet of the place, he told her about the elevated highway that runs around three sides of Grand Central. He treated her as if she were a queen. The woman smiled; possibly for the first time in years. And then, still in the matron's custody, she went away—went quietly to that asylum that was to be, in all probability, her last home on earth.

"An awful lot of human tragedy," as Ichabod would say, mixes in with things at Grand Central; and it's a melancholy fact that the Terminal Police have—of all things under the sun—a reputation for exceptional skill in managing psychopathic cases. That is not the whole story, of course. Under the sharp eye of Captain William V. O'Neill, they do very nicely, too, in the more usual forms of police endeavor. The New York City police authorities express high admiration of them, and the F. B. I. falls back upon their services from time to time. And it's well known that the criminal element generally gives Grand Central Station a rather wide berth. But still that one curious distinction stands forth—that reputation for skill in dealing with the mentally sick.

It argues a certain refinement of understanding not usually associated with police work. And better than anything else it marks the long way the Grand Central Police have gone since the old Commodore first organized them for service under the great glass roof of his beautiful train-shed at Grand Central Depot. The circumstances there were peculiar . . .

It was the autumn of 1871.

Grand Central was extravagantly admired by the generality of New Yorkers; largely, perhaps, in the mistaken belief that it was the biggest railway terminal in the world. But much as they esteemed it as a work of art, the people were annoyed, bewildered, and even angered by the Commodore's introduction there of two customs which, up to that time, had been peculiar to the English railways. The old man had put all his employees in uniform. (The New Haven followed suit.) And he had set up—though in a modified form—the English practice of inspecting and punching tickets before passengers were allowed to pass through a barrier to reach their trains.

The adoption of a "company livery" provoked a minor uproar, and among the city's noisier elements the indignation was widespread. They objected, they said, to the invasion of the men's right to dress as gentlemen; and the offense was reprobated all the more when it was discovered that conductors, for example, wore gold braid, while brakemen wore only silver braid and porters wore no braid at all. The critics resented this deeply; said "it ain't democratic," and stoutly assured one another that, as for them, *they* would not be took the liberty with. They raised a fatuous cry that no man should be compelled to wear another man's livery (meaning the Commodore's), and they espied in railway uniforms the beginning of the end of the American Republic.

They soon got over this though. As a matter of fact, the *New York Herald* had long campaigned for uniforms; for the situation aboard the trains had become intolerable. Thieves too often went through the cars posing as conductors; in which case passengers had to pay their fares twice. And train crews themselves had acquired a bad reputation for clubbing passengers with their brake-sticks and then swearing it "must have been somebody else." Almost of itself alone, the railway uniform cleared up serious evils.

But the popular resentment against the ticket barrier lasted for a generation. It was sullen, for the most part, but always liable to blow up wrathfully; for it was the gateman, barring the way to the train-shed, who forced people to go out into the street, even in the worst of weather, in order to pass from one station to another. (Especially in heavy rainstorms, cab drivers made a point of delivering their fares to a wrong station, thus making trade for other drivers who charged high prices—half a minute before train time—to carry passengers from one Grand Central station to another.) The direct and easy way, as well as the comfortable way, would have been to cut through the shed. Often, too, that was the only way, if a passenger was to catch his train. And the public, of course, was well aware of this. But the gateman said no.

When the gate was closed, nobody at all could pass through; and when the gate was open, nobody could pass through except on presentation of a ticket for a particular train that was then receiving passengers. And that rule was not relaxed for anybody. When the President of the United States was on his way to Massachusetts for the

Lexington-Concord Centennial Celebration in April, 1875—when he swept grandly through the New Haven Station, doffing his hat and bowing to the left and right—even he was stopped at the barrier; and Grant, who for seven years had traveled all over the country without paying any fare, stood meekly waiting while one of his party rushed back across the room to buy the necessary tickets to Boston.

The gateman had arrived on the American railroad scene—and he was a formidable fellow. And did the railroad apologize to Grant? Devil a bit. In a book published as recently as 1938, a former publicity chief of the New York Central Railroad described the episode as a "noble victory" for the barrier system.

Nobody liked that system at the old Grand Central. But when they saw how the terminal was being worked, the fair-minded ones decided that Old Man Van Derbilt was mighty clever after all. As a matter of fact, it was the cleverest piece of work the American railroads had seen till then.

It was a magnificent train-shed the gateman so zealously guarded. Under a single roof of iron and glass, under an array of arches that sprang with easy, effortless grace to a crown-line a hundred feet above the floor, it was a kind of sun parlor 530 feet long and 200 feet wide. It was closed in at both ends: at the south end by the New Haven station, and at the north end by an immense wall of glass, with doorways at the bottom where the trains passed in and out with hardly any room to spare. There was two-thirds of an acre of glass in that north wall; there were two acres of glass in the roof. And the place, we are told, was always airy, and remarkably clean and bright—for the locomotives were kept out of it.

The floor had a quite considerable pitch to the north; Grand Central was just what Shakespeare had in mind when he spoke of a "station . . . on a heaven-kissing hill." Civil engineers describe it differently, but their ideal is the same. The best possible place to build a terminal, they tell you, is on a "summit," so that every train may leave on a downgrade, enabling her to start quickly, and enter on an upgrade, enabling her to come in quickly with the assurance that she can stop quickly. At Grand Central Depot, the brakemen simply released their brakes, and departing trains coasted out of the train-shed, to meet their locomotives and couple up on the outside. And coming in, of course, it was the reverse of that—more or less.

On the approach track, the incoming train speeded up. At a given point, the engineman braked his locomotive slightly (to create slack at the couplers) and sounded a blast on his whistle, whereupon the head brakeman pulled the pin, uncoupling the train. With a quick burst of speed, then, the engineman dashed forward and over to a parallel track, moving around an open switch that was instantly closed back of him. And a moment later the train came coasting through the closed switch, and into the train-shed, in charge of the brakeman. It was before the days of the Westinghouse brake. These trains were equipped with Armstrong brakes—everything depended, that is to say, on the strong arm of the brakeman.

But the method was not unusual. It was, in fact, the grand old way in the grand old days. It was called "switching on the fly," or simply "fly-switching"; and out along the big pike, where there was room enough, it was often the way of changing locomotives without stopping a train. Having slipped one engine, the fast-moving cars gradually overtook the other, which was out on the iron ahead of her, running forward at only a slightly lower rate of speed. As they drew together, the links were lifted. The pin was dropped as the bump occurred. And with a "Come-along" toot on his whistle the engineman gave her the steam, and the train was on her way again. With a good, responsive locomotive, and a good, sensitive man controlling her, the maneuver was carried out so flawlessly that passengers were hardly ever aware of it; and it used to be the mark of a good engineman that he picked up a "flyer" with less jar at the couplers than would break an eggshell.

In the end, though, a new generation of railroaders fumbled the play too often. There were many reasons for this, but mainly, perhaps, it was the fault of the new locomotives that began to dominate the rails at the beginning of the twentieth century; massive and brutish, they had no "understanding" of a throttle touch, they were not responsive to close and delicate handling, and fly-switching was not their meat. In any case, fly-switching became a "fancy" operation —when it succeeded. And so it was outlawed.

But it was standard practice at the old Grand Central Depot; and, so the story goes, never an accident resulted. As we have seen, it kept the train-shed free of smoke, and that was worth considering. The real reason for it, however, was that it solved a serious operating problem: it freed the locomotive immediately on her arrival, instead of trapping her between train and bumper; in a desperately crowded terminal, it saved a host of operations that would otherwise have been necessary to provide for locomotive escapement.

On the other hand, it gave rise to another problem. There were twelve tracks in the train-shed. The floor was paved, even between the rails; and the passengers were not confined to platforms as they were in English railway terminals, but went trooping cross-tracks in the most direct way to and from their trains. This was the usual way at American terminals, and the Commodore intended it to be this way. After all, the Central-Hudson station was at the northwest corner of the train-shed, and Central-Hudson passengers could not have been expected to walk a quarter of a mile, via the perimeter, in order to reach a train on Track 1, less than two hundred feet away.

But the engineless trains came spinning in with a burst, and the problem of keeping the crowds out of their way was a problem of serious magnitude; and that was why the Commodore had borrowed the barrier system from England, and why he had posted gatemen at the barriers with orders to let nobody through but actual passengers, with tickets, and to let them through only when pathways to their waiting trains were safe.

There were three separate stations at Grand Central, but the twelve tracks in the train-shed were used indifferently by the trains of all three railroads. In a bay window high up on the south wall of the shed, a single "stationmaster" in his gold-braided uniform called every move. Outside the shed, he had the towermen establish avenues through the switch-work. In the proper sequence he dispatched all trains, each at the proper minute and each with the proper route laid out before it.

And he so ordered his work as always to have a track available for each incoming train. At the right moment, he directed the towermen to set up this route, too. As the train crossed the Harlem river bridge, he was notified by an electric signal; one of the earliest in American railway service. That gave him eighteen minutes to clear and make ready a receiving track. By the twentieth minute she was on it and coming to a stop. It was a hard enough job. It called for quick decisions.

And yet his work was further complicated by his having also to call each move of the crowds. Before each train was due to come bursting in from the fly-switching, the stationmaster gave orders to the gatemen, and all the barriers were closed. And before each train was due to release her brakes and start coasting out, the barriers were closed again. And so it was, in the end, that the crowds could freely and safely swarm across the tracks, once the signal was given; but the floor was always clear of people for every train movement.

By adopting the barrier system, the old Commodore had done all this; and he had also done three things more. At long last he had made it possible to dispatch trains "on time"—not within a minute or two, but dead on the sixtieth second, so as to clear tracks for the in-coming trains. (You could not delay an in-coming train, or she would lose the momentum relied upon to carry her across the fly-switches.) Next, the Commodore had set a remarkable record for safety. And, finally, by keeping out people he had been able to crowd twelve tracks into a train-shed that would normally have contained eight. . . . And that, preserved, is a principal characteristic of Grand Central Terminal today.

In those days they were policemen in the original sense of the word, having little or nothing to do with crime or criminals. To deal with crime, the Commodore had his *watchmen*, a plain-clothes force organized as the Protection of Property Department. But his policemen had only one duty, and that was to control the movement of people in the train-shed—to usher them cross-tracks when the coast was clear, and to keep them off the tracks when the trains were in motion; to watch the stationmaster in his bay window high up on the south wall of the train-shed, to obey his every signal, now to hurry the crowds along and guide them to their trains, now (with the closing of the barriers) to bring all movement to a dead stop. It was of the essence of police work, because it implemented a policy.

But the day came, of course—though it was long after the Commodore's day—when the Grand Central Police became the New York division of the P. P. D.; and the Grand Central policeman became the figure he is today, a policeman in the modern sense, called upon to deal with every kind of problem that vexes the administration of a city, every sort of ill that plagues humanity. He stands guard today over a city within a city; over a shifting population that averages 350,000 persons in the course of every twenty-four hours. And, if Grand Central today is moderately free of crime, it was not always so. Since the present station was opened on the second of February, 1913, swindlers and pickpockets, bag thieves and armed robbers have all had their innings here, and these buff-colored walls, which have seen so much in their day, have also looked upon suicide, kidnaping and even murder.

As the years went by, the picture passed through many changes:

1913 to 1917: The swindler was in his heyday, and "there was hardly a week" when the building was not sold. "Some smooth talker," said the captain, "would get hold of a hick, show him around the place, point out its values, and talk him into buying Grand Central Terminal." It confronted the police with a major problem. In the end, however, the problem gradually cleared up of itself, and by 1929 the police had heard the last of it. "During the First World War, and in the years immediately after it," said the captain, "people began to travel as they had never done before, and they got wiser. The old-fashioned hayseed gradually disappeared. The public became less gullible."

1917 to 1922: Now the bag thief was the principal enemy. "A good detective is always able to spot a bag thief: he has a peculiar bearing; he studies the situation; he'll take anywhere from twenty minutes to five hours to pick out the bag he wants, and he has a way of approaching the bag and walking off with it. Each one," said the captain, "has a style of his own. But you know it *is* a style.

"And if he gets away now, we get him the next time, for he always comes back. . . . We never had but one woman bag thief. She got away with four bags before we nabbed her. There was something psychic about that woman. She never picked up a bag that didn't have jewelry in it."

1922: In the spring the pickpockets came in with a rush. "They didn't care what they did with their fingers." The police began a counter-offensive, and in the first two weeks trapped eight of them.

Before the year was out, the nimble-fingered gentry were so badly beaten that they've never come back—professionally, that is. The story goes that if you should ever see at Grand Central a man with his hands folded in front of him and a railway ticket held between his two thumbs, *that* man is a pickpocket proving his good-behavior while passing through on his way to a train.

1923 to 1941: The bag thief was back in first place again. The police laid traps for him, and many a scatterbrained girl who impulsively dashed off to buy a magazine, leaving her suitcase "where it could be stolen," was only a railroad employee planting a decoy for some thief known to be working that day. But the thieves knew that too, of course.

"Once, back in the summer of 1930," said the captain, "we had grips and suitcases all over the place every day for a week, but the man we were after stayed clear of them all. He was on to us. We kept it up, though, till we hurt his pride. Then he deliberately picked one up, just to show us he could do it and get away with it. And he thought he did get away with it."

But they followed him halfway across the city to his furnished room—for they can go anywhere, these Grand Central policemen, and by virtue of their commissions, signed by the commandant of the State Troopers, they can make arrests anywhere in the entire State of New York. They found the place loaded down with loot. The fellow went to Sing Sing after that—by way of Grand Central Station.

1941 and 1942: It wasn't anything that happened at Grand Central. It was just a series of false alarms. Four times in the space of two years the New York City police were notified that Grand Central was about to be blown up. It happened first on the day Fritz Kuhn, the leader of the German-American Bund, appeared before the New York County Supreme Court on a writ of habeas corpus. It was said that ever since the German armies had begun their march in Europe, Kuhn had betrayed a marked anxiety to be out of jail; and the report was that others too were anxious to see him at liberty. In any case, the Court denied his petition, threw him back into the Tombs; and within the hour the police intercepted a message, ostensibly addressed to Kuhn, announcing that "the bomb will go off at Grand Central Station at six o'clock tonight."

Within one minute's time, the emergency trucks, the bomb truck and half a hundred police cars, with all their sirens screeching, wer closing in on Grand Central. The city policemen came tumbling i just after five o'clock, when the evening rush to the suburbs was at it height; and while detectives of the Alien Squad combed through th immense crowd of commuters, more than a hundred city patrolme ransacked the whole premises in search of the bomb.

And so it was each time the scare was reported. They went throug all the baggage in the baggage room, they went through every car an locomotive, they searched the tracks far into the tunnel. And in al their searching they were led, step by step, in swift, methodical orde by the officers and men of the Grand Central Terminal Police, whos blueprints show the points at which an exploding bomb could do th greatest damage—and who looked there first.

They never found a bomb, for none was ever there; but once the found a "suspicious object," the heart's delight of every policeman. I the baggage room they found a suitcase; a man had left it there tha morning and dashed away without waiting for the check. That obviously, was a very suspicious circumstance.

Gingerly the suitcase was lifted up. Gingerly it was immersed i oil. Then a way was made clear, and the thing was got up the baggag elevator and safely into the bomb truck, a huge vehicle with twelve inch-thick walls of basket-weave laminated steel. At the nearest ope space, the truck came slowly to a halt, and the crew got out the equipment. First came the fluoroscope—and last, too, for that matte for what the X-rays revealed inside that suitcase were four new starched white shirts, three neckties, and two pairs of socks, a thoroughly saturated with oil.

1942 to 1946: These were the war years. Grand Central was a vit communications point; so the authorities laid down emergency law for its protection, and—for a time—even Ichabod was prevented fro walking down the tracks to the signal towers.

Troops came pouring through; the Military Police and the Sho Patrol came in to take charge of them, and—to protect them—th city police posted inside of Grand Central a battalion of polic women. Coming just when a first batch of college girls had taken ov the work of drafted ticket clerks, the lady-coppers were widely a umed to be just so many other girls bent on doing war work. Their badges told a very different story; but people are very unobservant. They decided it was just a pretty show. They called it the "Grand Central Follies."

Unobtrusively, the Grand Central Terminal Police went on with heir ordinary work—save that it was never ordinary. With the ex-itement of the war, hysteria cases increased, and thieves were quick o profit by the fact. "For example," said the captain, "there was the irl who came to the Concourse expecting to elope. She stood below he Clock, waiting for the boy who failed to keep the rendezvous. She stood there for hours, waiting; and then, distraught, she ran to a elephone to call him up. She closed the door of the booth, leaving er suitcase outside." She didn't realize; perhaps she didn't care, she vas so distressed, so overwrought. But for two hours the thief had een watching her, knowing that she would do just that. "He knew it ll in advance," said the captain. But what he didn't know was that, ll the while he was watching the girl, a Grand Central Police de-ective was watching him.

"Right now," said the captain, "there's a case in the Waiting Room. . . . It's a mother, an unfortunate mother. . . . The men ay she's planning to abandon her baby. A thing like that takes time, ecause no woman can bring herself to do it easily. . . . Two men re down there now, keeping an eye on her; uniformed men. Maybe he'll see them watching her; that's what I hope. Maybe it will pre-ent her from carrying out her plan and doing what she could only e sorry for later. . . ."

Captain Bill O'Neill is probably one of the hardest-working police fficers in New York. He's rather on the handsome side, combining eavy black eyebrows, dimples and a serious young face with a great nock of snow-white hair. And the contrast hardly ends there; for ith the size and bodily strength of a pugilist he combines a swift and owerful intelligence, which enables him to attack with unflagging nergy an amount of work that would appall the minds of two-thirds f New York's big corporation executives. He goes over the work of ll his detectives, coaching them in sheer adroitness before they go ut and cross-examining them on every minor point when they come back. His strong point is said to be his ability "to see around corners" —which is only another way of saying that he sees the cause, or the motive, where other men see only the effect. Above all, he has the gifts of a great general, or a great fireman, the powers of instant realization and instant decision.

Criminals are always being tracked. Telegrams from police departments all over the State and country are always pouring in on Bill, requesting the apprehension of such-and-such a person believed to be arriving at Grand Central on such-and-such a train. And reports of men leaving town in a hurry are never-ending. Three times in forty minutes, while we were talking to Bill, the F. B. I. was on the telephone; and several times a day it's a question of intercepting a man within as little as half a minute. Then—around the base of the Golden Clock, at the center of the Concourse, red lights flash on.

You may never have noticed those lights; after more than a genera tion, the crowds in the Concourse have never betrayed an awareness of their going on. But they are, in fact, the main police alarm at Granc Central. When they flash white, it's one of the clerks at the Informa tion Desk summoning help; in which case, nine times out of ten it's only a question of persuading the inebriated one to board his trair and go home quietly. But when they flash red, it may mean trouble All normal patrolling comes to a stop, and swiftly, silently, the uni formed men move to action-stations; they're on guard now, alert anc ready. And the red caps and the gatemen all know the signal too of course. Something has happened; and while the crowds, incredibl purblind, continue about their business, all these men are tense witl excitement. The plain-clothes detectives at once begin combing th crowds, outward; from the train gates, that is to say, to all the variou entrances and exits. And the sergeants and lieutenants, as unob trusively as possible, rush to the nearest telephones and call headqua ters—to learn the cause of the emergency and to receive their orders.

Sometimes, though very seldom, the wanted man makes a dash t escape; and then, for a moment, there's an uproar. But for the mos part there's never a sound or a sign to attract attention. And in th end, of course, the red lights below the Golden Clock blink out agair The uniformed men resume the pacing of their beats. The crisis i ended.

BACK OF THE TICKET WINDOWS

"YOU'LL NEVER know Grand Central," said Ichabod—

It was 3:10 by the Golden Clock, and the tall fellow, back-from his classroom, had found us again.

"You'll never know Grand Central," he said, "unless you see it broad-side as well as lengthwise; unless you see it as the workaday place it is today as well as the embodiment of so much railroad history. . . . You can't deny history and forget old Commodore Van Derbilt. But you can't forget, either, that today Grand Central is also the big sister of all the small-town railway stations in America. That's one more surprising thing about it.

"There are differences," said Ichabod. "Slim, the agent, is all alone in the village depot. He sells the tickets, smashes the baggage, loads the milk, makes out the waybills and watches the telegraph. He flags down the limited to pick up a change of running orders; and when No. 8 arrives from the city in the evening, he unloads the empty milk cans and, occasionally, a bit of freight. Also, he does all his own housework; and . . . you feel all the more at home because the windows need washing, and the floor could do with a good sweeping, and there's a comfortable scattering of ashes about the big-bellied stove in the waiting room.

"In a way, Slim has too much to do, but he can't ever explain that to the company. The company doesn't take into account that, besides all his official duties, Slim also has to pass the time of day. . . .

"That's the point about Slim," said Ichabod; "he's the busiest, friendliest, most helpful fellow in town. He's a pillar of the community. He's everybody's friend; and he's the helper and advisor of more people than the village doctor ever sees. America owes an awful lot to Slim . . . and you find Slim, or a fellow who's the spitting image of him, in every small-town railway station in the country.

"But you also find him at Grand Central—the same old Slim. And that's the point I've been wishing to make. If you equate Grand Cen-tral with Commodore Van Derbilt on the vertical scale, you have no choice but to go the additional step further and equate Grand Central on the horizontal scale, with Slim. . . .

"For example," said Ichabod, "there are ninety-one ticket sellers a Grand Central; fifty-odd (including a dozen girls) employed by th New York Central, and the rest (all men) employed by the New Have Railroad. . . . A few have worked here all their lives, but most of them have come up from little stations out along the line, and they'v brought the spirit of those little stations with them. . . ."

Slowly, deliberately, Ichabod consulted his watch—and the tickin could be heard at seven feet. It was 3:14.

"We'll see Bill Hood," he announced, as if that settled everything "Bill's a ticket seller for the Central, and a Kentucky colonel, and member in good standing of the Brotherhood of Railway clerks.

"We'll also see—we'll pay our respects to George Philips," sai Ichabod and, in that abrupt way of his, he was off toward the ticke windows.

He showed the way to a door between Window No. 1 and Windov No. 29. No. 1, of course, belongs to the great array of windows facing th Concourse. No. 29 faces upon the ramp that connects the Concours and the Waiting Room. Between them, unnoticed by thousands c people who pass it daily, is a not too noticeable door. Ichabod reache almost to the top of the inside face of the doorpost, where he lightl touched the most inconspicuous of doorbells. George Philips answere the door himself.

George is Ticket Agent for the New York Central Railroad, and responsible directly to that company's passenger traffic manager. He i not one of the Stationmaster's men, and the Terminal Manager has n control over him. He is not one of the neutral officials who operat Grand Central on behalf of both railroads equally. He works for ju one of those railroads; and when you enter his office, you step out c neutral territory, you enter the ticket offices of the Central. And it's th same way, of course, across the ramp. There, between Window No. and Window No. 30, you would enter the offices of the New Have Railroad; and there you would meet Charles Tienken. Ticket Agent fc hat company. Outside the hierarchy of Grand Central officials, Charles Tienken and George Philips are straightforward railroad men.

It was George Philips who bade us enter his domain; a heavy-set man of more than middle height, who looks sharply at you through very clear blue eyes. He's a man in his early fifties with a good head of hair; a softly spoken man who looks the part of a successful banker; a man who dresses well and keeps the lenses of his eyeglasses polished to the last degree of gleam and glitter. No need to ask, he isn't a man to pass the time of day. He's brief. But he has a good smile, that somewhat tempers a stern and businesslike demeanor. That's about the size of George Philips—a man who knows his job and knows he knows it.

"Including stock-room clerks and others, I have a staff," he said briefly, "of 130 people. Forty are women, of whom thirty-nine came in during the late war to take over the jobs of drafted men. The fortieth—May O'Connor—came here in 1917, during the other war. She's been here ever since.

"As ticket sellers—" George Philips has the answers instantly at the tip of his tongue. "As ticket sellers," he said, "women are either very good or very bad. We've had some very bad ones, but I've noticed that the woman who did poorly at the window was, in most cases, the wife of a man on service overseas; she was worried, her mind wasn't on her job. . . . We still have women who are exceptionally good; largely widows or unmarried girls who are anxious to make careers for themselves in the transportation industry. . . ."

"And now," said Ichabod, "I want you to meet Bill Hood. As I said before, Bill's a crack ticket seller; knows everything about tickets. In fact, Bill practically invented tickets . . . or that's what some of the boys and girls at the windows say. And he's even better at tariffs—which is the railroad term for what the layman calls fares. You'd hardly believe it, but when you delve into American railroad tariffs, you can lose yourself in a forest of complications. . . . There's a growing science that deals with this subject, and Bill Hood is an outstanding figure in that field of endeavor. At the windows here they call him the Tariff Encyclopedia."

At Ticket Window No. 5, a relief man took over, and Bill Hood came toward us—a tall and lanky man with blue eyes, a pale, thin face, and a quite remarkable grin. He's a man in his middle forties, and if you called him Slim, he'd answer you, the chances are, as quickly as if you had called him Bill.

Where was he born?

"Louisville, Kentucky!" It was a declaration rather than an answer; and there was in it more than a note of pride, there was in it—no doubt for some excellent reason—a ring of triumph.

With a grin that was good for the rest of the afternoon, Bill stretched his legs out a mile and a half in front of him, and leaned his head back on his chair; comfortably.

Hobbies? Sure; Bill's an entertainer—song and dance. He imitates Al Jolson. His best act, though, is his imitation of George M. Cohan.

Thomas Hood? No relation of Bill's—so far, that is, as Bill knows. Bill once read "The Song of the Shirt," though. Pretty good. And there was that other one that Thomas Hood wrote—yeah, that's it, "The Bridge of Sighs." Bill's always wanted to read that, but he's never come across a copy. Funny.

Been around a bit? Sure; Bill's worked on the Pennsy and the B. & O. in his day; and during the First World War he was a chief clerk for the United States Railroad Administration, which had its headquarters, you may like to know, right here in Grand Central; and which conferred on Bill a certificate of commendation. When demobilization was the big excitement, back in the early months of 1919, Bill helped clear out of Camp Upton in one day fifty-eight trains loaded with 66,000 men; and that was a piece of railroading any man could be proud of.

After the war, Bill joined a travel agency; then, for three years he was "production man" for a New York firm of railroad printers specializing in timetables, tariffs, waybills *et cetera*. That's how he came to know so much about tariffs. And when the firm he worked for gave up the ghost, Bill went into the railroad printing business on his own account; but he ran into a streak of bad luck, and after a year's effort to make a go of it, he cashed in his chips and returned to railroading.

"I came to Grand Central as a ticket seller on the twenty-second of November, 1926 . . . and, well, you see, I knew the tariffs pretty well

Grand Central from the South: In the foreground the ramp that carries the middle lanes of lower Park avenue over Forty-second street. In the distance, straddling the railroad tracks, the New York Central Building.

The Golden Clock and some of the late morning crowds in
as they are seen from a point near the East end of the Nort

High above the Concourse: The painted sky, showing the ecliptic and the celestial equator intersecting at the Vernal Equinox; showing also a left-handed Orion and constellations of the winter zodiac in reverse order.

The Big Fellow out front—and, of course, the official title of Grand Central, which ought to prove something.

And here, high up in the attic of Grand Central, just back of the Big Fellow, is Jake, the Clock Master, ministering to the works.

This is the Commodore as he stands out front; as for sixty years he stood above the freight-house on the Lower West Side of the city. The old gentleman, who likewise appears in the inset, saw and approved this statue of himself and dedicated it as part of his own memorial.

This is the Depot the Commodore built—

and this is how Wilgus transformed it, back at the turn of the century.

This is the Commodore's train-shed, with the Station-master's bay window high up on the South wall, and—at the lower left-hand corner—the opening in the wall through which the Yankee trains for many months continued running straight on down to the former terminal at Twenty-sixth street.

And this is what those wrought-iron arches really looked like against the red brick of the East wall of the train-shed.

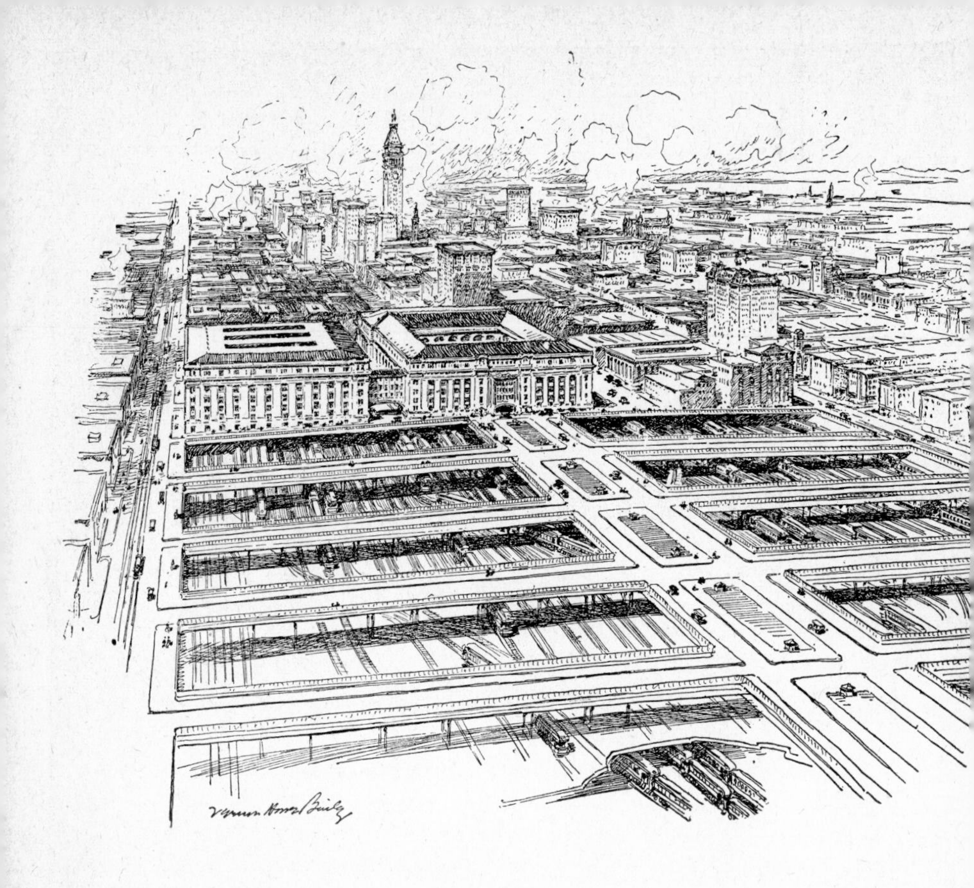

Two levels of track-work below the bridges which today carry the streets. In this sketch, long before the work was done, Vernon Howe Bailey *visualized for the readers of* Munsey's Magazine *the boldness of* Wilgus's *undertaking. Above the open spaces, from bridge to bridge, tall buildings now stand cellarless, founded on rows of steel stanchions that reach down between the tracks to bed rock. Below is an illustration of what's meant by the compactness of things at* Grand Central. *Nobody has ever been found to explain the beam of sunlight which apparently passes straight through the* Grand Central Art Gallery *at the upper right.*

Above, looking West, is the Waiting-Room; and below, with the ramp over at the left and the train gates to the right, is the Lower Concourse at 4 o'clock in the morning.

Here at the left is W
liam Smith making se
out of the jottings of t
telautograph—
And below (right)
William Walsh, the
formation chief.

"I'll meet you at the Golden Clock"—and every day and all day long you see people standing in a rough sort of ring, well back from the Information Desk, waiting to keep their appointments. At noon, when the sun strikes the clock, they aren't many, but still you can see something of the pattern . . .

On the marble stairs is Chief Williams, head of the red caps at Grand Central, and at the counter in Station-master's office is Joe Guardino, signing a slip to let somebody out on the platform to meet an arriving train.

Bill Keogh calling a train over the loud-speaker in the Arrival Station.

This—at the left—is Bill Hood behind his ticket window; and this—at the right—is what can happen at Grand Central when half New York suddenly takes a notion to spend the Fourth of July week end out of town.

And this is Kathleen Mullady of the cashier's desk, office of the Ticket Agent, New York Central Railroad—the prettiest girl at Grand Central.

At the left, above, is genial Jimmy Mahoney; at the right is that ancient legend that no more appears above the gateways of the Concourse; and below on Track 20 lies the Twentieth Century Limited on the day of her first "flight." The train board tells the story: First stop Chicago.

Here we have Andy Durkin and his two faithful dispatchers, Sol Schultz (left) and Harold Stegman; Harold in the very act of O S'ing a train. Below, a leverman watches the board in Tower A.

Above, the morning sun strikes the marble pavement of the Concourse and is reflected upon the ceiling. Light of a different sort is brought to Grand Central by the man at the right—for this is Ralston . . . preacher and, by the grace of God, a red cap.

because I was the fellow who printed them. . . . I selected ninety or a hundred of the most important places in the United States, and I worked out the tariffs—one-way and round-trip, day-coach, first-class and Pullman—to each of those places from right here at Grand Central; I arranged them in geographical order, and when a passenger wanted to go to one of those places, I just flipped over a page and told him the principal things he wanted to know. That way I greatly reduced the amount of time a ticket seller ordinarily spends in thumbing his way through the tariffs; so I got a lot of work done at my window. . . .

"Then the Ticket Agent came round to see how I did it—not George Philips; this was before his time. So I showed him my notebook, with all the arithmetic worked out in advance; and he had similar notebooks made for all the windows. . . .

"I wrote a long article about tariffs. . . . It was called 'The Great Experiment,' and it was published in the January (1940) number of *The Ticket Agent*—that's the magazine of the American Association of Railroad Ticket Agents. . . . I took the ticket seller at New York, and I took the case of a passenger who wants to go to Seattle. The ticket seller consults the tariff, and after reading seven or eight footnotes and wading through pages of supplementary tariffs, he floors the passenger by quoting nine different prices for a round-trip first-class ticket; and that's just his railroad fare, his Pullman is extra.

"There are nine different tickets to choose among. The first is good for a year, the second is good for only six months . . . the last is good only in the mid-winter season. The difference amounts to almost fifty dollars. . . .

And it's terribly confusing for the ticket seller, who always runs the risk of overlooking some small line of type in a supplementary sheet . . . changing a tariff or canceling a particular type of service. . . . The ticket seller can only do his best. If he does one thing, he may be overcharging the passenger; and if he does another thing, he may get his own fingers burned—he may undercharge the passenger, and then one of the railroads will bill him for the difference.

"The tariffs are too complicated for any one person to know much about them. At the windows we have only a short-form tariff, and that's about six times as big as the New York telephone directory, and supplementary pages are always coming in. . . . When we really meet a problem, we call up the Rate Room, where all four walls are filled with tariffs. . . . But not even the Rate Room clerks can know it all. So it's an experiment, no matter how you look at it. And that's what I called it—'The Great Experiment.'

"I made a suggestion that the carriers get together on a standard tariff structure from gateway to gateway over the whole United States and Canada; a *gateway* being a city like Chicago, Saint Louis, Kansas City . . . where different railroads come together and through coaches are swung over from one line to another. If that was done, I said, the ticket seller would know where he's at . . . and millions of dollars a year would be saved on printing alone . . . Well, sir, I got a flood of letters in reply to that article . . . and, to some extent, the tariffs have been simplified . . . but then Pearl Harbor came along. . . ."

Still grinning, Bill Hood untangled his long legs, wrapped them together again the other way about, and readjusted himself in his chair.

"After Pearl Harbor, the girls came in to take the place of the drafted men . . . and I was chosen," he said, "to teach them the job of the ticket seller. . . . I began easy. I wanted them to learn their railroad geography—what the gateways are that you pass through to get to various parts of the country, and where they lie. So I began with American history . . . and showed how the country grew, because there was timber here and corn there and cattle somewhere else; how the railroads were laid to tap these resources, and how the settlers drifted like loose earth in a windstorm till the railroads came and gave them something to cling to, and how the towns grew up along the railroads.

"It was history, I said, that laid the tracks down where they lie today . . . and the tracks ran east-and-west, as Lincoln discovered to his sad dismay; and Scott of the Pennsylvania Railroad replied that if only the tracks ran north-and-south, there wouldn't be any Civil War. I told 'em all that railway history, you know; figuring it would help 'em remember their railroad geography when they got to the ticket windows.

"And I told 'em about the tariff wars, and all the cut-throat competition that went on till 1887, when the I. C. C. was set up. . . . And I told 'em all about Commodore Van Derbilt. . . ."

"Only this morning," said Ichabod, "I was telling how the Commodore's ghost still haunts Grand Central."

"Hey!" said Bill Hood, "let *me* tell *you* about the old man's ghost . . ."

At the opening of Grand Central Depot in 1871, the Commodore was already in the seventy-ninth year of his age; but exploits famous in history still lay ahead of him. In 1873 Wall street felt the tensions of another battle, and the old man came out of the scrimmage with absolute control of the Lake Shore & Michigan Southern Railway, which connected with the Central-Hudson at Buffalo, and which gave him, therefore, a clear track all the way from New York to Chicago.

Almost at once, then, as president of the Central-Hudson, the old man conferred with himself as president of the New York & Harlem; and the Harlem leased all its real estate, trackage and other physical assets to the Central-Hudson. The lease was drawn for a term of 401 years, and is subject to renewal by majority vote at the annual meeting of the Harlem stockholders in A. D. 2274; it was made subject also, of course, to the perpetual rights previously acquired by the New Haven.

Thus the Harlem Railroad, with its 124 miles of line from Grand Central Depot to Chatham, became to all intents and purposes an integral part of the larger railroad; became, indeed, the present-day Harlem Division. And thus, too, the Harlem acquired its present status, which is that of a landlord company, the owner of much of the land on which the present-day Grand Central Terminal stands. That was an achievement for the old man, too, for it lifted the Harlem stockholders clear out of the railroad picture, retiring them to a different role and leaving him responsible, in railroad matters, to just so many fewer stockholders.

For all that, though, the signing of the lease was not unconnected with other plans and other events. In 1873, only four years after Black Friday, the country was again in the grip of a serious depression. There was unemployment in the city, there was danger of food riots; and in a crisis—since it was a question of creating work—a long and bitter quarrel came abruptly to a head. The quarrel was between the

Harlem Railroad and the city, and it culminated in the city's peremptory order to the Harlem to eliminate all grade-crossings from Forty-fifth street to the Harlem river. To avoid legal questions, and to get the work started quickly, the city agreed in advance to pay half the cost. However, it was still a project that would cost the railroad millions to carry out; and the Harlem's treasury could not have stood the gaff. And so in the end it was for this, the most urgent of many reasons, that the Central-Hudson took over.

The negotiations were not long—and in the course of them the city fathers made the acquaintance of the Commodore's new attorney, a political lawyer and Republican party orator called Chauncey Depew. It was a double-tracked line as it stood. The city, of course, would pay half the cost of depressing it below the grade level. And the railroad would cease operating till the job was done? Or would the railroad build two additional tracks and, later on, abandon them? As finally agreed upon, the scheme called for the closing of four streets below Forty-ninth, and the construction of a four-tracked railroad that would pass under Forty-ninth street and remain below the surface of Fourth avenue—save where it crossed the Harlem Flats—from that point on. It was a little more than the city had ordered, really. It not only doubled the number of tracks, but by further smoothing them out, and permitting of higher speeds, it increased their train capacity by 333 per cent.

There was a cry of "Robbery!" but the Commodore was stubborn; at times, perhaps, appallingly profane. And Chauncey Depew—the first of a long and notable line of Yale graduates to enter the service of the Van Derbilt railroads—was a grand negotiator. The city stood by its promise to pay half the cost.

The work went forward. And the old series of cuts, fills and tunnels were merged in a single tunnel that extended from Forty-ninth street north for the better part of three miles.

This was the famous brick-arch enclosure known for a dozen years to engineers all over the world as the New Fourth Avenue Tunnel. Then, in 1888, the 140-foot avenue that ran along its roof—with the smoothest, easiest grades of any of New York's great thoroughfares—was renamed Park avenue; and so, inevitably, the New Fourth became the Park Avenue Tunnel. For years it was to prove the bane and torment of the railroad; and at the beginning of the twentieth century it was to fix the inexorable and almost impossible limits within which the builders of present-day Grand Central had to do their work.

At the beginning, anyhow, its building partook of the nature of a work-relief project. The Commodore made it the start of a vast program, which included the four-tracking of the Central-Hudson railroad all the way to Buffalo, and corresponding improvements to his new pike, the Lake Shore & Michigan Southern. And all that work was under way when the Commodore, in 1875, insured the future prosperity of the Lake Shore by purchasing control of the Michigan Central and taking over, merely for its debts, the Canada Southern Railway. It was the old man's last great triumph. He was eighty-two years of age.

Less than two years later, on the fourth of January, 1877, just as the first flakes of a heavy snow had begun to fall, the Commodore died, surrounded by his children, his grandchildren and his great-grandchildren—to the number of sixty-two. It was less than fourteen years since he had turned his back upon steamboating; and in that short space of time he had built a railroad empire. It was only forty-four years since the Harlem Railroad had begun operating its first horse-drawn car. And it was only forty-eight years since the *Rocket*, by her great run at Rainhill, outside of Liverpool, had roused the world, and the age of the steam locomotive had begun. . . .

"He died," Bill Hood repeated, "just as the snow had begun to fall. He died in his mansion over there on Fifth avenue, hardly a block away from his great big station. I knew a fellow once was a brewer, and he built a marble mansion right next door to his brewery. . . . Anyhow," said Bill Hood, "it was snowing . . . and the snow that began before the Commodore died, in the morning, grew heavier during the day. It lasted an unusually long time. It became an historic blizzard. And, before it ended, the great glass roof at Grand Central Depot came crashing down."

Bill looked very solemn for a moment; then he shrugged as if to say that those were the facts and we could make out of them what we could. Obviously, this was Bill's contribution to the lore and legend of the Grand Central ghost.

"With you for a teacher," said Ichabod, "the women must have been exposed to a lot of good railway history."

"Of course," said Bill, "I didn't go into it as deeply as all that."

"What else did you teach them?"

"Salesmanship," said Bill. "A ticket seller occupies a special position. . . . It's a very solemn moment when a person steps up to the window to buy a railroad ticket. The American public is not so used to traveling as a lot of people say; and the longer you work around here the better you know that. The average person who comes to the window at Grand Central is inwardly shaking. . . .

"I know all about hardened travelers; see lots of them. But they aren't average. . . . And you can't ever guess what the cause of a journey is. It may be trouble; it may be a mother dying back home in Ohio; as I told my class, it may be a mission of sorrow. So the first rule is, your approach must be serious—no joking, nothing jolly; just serious.

"But if the passenger is jolly and cracks a joke, then the situation is different, and you meet him on his own ground. . . ."

Bill once more unwrapped his long legs and, after making himself more comfortable in his chair, wrapped them up again.

"Grand Central? I'll tell you how it is," said Bill Hood. "You've heard of the New York newspaper man who dreams of running a country weekly of his own some day. Well, that's the way it is with some of the ticket sellers here. Many a one will tell you, if you know him well, that he looks forward to becoming an agent some day in some small town out along the line. . . . There's many a man will tell you that's the best job on the railroad.

"In a small community, the company's agent is a big man. And if he knows how to build up business, he's liable to have a better income and live in a better home than the small-town banker. Sure, it's only the exceptional agent does that; but what I mean to say is, the chance is there and it's up to the man to make good.

"Also, the small-town agent is closer to the railroad. He sees the trains, he hears the drilling in the freight yard, he smells the smoke. And that means a lot to a man who's really got railroading in his blood. . . . Out in a small town like that," said Bill Hood, "you do your work and you get all the credit that's coming to you . . . and you have a chance to be human. You meet people man to man. You have time to be friendly and pass the time o' day."

"I wouldn't go so far as to say that Bill Hood is the typical Grand Central ticket seller," said Ichabod, "but he's typical of a great many of them. He's typical of the crowd of up-from-the-small-town ticket sellers; the fellows who miss at Grand Central the clangor of locomotives and the smell of soft-coal smoke. . . .

"They can neither see nor hear the trains here, and I've heard some of them say they might just as well be working in a bank. . . . But they're a kind of leaven, and they leaven the whole lump. . . . Grand Central wouldn't be the same without them; and, by the magic of their full brotherhood with Slim, the small-town agent, Grand Central remains, as I said, the big sister of every railway station in America. . . ."

LADY TICKET SELLER

EACH AFTERNOON at 3:45 you can see her come in by the West Balcony, from Vanderbilt avenue—a slim, good-looking, stylish woman with eyes that haven't lost their shyness.

Name: Mary Sweeney. *Address:* Princeton, New Jersey. *Training:* Bachelor of Science in Education, Rutgers University; one year's graduate work at Columbia University. *Prior Experience:* School teacher. *Job:* Ticket seller, New York Central Railroad, Window 13, Night trick (4 P. M. to midnight). *Observations:* Well, it's somewhat special, isn't it, to find a former school teacher at the ticket window?

"It was the war, of course, that supplied the opportunity. . . . Now that the war is over I intend to stay on. . . ."

Miss Sweeney speaks with unusual preciseness, and just a bit of a Scottish burr.

"I was born in Glasgow," she said. "My mother also is a native of that city; and she was a Sweeney, too. My father came from Ireland. . . . We immigrated to this country when I was five.

"We're a big family, Father, Mother and six children—four boys and two girls. During the war two of my brothers served overseas. My sister was a first lieutenant in the Wacs. . . . We're all together again now. We've lived in the same house in Princeton for all but two years of our life in America. . . .

"I go there every week end. Through the week I stay in the city. . . . I read a good deal; mainly autobiography. I play the piano . . . not ambitiously; just for my own delight."

And how did she turn railroader?

"In a casual sort of way . . . I had been teaching in a private academy here in the city; and at the close of the spring term, 1942, the school transferred itself to a large country estate, far out of the city. . . . I would not have been able to spend my week ends in

Princeton. So I resigned . . . and went off to Cape Cod for a brief holiday before looking for war work.

"On the train returning from Cape Cod, I had difficulty with my suitcase. . . . A young man lifted it off the rack for me. I had no recollection of having seen him before, but he addressed me by name. It turned out that he was a friend of one of my brothers in Princeton . . . so we changed trains together at Princeton Junction and talked as we rode in to town. He told me that the Pennsylvania Railroad was looking for women to take over the jobs of drafted ticket sellers, and I was out looking for one of those jobs early the next morning. . . . I spent fourteen months on the Pennsylvania. . . . Then I worked for the Atlantic Coast Line Railway. I joined the staff here at Grand Central in May, 1944. . . .

"There's a dreadful monotony about a teacher's life, and the parent-teacher relationship is not pleasant for the teacher, nor is it very capable of improvement. In their demands upon teachers, parents are everlastingly the same, and each one poses a problem that lives with the teacher for months and months.

"But the people and the problems at the ticket window are everlastingly different. The ticket seller has, of course, his stock of tickets and his cash account, and the one must balance the other, and that's all very easy. The problems, mainly, are how to get the passenger from Grand Central to his destination, which may be any railway stop in Alaska, Canada, the United States or Mexico. The ticket seller must map the itinerary, arrange for all the stopovers required by the passenger, work out all the train connections. The ticket seller must know things the traveler does not know, must supply information of a highly specialized nature. And this service to the traveler is not only interesting in itself, it yields a certain sense of satisfaction. . . .

"We have printed tickets, New York to each of 105 different stations on the New York Central System, to forty-nine more stations on other lines, and to fifteen pullman destinations; that is to say, we carry in stock 169 different tickets. But we also have our Blank-to-Blanks. These are tickets on which we have to write in the names of stations. Using them, I can sell you transportation between any two points on the North American continent. . . .

"The first essential I had had before ever I became a ticket seller.

That was a good, clear knowledge of the geography of the United States. . . . The work was never bewildering because, when I was new, I stuck to the routine that was mapped out for me. But when I had been at the window for just about four months, very suddenly one day I saw through the routine. I saw my job in relation to the whole work of the Ticket Agent's department; saw very suddenly and very clearly how my job articulates with the jobs other clerks are doing, and how all these jobs fall into a pattern. It isn't only a balance of my ticket inventory against my cash account; there's also a balance between my ticket inventory and the stock-room inventory, and there's another balance between my cash account and the auditor's account—and so it all goes on through a cycle of checks and counter-checks, and the sale of one lowly ticket to Yonkers is the beginning of a quite remarkable process that's completed and registered when the Ticket Agent certifies the daily sheet, debiting Cash and crediting the New York–to–Yonkers Passenger Account. . . .

"All this, I say, became clear very suddenly," said Mary Sweeney, "and the effect of that was to take all the worry away from the job. And you *do* worry, a bit, while you're still blindly following a routine. . . .

"I wouldn't know when ticket inventories are taken by the auditors. That really doesn't matter. If your work checks day by day, it will have to pass inspection when the auditors come around. . . . On the other hand, we ticket sellers are all bonded. . . .

"An inventory is easily taken," Mary Sweeney continued, "because of the railroad's method of numbering tickets. They're numbered serially, of course, but they do not begin with No. 1. They begin with No. 0, and No. 1 is therefore the second ticket. As a result . . . you simply read the number of the top ticket in each rack, and that shows you the precise number of tickets already sold from that particular rack. . . ."

And how did she ever land at Window 13?

"I took it. How long I'll keep it, though, I don't know.

"You see, each clerk owns his job—under the contract with the Brotherhood of Railway Clerks. But he acquires his right to it by seniority. . . . Well, I preferred the Window 13 job to the job I had been doing. I looked up the seniority list and found that I stood higher than the girl at Window 13; so I claimed her job, and she had to give way to my seniority. In railroad slang, I 'bumped her off.' . . . She looked at the job I was relinquishing, decided she wouldn't care for it, and bumped somebody else off a job she liked better . . . and the process was repeated till water had found its own level all around, and my old job was filled by a clerk who had less seniority than would buy a better job.

"Of course, in my time too," said Mary Sweeney, "I'll be bumped off No. 13. The men are still coming back from the Pacific—or still getting out of the hospitals—and they have mountains of seniority to bid in good jobs . . . for every day spent in the armed forces was added to the seniority totals of railroad men."

Any further questions?

"Yes, I have a serious question"—this from somebody's maiden aunt far back in the audience. "Last week I was standing in a long line before your window, Miss Sweeney, when a person thrust himself in front of everybody else and shouted at you: 'Hey, Sweeney!' (He did not say *Miss* Sweeney.) 'Hey, Sweeney!' he said. 'Look after everybody tonight! Don't turn anybody away! Wait on everybody who comes along!'

"Now I would like to ask, Miss Sweeney, is it customary for the clerks at Grand Central to wait on one person and refuse to wait on another?"

In a calm sort of way, Mary Sweeney thought for a moment; then she said: "Do you recall the illuminated sign over my window? It says: PULLMAN TRAVEL. It means that my window is reserved for those who intend to travel by Pullman. And every night, up to nine o'clock or so, I always have a line of five or six persons waiting to be attended to.

"A Pullman line is always slow in moving, because the clerk has to call up the Reservation Bureau on almost every ticket. That's why the Pullman windows are separated from the rest—so that people can get faster service at the day-coach windows. . . .

"But every hour of the day somebody turns up in my line asking for a day-coach ticket—and three times out of four the ticket asked for is not even a New York Central ticket but a Yankee ticket—New Haven Railroad ticket. Now the standing orders are that I must direct such a person to the proper day-coach window; and, after all, he has no one but himself to blame. Often, though, after standing in a Pullman line for twenty or twenty-five minutes, a passenger has hardly any time left to catch his train—and if it means a difference of many hours' waiting for the next train, a ticket seller will stretch a point and wait on him. But the rule is otherwise. . . .

"And then, every once in a while, we experience one of those strange nights—they come in cycles—when a kind of waywardness seems to take hold of the people in the Concourse, and they don't pay any attention at all to what they're doing. It's usual at No. 13 to have to turn away eight or nine day-coach passengers every night; it's that way steadily for week after week. And then, one night, for no apparent reason, the figures soar; and we have the thin edge of Bedlam breaking in on us. On a night like that the rule is lifted. The word is passed around among the ticket sellers: Wait on everybody. Don't turn anybody away. Sell the passenger anything he asks for.

"The gentleman you overheard last week," said Mary Sweeney, "was probably another clerk passing that word along from window to window. . . .

"Or," she added, "it could have been one of the ticket sellers from the Airlines Terminal across the street. Most of them come over to Grand Central for supper, and often they say things, just for fun, to mystify our passengers. Several of them had windows at Grand Central once, and there's a lot of kidding between us. We tell them it's shameful, their selling space on airliners. They're all members, you see, of the Brotherhood of Railway Clerks."

Further questions? Dozens of them. But Mary Sweeney had a night's work ahead of her at Window 13, and so—

Anyhow, you see the sort of woman who came into Grand Central when the war drew men away from the ticket windows.

Another is twenty-year-old Kathleen Mullady who left the windows in 1945 to become night cashier of the Ticket Agent's Department. She has brains in combination with astonishing good looks. The New York Central once made use of her photograph in a four-color magazine advertisement; and Miss Mullady's photograph has since figured in the advertising of a very famous cosmetics firm.

"THE PUBLIC BE DAMNED!"

By the Golden Clock it was 4:01. The crowds in the Concourse were becoming numerous again; and once more the look of hurry was in their faces. And there was crossness in their voices, the mark of fatigue. It's astonishing the way the mood changes from one part of the day to another.

Just now they were women, largely. Hundreds of suburban wives on shopping tours to the city were hastening home to prepare the dinners of hundreds of Grand Central commuters. Children were numerous. Some of the smaller ones broke away from their mothers, gleefully, to slide upon the marble floor as if it were ice. But their shrieks of delight only emphasized the ill-humor of the adults.

"The train leaves in half a minute, hurry!"

"Don't give me that stuff!"

"What did he say, Track 29?" "Twenty, *twenty,* he said Track *Twenty!*"

"I have to get my tickets yet."

"All these girls wearing Polack shawls over their heads give me a pain."

Unlistening, Ichabod went merrily forward with still another of his tales.

"What you've now got to see," said the pedagogue, "is that Grand Central is more than a building, more than a concourse of people, more than the New York terminal of the *Commodore* or even the *Century.* It's all that, of course. But, transcending all that; it's also an idea.

"Grand Central is an idea," he said, "like Wall street, or Hollywood. . . . Not just a symbol, it's a principle; a dynamic force. For a time it was a militant force in the shaping of this country's history. It was New York fighting for the commerce of the Middle West and capturing the commercial leadership of the Continent. At a critical moment," said Ichabod, "Grand Central station was power personified. And you're not likely to forget, of course, that in the eyes of millions of people, Grand Central Station was 'The public be damned!'

"It was known all over the world . . . and Chauncey Depew was its ambassador to England. You remember Chauncey Depew; he was the Yale graduate who succeeded so well as the Commodore's attorney, and attracted so many more Yale graduates to the Vanderbilt railroads. Time was when they called the executive offices at Grand Central 'the Yale Club.' Today, of course, the real Yale Club is just across the street, at Vanderbilt avenue and Forty-fourth street . . . on railroad property, straddling the tracks, right next to the Biltmore. And today, during the luncheon hour, the Yale Club looks like a meeting of the board of the New York Central Railroad. . . .

"Anyhow, Chauncey Depew was the lawyer who negotiated the agreement under which the city paid half the cost of building the Park Avenue Tunnel. He became a United States Senator in his day . . . Republican, of course. He turned down the post of American Ambassador to Tokyo in order to become the railroad's ambassador to the English investing public—to dine with Gladstone and the Prince of Wales, to bow before the Queen, above all to win and keep the confidence of the banking and brokerage houses of Throckmorton street and Threadneedle street. The public never quite understood these points," said Ichabod.

"But it was well known, of course, that an awful lot of English money was being poured into the Central-Hudson Rail-Road. People resented it . . . on patriotic grounds; and wherever they turned at Grand Central they saw—or they imagined that they saw—fresh evidences of English influence and control. When the railroads changed over to left-hand operation, the super-patriots foamed at the mouth. . . .

"There were all kinds of stories told," said Ichabod. . . .

When the Commodore died amid falling snow in the New Year's week of 1877, his place was taken by his eldest son, William Henry, who was already fifty-six years old. A modest man, whom his father had scorned for twenty years, William H. had married a finely cultured wife, the daughter of a Church of England clergyman. Notably, too, he was the first of his family to write his name in one word—Vanderbilt. And he was excoriated on the unsupported word of a Chicago reporter who quoted him as saying: "The public be damned!"

He was an extremely dutiful son. When his father, in a passion of curse-laden abuse, denounced him as too lacking in ability to be anything but a farmer, he took over the family farm on Staten Island and ran it for the first twenty years of his married life. He was forty when his father deigned to pull a few political wires on his behalf and had him appointed trustee of the bankrupt Staten Island Railroad. Abruptly, then, he turned the railroad into a highly prosperous enterprise, and astounded his father—who promptly "bought Harlem" and gave "Billie" a chance to try his hand at railroading on a bigger scale. And from that hour forward, William H. was the Commodore's right-hand man. The son of a genius, he was a genius, too; one of the ablest financiers in American history. But their partnership was always the partnership of a father and a son, and the father was master every minute of the time. "If you tell me not to smoke, I'll obey you," said William H., who was then forty-two years old. The old man grunted; and Billie threw away the offending cigar—gave up smoking forever.

After the death of his father, William H. had only eight years more to live, but in that brief hour he changed American railroad history. He acquired running rights over the Wabash and began operating a through sleeping car from New York to St. Louis in thirty-five hours—with unhurried half-hour stops for breakfast at Rochester, luncheon at Erie, supper at Toledo and breakfast at Mattoon. He reduced running time between New York and Chicago from thirty-six hours to twenty-six hours and twenty minutes. He consolidated the Canada Southern with the Michigan Central. He adopted the English plan of railway organization, and two years later transferred the bulk of Central-Hudson stock to English ownership. Notably, he fought his great duel with the Pennsylvania Railroad. And this last was a gigantic struggle, a campaign for an empire. People and railroads got hurt.

The old Commodore himself, as we have seen, had long ago laid plans for dividing the outstanding shares of Central-Hudson stock between the New York and the Royal stock exchanges. In 1879 William H. carried that scheme into full effect. It was given out at the time that he had disposed of those 250,000 shares—representing 62.5 per cent of his holdings—in deference to a widespread prejudice in the United States against personal ownership of railroads; and that he had disposed of them in England because he could not have thrown them into Wall street without wrecking the market. Both assertions undoubtedly were true, but they were hardly a tenth of all the reasons that lay back of that huge transaction. Actually, Vanderbilt had lifted his company's fate out of the hands of Wall street, and, by avoiding too large a dependence upon the London bankers either, by dividing the shares, he was insuring against shock from fortuitous raids and booms on either exchange.

Again, London paid 133 for the whole gigantic lot, whereas the bid price in Wall street was only 130 to begin with, and would have tumbled rapidly. So Vanderbilt actually got an immensely better price in London; and he got one thing more that, from his point of view, was priceless. By selling that quarter of a million shares in London rather than at home, Vanderbilt retained virtually full control—for he, personally, would continue to vote the shares owned in England. That was to be Chauncey Depew's great work. For years to come, Depew was to make those annual trips to London that were so to mystify American newspaper readers. Their purpose, of course, was to report, elucidate, explain; to hold the confidence of the English stockholders, and every year—like a Prime Minister appealing to Parliament—to win the renewal of their proxies.

There were these and still more reasons for the stock transfer; and the most urgent of all was that in 1879, when the transfer took place, a battle was brewing and Vanderbilt needed cash—and more cash than the Wall street of that day had ever seen all at once. Wall street was divided, anyhow, between his friends and his enemies; and, with few exceptions, he could never be sure of his friends. But it was part of his inheritance, one of the fruits of his father's planning, that the London bankers had conceived a great admiration for Billie and were willing to trust their money in his hands.

It was a fight of long standing. To trace it to its remote origin, let us say simply that it began the hour the Pennsylvania Railroad and the

Central-Hudson first became aware of each other's existence; they were rivals, and they disliked each other at first sight. It was a battle of men, of course; but it was also a battle of forces. It was a clash of great enterprises, and of the hopes and expectations of men. It was on both sides the usual sordid fight for riches; but on both sides, too, it was also a struggle to create and build what men had set their hearts upon. Therefore it was a passionate struggle.

We can overlook all that took place prior to 1881—the mad racing of trains to Chicago, as each road attempted to cut half an hour off the other's running time; the cutting of fares; the cut-throat slashing of freight rates. We can overlook their scramble for control of small but strategic railroads, and their fierce rivalry in the coal fields of northeastern Pennsylvania, which both had newly penetrated, which neither could quite claim as its own. By 1881 their battle had come to a new stage, and if you had had need of a surveyor that year, you would probably have had a hard time to find one within miles of New York. They were otherwise engaged; they were off in the mountains.

And by 1883 it was open war. The railroads were invading each other's territories. Striking at the heart of the Central-Hudson's monopoly of the Hudson and the Mohawk valleys, the Pennsylvania was furiously building a new line to Albany and Buffalo; and Vanderbilt was just as furiously building a new trunk line between New York and Philadelphia, Harrisburg and Pittsburgh. Technically, perhaps, we ought to say that the Pennsylvania was financing the construction of the New York, West Shore & Buffalo Railroad, the actual building of which was in other hands; but to say this is to be merely technical, for the power back of the West Shore, and the only power that made it possible, was the Pennsylvania Railroad. And, technically, we ought also to say that Vanderbilt had bought his way into the Philadelphia & Reading and the Central Railroad of New Jersey; and that he was building the South Pennsylvania Railway through the mountains from Pittsburgh to Harrisburg, where it would meet the tracks of the P. &. R. As a final step, he was planning to push the south Penn road straight on in from Harrisburg to Philadelphia; and to operate between Philadelphia, Baltimore and Washington over B. &. O. tracks, between Philadelphia and New York over the tracks of the P. & R.–Jersey Central combination.

The West Shore began operating on the fourth of June, 1883, when its first passenger train pulled out of Pennsylvania Station, Jersey City, for Newburgh, N. Y. By the ninth of July, the Pennsylvania was running a through service from Washington to Albany and, beyond Albany, to Saratoga—then at the height of its glory as America's finest summer resort. By the first of October, the West Shore had entered Syracuse, and before the year was out it was "a major trunk-line railroad" running over a well-constructed roadbed from Jersey City to Buffalo. And three weeks later—as the result of a fearful reduction of passenger fares and freight rates on the Central-Hudson—the New York, West Shore & Buffalo Railroad was in the hands of a receiver.

Fifty million dollars had been spent on building it. Now additional capital was pumped into it, in a campaign to enable it to take breath and live. And there was, of course, a lively reaction. In a spirit of lusty, boisterous good health, the West Shore undercut the Central-Hudson's rate schedule. Accepting the challenge, the Central-Hudson again reduced its rates; and Vanderbilt—apropos of nothing at all, of course—announced: "I am the richest man in the world. . . ."

He drove his engineers, and work went forward a little faster on the South Pennsylvania Railway. "Vanderbilt's Folly" men called it, but the South Penn was planned with the greatest care ever lavished upon an American railroad. From Harrisburg to Pittsburgh, it was laid out upon a line 215 miles long with easy grades, whereas the Pennsylvania's line was 249 miles long with very difficult grades. And as the builders pushed on feverishly, straight across the Alleghenies, tunnels were cut through four and a half miles of granite; great stone piers and abutments rose towering above the rivers; and by the first of December, 1885, a total of 164 miles of grade had been completed, ready for the laying of the ties and rails. Possibly sixty miles of it were curved. More than a hundred miles were on the tangent. A single stretch forty miles long was straight as a shaft of light.

It was a magnificent achievement, even as it stood. And—watching its progress—the Pennsylvania Railroad crowd passed from disbelief to anxiety, and from anxiety to painful recognition that something had to be done. In the end, they came to a decision, and on the afternoon of that fateful first of December, 1885, J. P. Morgan conveyed their message to Vanderbilt.

And that was the end of many things. It was the end of the Pennsylvania's invasion of Central-Hudson territory; abruptly the New York, West Shore & Buffalo collapsed and was handed over to the Vanderbilts, who paid for it not a single dollar—who simply accepted it, lock, stock and barrel, in return for their guarantee to pay two million dollars a year interest on its bonds. It was also the end of the South Pennsylvania Railway; when the whistle blew that night, the laborers laid down their tools—and never went back to pick them up again. It was the end of unrestrained war; Congress was in a fighting mood, and two years more would witness the setting up (1887) of the Interstate Commerce Commission with power to fix the fares and freight rates and govern the business practices of virtually every railroad in the United States. In American railroad history, the first of December, 1885, marked the end of an era. It was abrupt and final, like the switching out of a light.

The South Penn Railway was sold to the Pennsylvania Railroad, presumably for a good price. For a certainty, it was sold without haggling, and without consulting the Philadelphia & Reading Railway crowd who, after all, had been Vanderbilt's partners, who had laid out a great deal of money in anticipation of great days to come, and who now loudly complained that they should have had at least a sporting chance to buy in the property; who even went so far as to suggest that they had been thrown to the wolves.

The P. & R. went downhill after that. And when the South Penn was no longer to be feared as a competitor, the Pennsylvania in 1890 allowed it to fall, still unfinished, under the sheriff's hammer. The B. & O. bought it and carried it on its books for forty-four years as an asset worth —one dollar! And then, in 1934, it was acquired by the Commonwealth of Pennsylvania. The bridges were completed, the tunnels widened, the roadbed stripped of its overgrowth of weeds, briars, and even trees. Then a concrete pavement was poured over it, and the magnificently laid-out line of the South Pennsylvania Railway became the present Pennsylvania Turnpike, the greatest so far of America's high-speed motor highways.

The New York, West Shore & Buffalo was transferred on the first of December, 1885, to a new company, organized at a moment's notice and called simply the West Shore Railroad. And four days later the West Shore Company leased all its properties to the Central-Hudson for a period of 475 years; and, while retaining its separate name, the West Shore became in fact a division of the now immensely powerful New-York Central & Hudson-River Rail-Road.

"And three days after that again," said Ichabod, "on the eighth of December, 1885, William H. Vanderbilt dropped dead. The president of the B. & O. had called upon him at his home. . . . They quarreled loudly. At the height of an impassioned outburst, Vanderbilt fell to the floor. . . .

"No other American ever wielded so much power, and for eight years all that he was was summed up in the expression, *Grand Central Depot*. The Pennsylvania Railroad crowd, down in Philadelphia, was Broad Street Station—Broad Street Station said this, Broad Street Station did that. Vanderbilt was an individual; but, just the same, he was Grand Central Depot. Vanderbilt's victory was the victory of Grand Central over Broad Street Station; and when Vanderbilt was dead, Grand Central still represented in the minds of the American people the power he had concentrated here."

It was 4:25. Ichabod looked as if he intended to go on with the story; but things are always happening at Grand Central, and even the best of stories are liable to be interrupted. This time it was two things happening in quick succession, and, as we afterward discovered, there was a connection between the two.

We were standing near the northeast corner of the Concourse. There was a commotion at one of the gates, and the word spread swiftly through the crowd that a woman had fainted. Ichabod bit his lips, but made no move. After all, the woman was being cared for, and he could only make things worse by rushing over to stare at her misfortune.

But two minutes later there was a commotion among the gatemen. And this time Ichabod, who seems to know so much about these matters, announced seriously that "somebody's in trouble," and dashed off to find out who it was. He was soon back.

"A train just hit the wall," he said; then he remembered and grinned.

"It isn't half so bad as it sounds," he told us. "A train arrived and discharged her passengers; and the passengers, when they arrived at the gate, found it locked against them. . . .

"You see, every gateman follows a timetable; every move he makes falls in with the pattern of train movements, and sometimes there's a tolerance of only thirty or forty seconds between his locking one gate, back of a departing train, and his opening another gate in advance of an incoming train. It's all worked out, elaborately—and that, by the way, is one reason why the gateman can't afford to hold the gate for you if you aren't there dead on the second. . . .

"This fellow closed his gate at 4:25. . . . At 4:25:05 a woman came running up—they say she's sixty if she's a day—and, when she found the gate closed, she promptly collapsed; and the gateman tried to help her. . . . That's why his next gate wasn't open at 4:26½; and that's why the train hit the wall.

"He'll probably be on the carpet for this. Maybe they'll accept his excuse, and maybe he'll get a tongue-lashing and a fistful of brownies . . . for the laws of the railroad are strict, and excuses cut no ice. Each brownie is a demerit; it takes away from a man's seniority standing. . . ."

The tall fellow was silent for a moment. Then he announced abruptly: "Well, since we're on the subject, maybe I'd better tell you next about the gates. . . ."

SCARS UPON THE MARBLE

"THE GATES are important," said Ichabod. "Also they're imposing, and they pose—"

Ichabod again stopped short, again fished out his beautiful watch. "It's nearly half past four," he said. "Before it's too late, let's look at one of the gates. And let's consider a point of politeness.

"You remember Bill Walsh, the information chief who looks so much like Mr. Pickwick. You remember his words: 'The public is my friend.' Maybe you smiled at them. . . . But keep them in mind for a moment. There's something about these gates," said Ichabod, "that may surprise you."

To reach the gates—in the wall that separates the Concourse from the train platforms—you pass a few yards under the North Balcony, the Philosophers' Gallery. There the wall is all of marble, and each gateway is framed in marble. It is, in fact, a marble arch, drawn upon a long radius; therefore a low arch.

"Nothing in all the history of architecture," said Ichabod, "was ever more severely plain. . . . But if you like the Classic, you like this.

"And now," he continued with the air of one about to pull a rabbit out of a high silk hat . . . "And now," he said, "I'd like you to notice the marks on that marble. You can still read the words that used to be there in bronze letters, till the day after Pearl Harbor when the company ripped them out and turned them in for scrap. The words are still faintly visible, you see—where for twenty-eight years the marble was protected from the cleaners' soap and water; where today it shines with just a bit more of its original polish. The words are clear as day: 'All Passengers Will Be Required to Show Their Tickets at the Gates.'

"For New York," said Ichabod, "that was a remarkable legend. We can overlook the use of bronze, which was, after all, in keeping with the whole scheme of things. The important thing is the wording. You'll notice a British touch about it . . . you'll notice the deliberate avoidance of the imperative. Everywhere else in New York, you get a curt command: 'Follow the Green Line,' 'Have Your Fare Ready,' and 'Show Your Tickets.' But the New York Central Railroad carefully avoided saying: 'Show Your Tickets.'

"It's only one of a thousand instances of extreme politeness on the part of the Central. You can trace it through fifty years of their history following the death of Billie Vanderbilt.

"You remember Billie; he was the Commodore's son; the one who fought the great battle against the Pennsylvania and was supposed to have said, 'The public be damned.' It caused an awful lot of trouble; and, looking at these doorways, we can say it left its mark on the present-day Grand Central.

"And the funny thing is," said Ichabod, "that—"

It was in 1882 that William H. Vanderbilt—according to the reporter of the Chicago *Inter-Ocean*—uttered the words for which he and his railroad have been excoriated ever since. It would seem, however, that nobody knows, or ever did know, either the context out of which these four words were lifted, or the circumstances in which they were spoken. Many versions are given. Most commonly heard are two:

1. Vanderbilt was sitting alone at breakfast in his private car when the reporter burst in upon him, demanding an immediate interview. Vanderbilt asked him to wait in the reception compartment. The man refused. He laid it down, in effect, that as "the public's representative," he had a right to attention which overcame Vanderbilt's right to finish his breakfast in privacy; whereupon Vanderbilt, a powerfully built man, picked the fellow up bodily and threw him out of the car with a wrathful: "You and your public be damned."

2. Stealing a march on the Pennsylvania, Vanderbilt had cut half an hour off the running time of the *Fast Mail*, his best train, and was at Chicago to witness her arrival in the record-breaking time of twenty-eight hours. She was crowded with passengers, and, with a great deal of suppressed excitement, Vanderbilt had followed her progress as each towerman along the line telegraphed word of her passing. But

then, for several anxious minutes, she was unreported, and word got round that she had jumped the track and "piled up in a cornfield." Vanderbilt turned pale. Running up to him just that moment, the reporter demanded: "What shall I tell the public?" And, in obvious distress, Vanderbilt exclaimed: "The public be damned, I'm worried about all those people on the train."

There is a further story, that it was at no one time or place that Vanderbilt used the complained-of words, but that he had made a practice of using them to capsize the pretensions of some reporters of that period—pretensions that rose to their inevitable crest a few years later when a New York reporter solemnly declared: "*I* am the public."

In any case, the "Public-be-damned" incident, supposing that it had some basis in fact, was not what it was widely represented to be; and there are those who have argued that it might have been quickly forgot if Vanderbilt had not arrogantly refused to lay his cards on the table and defend himself. But the fact is that Vanderbilt was prompt and explicit in his denial of the story published by the *Inter-Ocean*. You can read that denial on page three of the *New-York Tribune* for October the eighteenth, 1882.

"Anyhow," said Ichabod, "a calculated campaign of politeness to live down the 'Public-be-damned' episode explains those marks in the marble over the gateways leading from the Concourse to the train platforms. . . . Folks like to know about such things.

"And now. . . ."

The tall fellow looked about him awkwardly for a moment. Then his face brightened up again.

"There's the next fellow I want you to meet," he announced—and led the way to where a man in blue stood, watch in hand, facing the gateway that leads to Track 20. He was a tall man with white hair and a very placid face; and he wore the uniform of an assistant stationmaster.

In all, Stationmaster at Grand Central has seven assistants; they supervise the loading of the trains, and the trains are under their jurisdiction till the moment arrives when the green light is flashed and the conductor, taking charge for the first time, gives the two blasts on the air whistle—the signal to proceed. It's an arrangement not usually met with on American railroads. At Grand Central the conductor's responsibility begins when the train begins to roll; and instead of turning a train over to the conductor, the yard-master—when he places her on the departure track—turns her over to the assistant stationmaster.

"It's one more relic," said Ichabod, "of the system the Commodore set up at the old Grand Central Depot—where the stationmaster, you remember, was also the train dispatcher. . . . Once you understand this, though, you won't be surprised to know that instead of the Brotherhood of Railway Clerks, the seven assistant stationmasters at Grand Central belong to the Railroad Yard-Masters of North America. . . .

"Anyhow," the tall fellow said abruptly, "this—is Jim Mahoney. . . . Assistant Stationmaster James P. Mahoney."

Jim Mahoney never quite acknowledged the introduction. Instead, he carefully put his watch away and called over to the gateman: "All right, John!" As if he disliked formality, and was choosing his own ground of approach, he announced, obviously for our benefit: "All we have to sell is courtesy." Then he turned and looked fully upon us for the first time and smiled a very genial smile; and, having thus evidenced his good will, he gave a jaunty toss of his head—by which he meant, said Ichabod, that we were all to follow him through the gate.

On the outer concourse, Jim Mahoney gazed straight ahead, smiling and chuckling to himself, and looking as if at any moment he might burst with good humor. Presently he did. Warmed, it would appear, by his own genial glow, he suddenly bestowed upon us the remarkable confidence that he used to be a bartender.

"Thirty years ago," he continued, chuckling more heartily than ever, "I was in charge of the bar at the old Vanderbilt Hotel. . . . A lot of high railroad executives used to do their drinking there, and that's how I came to Grand Central. . . . They were having a little trouble. . . . They said to me: 'Jim, what we need is courtesy, and you're the man for the job.' So I quit the liquor business . . . walked across the street from the Vanderbilt to Grand Central . . . began working as a doorman . . . made my own way up to assistant station-master . . .

"The old Grand Central? I remember it. They used to have a big clock on the old Grand Central, and they had a lot of pigeons on the roof. . . . Behind the bar at the Vanderbilt, we had an honest clock, but a great many commuters—in the evening—insisted on going by the station clock across the street. They knew the station clock was always wrong, because the pigeons used to roost on the hands and slow up the works. But their wives didn't know that. And so they'd miss their trains . . . they'd have an excuse for a few more drinks. And then they'd go home and tell their wives with a clear conscience that they had two minutes 'by the station clock,' but the gate was closed when they got there."

Jim Mahoney chuckled again. Then he drew forth his watch. There was a train ahead of us—and below us, for the platforms at Grand Central are somewhat below the level of the Concourse, and are connected with the outer concourse by ramps; and the tracks, of course, are below the level of the platforms.

"From 2 P. M. to 11 P. M.," said Jim, "I have charge of all departures from all tracks of the upper level east of Track 25. That means I have the eastern half of the Concourse tracks; what we call the New Haven side. They begin with Track 11. There isn't any Track 12. . . . I just have Track 11, Track 13, Track 14, and so on . . . up to and including Track 24; thirteen tracks in all. And I'm out here to see every departure with my own eyes. . . .

"Now look!" he said abruptly. "In one second—*now!*—the gate closes!"

It didn't, though; and Jim turned upon the gateman a face dangerously wrathful. A girl came through with a skip, and the gate slammed shut. The face cleared up, and hardly two seconds later Jim was chattering on, as genial as ever.

"Now watch the light go on—way up at the head of the platform!" he said.

He had hardly spoken when a green light flashed, and the trainmen, out upon the platform, all at once began their cry of "All aboard!" The girl, the last passenger through the gate, stepped quickly into the vestibule of the rear car.

"And now," said Jim, watchfully, "they *are* aboard. Get out of town!"

The air whistle sounded. The train began rolling. Jim looked at his watch.

"Perfect departure," he announced happily.

"What would have happened if—"

"I'll tell you," said Jim, and he turned upon us what must have been the most placid face in all New York. "It's this way. That gate-man there is working for me. When he locked his gate he threw the switch outside, and so you saw the green light go on. That green light . . . was my order to the conductor to leave town. If he didn't—well, I'd have been down there pretty damn' fast to find out why!"

A cloud seemed to pass over Jim's face as he said this; and once more you got the impression that Jim is not a man to be trifled with, but one who can be as swiftly wrathful, when provoked, as he is genial, and even gentle, when pleased.

"I hear," said Ichabod, "that one of your trains hit the wall a few minutes ago."

"No!" said Jim incredulously. "Today?"

Solemnly Jim thumbed his way through his report book. Solemnly he shook his head.

"It ain't in the record," he said cautiously.

And you knew then that Jim knows how to be angry, but he also knows how to forget.

"Well," said Ichabod, "you've now seen something of the gates; you've seen something of how the gatemen do their work, and how an assistant stationmaster does his; and why the stationmaster at Grand Central belongs to the yard-masters' union. . . ."

We were now out on the Concourse again.

"As I said before," the tall fellow continued, "the gates at Grand Central are imposing, and they also pose— But maybe I'd better show you one thing more before I take up the subject of the gates. I'll show you the dedication of Grand Central."

We passed through the Waiting Room. Beyond the Waiting Room, halfway up the ramp to the doors that open on Forty-second street, we stopped, and turned about. And there before us, above the

Waiting-Room doors, we saw the inscription that confronts all who come in by this main entrance to Grand Central: "To all those who with head, heart and hand toiled in the construction of this monument to the *public service* . . ."

It was 4:48.

RIDDLE OF THE GATES

"As I tried to say," said Ichabod, "you've seen the gates at Grand Central—with their low marble arches, upstairs; and their high round arches and ceramic trellises and oak leaves, downstairs. Upstairs and down, Concourse and Lower Concourse, they're an imposing lot of doors; and they pose a question. Every door implies a question: What's back of it, what does it open upon?

"At Grand Central," said Ichabod, "there seem to be two different answers. You remember the 'Triumphal March' from *Aïda*, what a grand opening *that* has, with the drums beating and all the horns and trumpets blowing. But in the end, you know, there isn't much to it; there isn't much for the grand opening to open upon. And that seems to be the general opinion of this array of doors at Grand Central. In themselves, they're grand; but what they open upon is something else again. For the average person they open upon a kind of desolate nether world of tracks and trains . . . dreary and uninviting. As you pass through them, you exchange the bright sunshine of the Concourse for a semi-Stygian darkness. Nobody's interested in darkness," said Ichabod.

"But the truth is," the tall fellow hurried on to say, "that they open upon the most fascinating display of organized effort in all New York. . . . You can think of it as a dozen games of chess played all at once, with a network of tracks for a board and swiftly moving trains for chessmen. Or you can think of it as a kind of swift, harmonious interlacing of train movements. This—"

Ichabod paused for effect.

"This is the railroad," he resumed, with fine simplicity; "and when you see how this works, you'll know forever that the hero of the piece is not the engineman in the cab of his locomotive, but the white-haired tower director, alone with his clock and his great diagram of the tracks forever flashing with tiny green lights. He's Dispatcher' local deputy; he's the man in charge here. No wheel may turn till h gives the word; and, grouped in his control, four hundred signals ar a single instrument for the conveyance of his orders to the engine men. Tower Director calls the tune, and the trains move througl interweaving patterns in flawless rhythm.

"All this is what the doors at Grand Central open out on, and it' New York's greatest drama. It isn't just a dark cellarful of tracks; it' a rather wonderful harmonizing of simultaneous movements. That' the essence of it. All the rest is detail. I won't bother you with detail," said Ichabod.

"This," he continued, "is the real Grand Central Terminal, an all the rest is built around it. This is what mattered first, and wha presented to the builders their essential problem. When they ha solved this, the rest came easy.

"Fundamentally," said Ichabod, "the problem was a problem o granite, as I said before. The Commodore never settled that. An then came enormous crowds, and it wasn't that the old Grand Cen tral Depot couldn't house them well enough. The point is that ther wasn't trackage enough to handle the required number of trains. . . ."

The Commodore had done well to place his gaudy terminal i Forty-second street. He had foreseen the growth of New York, and th movement northward of people and of business. But two things h had not foreseen. He had not realized that this growth would com all in a rush; that Grand street would give way to Fourteenth, an Fourteenth would give way to Twenty-third street as the city's princi pal shopping center, all in less than a quarter of a century. He ha never expected that the upward surge of the city would overtake an overwhelm his Grand Central Depot before it was twenty-five year old. But that's what happened. And he had not foreseen the ever swifter development of his own railroad.

Really, of course, it was never a big terminal. The house was bi enough, but the terminal was small even for 1871; and for the bette part of forty years it was a never-ending battle to get trains in an out. In one way it was a good fate that placed Grand Central Statio where she stood, at the heart of New York; but it was an ugly fate that placed her with her back against the rocks, leaving her so little room for track development.

At the south end, within the Commodore's train-shed, there were, as we have seen, but twelve terminal tracks. At the north end began a double-tracked main line. And fused between these upper and lower elements, linking two main-line tracks with twelve terminal tracks, was a third essential element, the terminal fan—a more or less triangular layout of tracks and switches, the simple purpose of which was to make any terminal track accessible to either main-line track.

It was an unusual fan; for example, it had all those sidings required to make fly-switching possible, and it had facilities to enable the locomotives of three different railroads to pass directly from any terminal track to any of three different engine yards and three different roundhouses. But, when all is said, it was still a twelve-to-two fan; and how tiny it really was became apparent as early as 1874, when the night express from Albany pulled in double-headed—drawn, that is to say, by two locomotives—and with a "consist" of baggage cars and the usual number of coaches, plus *twenty-two* sleeping cars. She tied up the whole terminal. She had to be broken up into three sections, and when these were in the train-shed they occupied 25 per cent of all the terminal tracks. The railroad was growing fast, there was no denying that; and there was no denying, either, that Grand Central was a huge front with very little back of it.

But the old Commodore was quick to see the flaw, and the four-tracking of the main line from Forty-ninth street out, completed in 1876, was followed almost immediately by the construction of six more terminal tracks and the enlargement of the fan to fit the new situation. And one curious result of all this was to force the adoption of left-hand operation; the law was reversed at Grand Central, and the operating rule of the English railways was adopted.

The Central-Hudson station, as we have seen, lay along Vanderbilt avenue, to the west of the twelve original terminal tracks. It followed, then, that there was no place to put the new tracks but over to the east; and so they were laid there, parallel to the others, and a new train-shed was built over them, alongside of and flush against the older structure. The latter, of course, was still the big shed; the new one was "the annex," equally long but only half as wide, less lofty, and a great deal less impressive.

Fly-switching had to be abandoned; the fan was too crowded. The annex became an arrival bay. The big shed was reserved exclusively for departures; there, while receiving passengers, the trains would lie "tails in, engines out in the open air." And thus the terminal tracks were divided into two separate clusters, according to function. The departure bay, bright and sunny as ever, was there in the angle between the Central-Hudson and the New Haven stations; and the smoky arrival bay was well out of sight of either, and empied its arriving throngs directly into Forty-second street. As to all of which everybody was fairly well pleased.

But since the arrival tracks lay to the east, and the departure tracks to the west, it stood to reason that the outgoing trains would have to use the westerly pair of tracks through the tunnel, and the incoming trains would have to use the easterly pair. It was either that or else every possible arrival route across the fan would foul every possible departure route; simultaneous departures and arrivals would be impossible, and the working capacity of the fan would be reduced by 50 per cent. But that was out of the question; and so, as there was no escaping it, the left-hand rule was adopted. It prevailed for thirty years at Grand Central and all the way out to Spuyten Duyvil on the Central-Hudson and Woodlawn on the Harlem.

At Woodlawn and Spuyten Duyvil crossings were established; at those two points the main-line tracks crossed each other, and—at such a cost—the changes were effected, from left-hand to right-hand operation outbound, from right-hand to left-hand operation inbound. Each crossing was, of course, a danger-point. It was protected by semaphore signals, and these were interlocked with one another all around the circle, so that no signal could be brought to the *Clear* unless all conflicting signals were first brought to the *Stop*—where they froze and remained immovable as long as the first signal stayed at the *Clear*. It was a noteworthy example of signal engineering work.

And the new fan, for its day and age, was a noteworthy piece of trackwork. It was so designed as to make possible the setting up of alternate routes; if need be, arriving and departing trains, in dovetailed, simultaneous movements, could exchange a given terminal track for a given main-line track, passing each other on parallel tracks within the fan itself. And every switch was equipped with locking bars that rode against the inside faces of the rails; and these, when pressed home by the flanges of wheels, locked up the working parts; hence it became impossible for an absent-minded towerman to "throw" a switch while a train was passing over it. Again, the switches and the signals were all mechanically interlocked with one another, and if the towerman threw a switch, the same pull of the lever also threw an assortment of bars that locked all conflicting levers in position. From all these points of view, the reconstructed fan at Grand Central was one of the best things of its kind in America.

But from the operating point of view it had serious faults, deriving mainly from its very low altitude. The original twelve-to-two fan had been cramped enough. But here was a fan with eighteen tracks at the base; and you cannot increase the base of a fan very well unless you also increase the altitude. At Grand Central there was a limit beyond which the fan's altitude could not be extended, and that limit was where the tunnel began. The fan was squeezed within four hundred yards; and so it was a very low-speed fan, full of sharp curves that made the going tortuous. It was twisted and ugly; at one point warped about to avoid an upward thrust of granite that towered forty feet above the tracks.

Yet, such as it was, the Central-Hudson and the Harlem had had to rip out their roundhouses and engine yards and coaching yards in order to make room for it. (Once more recalling its lease, the New-Haven Railroad flatly refused to move any of its facilities away from the terminal precinct where they belonged.) The Vanderbilt roads had had to transfer their yards to Mott Haven, which is five miles out along the main line. And that was a great misfortune, which in swift order had the twofold effect of overcrowding the main line with locomotives passing to and from their engine yards, and of creating within the tunnel smoke conditions that were not less than appalling. It was a not unheard of thing, in the years that followed, for an engineman to be overcome by coal gas at the throttle of his locomotive; and it was not unusual for a fireman to lie flat on the footplates, during a transit of the tunnel, in order to escape the worst of the fumes.

On the other hand, it soon became so difficult in the tunnel to see the red and green lights of the block signals that traffic was seriously delayed. Unable to see it except at close-hand, the enginemen generally were down to "dead speed" as they approached a signal. And to help cure this situation, William Vanderbilt borrowed still another trick from England, introducing to the Park avenue tunnel the London fog system of torpedo signals—though that's another story. The torpedo signals failed only once, so far as the public ever knows; but once too often.

Judged by its results alone, it was a tremendous upheaval. It changed the whole tone of city life; for a generation it left the city to the very rich and the very poor, without the cushioning of a sufficiently large intervening middle class to take up the shocks and absorb the rancors of class relationships. Notably, it changed New York from a city predominantly of home-owners to a city overwhelmingly of rent-payers.

It began in the early Nineties, slowly. New York was getting too crowded, and too dirty, and the better-off middle-class families fell into the habit of living in the suburbs all the year round instead of just in the summer months, as they had long been accustomed to do. Presently houses in the city became a drug on the market. Then the boarding-house keepers came in and whole neighborhoods went headlong to the devil. Anyhow, the older families got out, and the private house—with the green shades, the white lace curtains and the high brownstone stoop—had seen its day. And the last years of the nineteenth century were marked by a mass movement to the suburbs of roughly two millions of people; so that, as compared with possibly forty thousand in 1890, half a million commuters in 1900 were entering New York every weekday morning and going back to their homes in the suburbs every night. "Forty-five minutes from Broadway" was a slogan for ten years before it became a play.

And the story of that migration is in great measure the history of the "second Grand Central." By 1898 the commuter tide was rising rapidly, and nobody could tell what the end of it was going to be. But this much was clear, that the Commodore's Grand Central, with its three separate stations, was working badly and would have to be enlarged and simplified in a very great hurry, or else the railroads using it would have to forfeit any further share in the new prosperity; and, instead of a magnet to attract people to Westchester, Grand Central would be, in effect, a barrier to keep out all above a given number.

It was even possible that things had come to such a pass in 1898. Anyhow, the bulk of the commuters were coming into New York each day by ferryboat from North Jersey and Long Island. Grand Central's supposed advantage in lying at the heart of New York didn't count for much in their eyes. Perhaps they enjoyed the sail across the water; they preferred it, certainly, to being jammed into one or another of the relatively few trains that could be warped in and out of Grand Central, and then gassed half to death in the Park avenue tunnel. Whichever way it was looked upon, the evidence was clear that the new commuter element did not love Grand Central, and a startled management came abruptly upon the question of what to do about it.

What they did, briefly, was to change Grand Central Depot into Grand Central Station. The work was begun in 1899, completed in 1901. The gawky mansard roof was taken down, and the red brick walls were stripped of their heavy load of cast-iron "masonry." The walls were then run up three stories higher and faced with granite; and then you had, outwardly, a subdued and rather handsome building six stories high, in spirit Florentine.

Inwardly, the three stations were made into one, and the former New Haven station, facing on Forty-second street, became a single, vast waiting room in which, however, all three railroads had their separate ticket offices. And out in the train-sheds too—the big shed and the annex—things were reorganized. Gone was the old way of allowing passengers to cut across the tracks; they were now confined to platforms and to a concourse that lay between the platforms and the Waiting Room.

By making these platforms very narrow indeed, the authorities crowded in three additional tracks, and so they now had twenty-one. They kept the gateman, but posted him in the train-shed, at the entrance to each platform, so that people could pass freely between waiting room and concourse, but, except on presentation of a ticket, could not go out on a platform. And they kept the annex for an arrival bay, and the big shed for a departure bay. The only trouble there was that, when the commuter trains came in each morning with a rush, many of them *had* to be received in the big shed.

When all these changes had been effected, when the work was done, when the scaffolding was taken down and the paint was dry and the city was called upon to celebrate the event, the rebuilt edifice was formally christened Grand Central Station, and the change of name was much emphasized. True, Grand Central Depot had been spoken of as Grand Central Station for ten years, even by the railroad companies themselves; but now, as it were, the change was made formal. It was intended to advertise the total transformation wrought at Grand Central; and that transformation was, be sure of it, tremendous. The work had cost five million dollars.

The opening was duly celebrated in 1901, but the event was not happy. For several months beforehand the authorities had realized their failure to solve the one essential problem at Grand Central, which was not to house the crowds in a bigger station but to provide trains in greater volume; and so they turned their attention back to the fan.

They studied the tracks all over again. Like men playing chess, they studied every move, possible or impossible. They tried out everything known to man, every train maneuver, every terminal operation, every possible combination of things heard of or unheard of. They pored over this problem for months and even years. They were searching for some latent possibility in that track layout which had theretofore escaped them; something which the designer of it never consciously put into it. After all, the designer of the chess board never dreamed of the skill with which a master makes use of it today.

"Well," said Ichabod, "all this lies at the other side of the doors at Grand Central—tracks and switches, and trains weaving in and out to the crack of the towerman's whip."

Ichabod paused; once more drew out his watch. It was already 5:15. As if he'd have to hurry now, the tall fellow looked about him briskly.

"The trouble with Grand Central," he began—but he was interrupted.

Upon his cap the little man wore the badge of the British merchant marine. He was a little man with a large head, a long face and sunken cheeks. He approached us diffidently. He begged our pardon, but he was a stranger in the land, and: "Whur's the Caledonian Club?"

Ichabod confessed he didn't know, but suggested looking it up in the telephone directory. The little man thanked him politely. For a moment, in a bewildered sort of way, the little man stood silent. Then he said, sadly: "I thought it would be known to everybody."

"The trouble with Grand Central," Ichabod began again, "is that everything comes to a climax at once. There's the evening rush, for example, and there's the departure of the *Century*. . . . Each one is an event, and we ought to see them both. . . . What's worse, this same hour from five to six o'clock is just the hour we ought to be spending at Tower A, to see how the towermen, with only a few seconds' play between operations, line up the routes—create the avenues through a network of switches—and cancel them again as fast as the trains pull clear. . . . Since I've told you so much about the tracks and how they form the fundamental thing at Grand Central, you'll have to see all this. From the point of view of the towermen, the track layout is a piece of mechanism which they operate. . . .

"I'll tell you what we'll do," said Ichabod suddenly. "First we'll see—"

But the tall fellow with the green eyes never did say what we'd do. He turned aside, as if to clear his throat; and, as if transfixed, he stood for a moment staring. There was a slow hiking up of one corner of his mouth; again there was that enigmatic tilted smile. And again there was that glitter we had seen before in those strange green eyes of his. A woman leading a wide-eyed little boy by the hand was being followed across the Concourse by a straggling family that consisted of (a) three wide-eyed bigger boys, (b) two equally wide-eyed girls, and (c) one wide-eyed husband, who brought up the rear of the procession—he was carrying two suitcases—but who seemed to be steering it by calling out directions to his wife, whom he addressed as "Mother."

Ichabod cleared his throat, as if to resume what he had been saying about the towermen, and about the track. But all he did say, almost under his breath, was: "Pete's sakes! Six kids!"

It was 5:19 by the Golden Clock.

EVENING RUSH

EACH DAY's return to the suburbs begins, perhaps, a little after four o'clock when the elderly and the well-to-do, the last to arrive in the morning, are the first of the commuters to leave the city at night. Then, little by little, the crowds grow more and more. But the "rush" comes later.

The rush begins a minute or two after five o'clock; and begins abruptly. The rush is somewhat of a spectacle. The rush is at its roaringest between 5:10 and 5:30.

It was precisely 5:20 when Ichabod led the way to the West Balcony, and we had just arrived at that vantage point when half a dozen men and girls burst through the Vanderbilt avenue doorways together, laughing, and then went tripping down the marble stairs to the Concourse. Crowds of others were going the same way; they poured across the balcony, they seemed to go cascading down the stairs. It was a whole minute before Ichabod spoke. Even so, he hardly said much. He nodded. He gestured toward the Concourse. He whispered that the "show" was pretty good tonight.

At the center was the Golden Clock—and stillness. There were, of course, the people tightly massed about the Inquiry Desk, but movement there was only occasional. About them in turn, facing inward, was the ring of people waiting to keep appointments. ("I'll meet you at the Golden Clock.") They formed an almost perfect circle the better part of fifteen feet out from the desk. Within that circle, except for the occasional ones who approached or left the desk, the floor was clear—astonishingly clear. And outside the circle, avoiding it as flowing water avoids the rocks, were the dense crowds of people.

These were the "fierce" Grand Central crowds you've heard about. They kept pouring in through all the entrances at once, and moving upon a dozen different train gates and ticket windows with a calm smoothness of movement that was fascinating. There was hurry; and once in a while, of course, there was a momentary hitch. But the dominating note was one of almost mechanical smoothness of motion.

There was a woman in a green hat; she swept through the crowd with the steadiness of a comet along its inexorable course. There was a woman in a red hat; she cut across the floor diagonally, not following a straight line but swerving now a little to the left, now a little to the right, without ever changing gait; and by that kind of interlacing path arrived precisely at the right gate. It was easier to watch the women, because their hats were so much more distinguishable; but the men were obviously doing the same thing. And then, suddenly, it became apparent that the women in the red and the green hats, and almost everybody else for that matter, were not quite on their own, but—wisely—were following currents.

The currents formed and divided and came together without awkwardness; and the crowd was not at all a "swirling, seething mass," but a kind of interweaving of many lines of hurrying people. Save at that strange empty core about the Golden Clock, the crowd was all in motion. Spontaneously, it assumed a pattern; and as the minutes passed, as these gates closed and those gates opened, the pattern changed. Once or twice it was lost, but only for an instant or so, till the crowd resolved itself differently and, out of a moment's blurring, a new pattern emerged.

Fundamentally, perhaps, all this is but a simple reflection of the commuter's eternal passion for following the same path day after day, month after month, and year after year. Commuters the world over are notorious for that. But here the tendency is emphasized. Here it's encouraged by the very plan of Grand Central with its ramps and corridors all pouring into a central "mixing basin"—which is precisely what the Concourse is.

"And what a spectacle it would make," said Ichabod, "if all the people carried silk flags—green, yellow, red, a different color for every entrance—to show where each of all these blending streams begins and ends!"

He paused for a moment, as if to give us time for wondering. Then he abruptly changed the subject.

"This is, in a way, the main thing to see at Grand Central," he said, "for it was a great rush to the suburbs—as I told you, it was a great and unexpected migration of people away from the city that broke the back of things at the Commodore's Grand Central, and posed the real problem which the present-day Grand Central solved. . . ."

The tall fellow again consulted his watch. It was 5:26.

"We'd better take a look downstairs now," he said briskly; and with a come-along toss of his head he led the way.

The Lower Concourse was alive with crowds. From the ramp at the center of the south wall, the lines spread out finger-wise to the various gates along the north wall; and from the stairs at the west other, and similar, lines of commuters cut across the first. There was more of a commotion here than upstairs. There was a great deal of actual running as the gatemen raised their warning cries of "All aboard!" But in general the movement of the crowds was smooth and orderly, and remarkably rapid. As fast as they came pouring down the ramps and down the stairs, they crossed the floor and poured through the gates. And when gates were closed, there was the same slight recoil, the same loss of definition we had observed upstairs, and the same working out of a new pattern as other gates were thrown open and the crowds adjusted themselves to a new situation.

And there was much the same kind of talk we had heard this morning:

"Expect to have a big garden this year?"

"Just sail away, that's what I'd do."

"Go on and catch your train. To hell with both of you!"

"Wasn't it a lovely day?" "A beautiful day, thank God!"

"Yes—if there still *is* a Europe next summer."

"Golf was in the air today."

"O. K., you make a hole in the crowd and I'll follow you through." "What? *Me* run interference for *you?*"

"Did you get that seed catalog?"

"If you find a seat at all, you'll be doing all right."

Grand Central has a reputation for its wild rush-hour crowds, but there's little enough to account for it. The fact is that Grand Central handles very great crowds with much less crowding than occurs at any of a score of other railway terminals; and what impresses you the more is not a mad crush of people, but the utter smoothness and swiftness with which the people pass through. For really oppressive crowding, Grand Central is not in the same class with—to cite but one example—Liverpool Street Station, London.

But Grand Central does have, of course, its moments of unusual crowding: they occur in regular order, Christmas Eve, the Friday before Decoration Day, the Friday before the Fourth of July, the Friday before Labor Day and the eve of Thanksgiving Day. It may be added, however, that Grand Central—Arrival Station, Concourse, Waiting Room and Lower Concourse—can hold 30,000 people all at once. And in all its history the present-day Grand Central has never been filled to capacity.

The all-time record crowd gathered on the eve of Thanksgiving Day, 1945, when a total of 240,078 railroad passengers alone passed through. The belief is, however, that not many more than 20,000 people were actually in the station at any one moment.

DEPARTURE OF THE "CENTURY"

It was 5:40 by the Golden Clock.

In the Concourse a new thrill of excitement was in the air. "The carpet's out." The *Century* was in her dock on Track 34, and the famous gray-and-red carpet lay beside her on the quay.

"Strictly speaking," said Ichabod, "the word is *quai;* which is the French word for a railway station platform. Like most other things at Grand Central, the platforms are French, being forty-eight inches above the rail-top. That's ten inches higher than English platforms; and quite different, of course, from the American type, which is little more than rail-high. The platforms at Grand Central are flush with the car floors; and, when Grand Central was new, the publicity department made a special point of calling them *quais.* The word was inevitably Anglicized, and then was forgot—except in the case of the *Century.*

"The *Century* is the only train in America, and doubtless the only train left in the world, for whose passengers a carpet is rolled out each day. As you know, she's the world's most extensively advertised train, and the carpet," said Ichabod, "is one of those little things involved in the publicity build-up.

"She's always paid a high return upon the advertising. She's an extra-fare train, to begin with—the last extra-fare train left on the New York Central Railroad. First-class fare to Chicago is thirty dollars, and the extra fare is three dollars. . . . Back in 1928 she set a world record, never since equaled, by earning a gross revenue of more than $11,000,000. That was nearly as much as the aggregate passenger revenue that year of entire railroads operating out of New York. . . .

"Otherwise, too, 1928 was the great year of the *Century.* She ran in 2,151 sections—roughly three sections eastbound and three sections westbound every day; six separate trains per diem—but from one year's end to the other she was 95 per cent 'on time.' . . . It was the year of the new locomotive. . . . In 1925 and 1926 the iron horse had passed through the most revolutionary phase of her history. The electric jack had proved a disappointment, and steam power in those two years was reborn; and 1928 was the first full year in which the *Century* was hauled by the new 4,000-horsepower Hudson-type locomotives. . . . The year before, in 1927, the *Century* had been broken up into 2,261 sections; but in 1928 the new engines drew a much greater number of cars in 110 fewer sections. . . .

"And that's another point to remember about the *Century*," said Ichabod. "For eighteen years she was the symbol of the steam locomotive's triumph over the electric jack. . . .

"They're using diesel power lately. A jack rolls her out of Grand Central, of course, and as far as Harmon, which is on the Hudson Division, as Andy said, just a little this side of the thirty-third milepost. There she's tied onto the tail of this new streamlined diesel job.

"She's a 4,000 horsepower diesel-electric job, turned out by the Electro-Motive Division of the General Motors Corporation and she has a ceiling speed of 98 miles an hour. So the old Hudson could outrun her in a race. But she's speedy enough, and powerful enough for the job along a water-level route. She's a two-unit proposition with double-end control," said Ichabod, "and her 24 cylinders are directly connected with her direct-current generators, her electric motors linked by gears to her axles. . . . And, of course, she's painted gray to match the rest of the *Century*.

"The *Century* runs every day in the year," said Ichabod, "including Christmas. Really, she's two totally different trains. She leaves Chicago every afternoon at four o'clock; and she leaves New York every evening at six. That's because of the time difference. Actually, she leaves Chicago at five o'clock, New York time; and she leaves New York at five o'clock, Chicago time. In each case, she arrives next day at 9 A. M., local time. . . . She's No. 26, eastbound; and No. 25, westbound. On the New York Central," said Ichabod, "all westbound trains have odd numbers, all eastbound trains have even numbers. . . .

"She looks," the tall fellow continued, "like a long, gray, metal tube, flattened on the sides. . . . The *Century* is a new and shiny article, not to be mentioned in the same breath with the *Fast Mail,* which—though she isn't much today—comes down to us out of the golden age of American railroading. . . . The *Century,* in fact, is less than half a century old. She began running on the fifteenth of June, 1902. . . ."

It was a Sunday afternoon. There was a Roosevelt in the White House, and there was a MacArthur in the Philippines. And, of course, there was a coal strike going on. In general, though, the times were rather good. It was the year of Lorimer's *Letters of a Self-made Merchant to His Son;* a great rumor was spreading over the United States that the truth of all things was known at last, and that salesmanship is what makes the wheels go round. It was the year of Ping-pong, and of the Buster Brown suit and of Dowie, the "faith-healer." And it was the year of *Floradora,* and of Maude Adams in *Quality Street.*

It was also the year when a man called Mussolini launched a Socialist crusade in the North of Italy; but, except to note that he was promptly locked up in jail, the newspapers paid no attention to him. The Sunday supplements of June 15, 1902, contained the portraits of two men who rejoiced in the name of Wilson. James Wilson had just left for London to represent the President of the United States at the coronation of the seventh Edward; and Woodrow Wilson had just been elected president of Princeton University. James received a great deal more attention than Woodrow that Sunday morning. Woodrow Wilson—it was only a name. The newspapers did well by James Wilson; but they did even better by the chief ornithologist of the American Museum of Natural History, who on this day, when the *Century* began her first run, gravely considered the question of the hour: Whether the possible spread of automobiles might not entail the extermination of the English sparrow.

We stood at the dawn of a new era, it was "glad, confident morning," and the *Twentieth Century Limited* was not only named for, but was intended to typify and symbolize, the great things that lay ahead of us. She was to be what the world had never known before, an all-Pullman train; and she was to cover the distance between New York and Chicago in the record-breaking time of twenty hours. So there was great celebration the day she began her first "flight."

But the celebration, curiously, was not all for her. On the Pennsylvania Railroad, oddly, the *Broadway Limited* began her first run also on the fifteenth of June, 1902. And down to the last minor detail she was the "opposite number" of the *Century*. She too was an all-Pullman train, and she too was on a twenty-hour schedule. Half the people of America lifted up their heads, expectantly. The old rivalry had broken out again, it seemed, and the racing to Chicago was about to be resumed. It wasn't, though.

In 1905 the *Century* reduced her running time to eighteen hours. On the same day the *Broadway* did likewise. There was a disastrous wreck; and in December, 1907, both trains changed their operating time to 19 hours and 30 minutes. A month later, in January, this was reduced to 18 hours and 30 minutes; but in the spring it was extended again to 19 hours and 30 minutes, and there was no change that was not made simultaneously on both railroads. Nearly five years later, in November, 1912, both trains went back to the original twenty-hour schedule, and this continued unchanged for twenty years.

Then, on the twenty-fourth of April, 1932, eighteen-hour service was begun again; just twenty-five years after it had been given up as unsafe. In 1933 the *Century* and the *Broadway* were both streamlined, and except for the decorative scheme, each train was a duplicate of the other. On the twenty-eighth of April, 1935, seventeen-hour service was begun, the fastest ever attempted over so great a distance. On the fifteenth of June, 1938, the *Century* was streamlined a second time (so was the *Broadway*), and to celebrate the event (it was also the old girl's thirty-sixth birthday), running time was reduced to sixteen hours.

Now sixteen hours is 960 minutes; and the distance from New York to Chicago via the New York Central Railroad is 961 miles. So the *Century* had to cover the entire distance at a start-to-stop average of just a shade more than a mile a minute. That meant a cruising speed of eighty-five miles an hour, and a maximum speed along the tangents, of almost a hundred miles an hour. And it wasn't any easier for the *Broadway*. True, the distance from New York to Chicago via the

Pennsylvania Railroad is only 902 miles; but the Pennsylvania tracks are steep and forbidding where they cross the Alleghenies, and the Central tracks, following the pre-historic Indian trails, are never far from water-level all the way along.

The Second World War brought about a suspension of the sixteen-hour schedule. Performance data revealed that one hour's additional running time would enable the locomotives both to save fuel and to haul substantially longer trains; and so, by order of the Office of Defense Transportation, the *Century* and the *Broadway* went back to a seventeen-hour schedule on the seventh of December, 1942, the first anniversary of Pearl Harbor. That arrangement lasted three and a half years; and then, on the twenty-eighth of April, 1946, they resumed their sixteen-hour schedule—both trains together. It's the curious truth that in her whole history the *Century* has never changed her schedule, or style of equipment, but that the *Broadway* did the selfsame thing on the selfsame day.

"It's curious," Ichabod repeated; "it becomes understandable, though, when you recall the all-Pullman character of both trains.

"The *Century* and the *Broadway*—in each case the railroad owns and operates the dining cars; and aboard the dining cars there's some right smart competition between the Central and the Pennsylvania. There's competition, too, aboard the locomotives; for there's prestige to be won by an outstanding record of on-time arrivals. Finally, there's competition in the advertising columns of the newspapers . . . and the Central is always advertising those three magic words, *Twentieth Century Limited.*

"Nobody has ever estimated the value of that name. It must be worth. . . ."

Ichabod was about to repair the omission by doing the estimating himself when a clerk from the terminal manager's office appeared before him with a number of yellow forms which all of us had to sign before we'd be allowed to visit Tower A. We signed them, acquitting the railroad in advance of any responsibility in the event of misfortune's befalling us; and thereupon the clerk, nodding to the gateman, led us through the gate to the carpeted Platform 34—one of the longest platforms at Grand Central.

"She looks like a long, gray metal tube, flattened on the sides," Ichabod had told us. And that's just what the *Century* does look like as she lies in her dock at Grand Central. The old-fashioned idea of a train of cars has been almost obliterated; the whole contraption has been rubbed over and smoothed over and painted over till the cars, as separate entities, are easily lost sight of. The vestibules are not tapered; the cars are coupled very closely together, and the gaps between are bridged by opposing pairs of bellows, car-high and car-wide, so that roofs and sides present more or less unbroken lines; and the train herself looks like one long tube—segmented and jointed, to make it flexible; but a tube just the same.

At the rear, of course, is the observation car, with its rounded end, its great show of glass. At the head end, just abaft the mail car, is the dormitory car, where the waiters sleep. And in between are the lounge cars, the dining cars, and the sleepers. There are no berths aboard the *Century*, but only private bedrooms furnished with chairs and sofas—and beds that disappear into the walls by day. A master bedroom, the largest available, has two double beds and a shower bath, and is large enough to serve by day as a private lounge for a family of four plus two or three visitors. The carpeting is gray and red —the same as the carpet on the quay.

"And to make up the *Century* day after day," said Ichabod, "the company has a pool of sixty-two cars and ten locomotives. The locomotives are painted gray to match the cars; and they, too, are streamlined, I'm sorry to say. They're good, powerful, high-speed engines, each able to haul, if need be, a train of eighteen Pullmans. . . . And they're dressed up to look like sissies.

"But you won't see one of them today," said Ichabod. "Any old electric jack at all is used to pull the *Century* from here to Harmon. . . ."

It was six o'clock; possibly two or three seconds later. At the north end of the quay, visible to the conductor but not the engineman, the green light flashed, signal that the Concourse gate was closed. Instantly the conductor called the "All aboard!" The cry was taken up by the trainmen ranged along the entire length of the quay; and, just back of the observation car, a yard man dropped quickly to the tracks, and began rapidly "cutting her loose." Swiftly—one, two, three, four—the train valves were closed. The valves were closed upon the station reservoirs, and the air pipes were disconnected. The valves were closed upon the station boiler, and the steam pipes were disconnected. The switch was drawn, and the electric cable was unhooked. The *Century* henceforth drew light, heat and air-pressure from her locomotive.

It was 6:01. Slowly, smoothly, dead on the second, the *Century* began to roll. The yard man stood up and watched her move away. A last remaining cable, a thin flexible wire, was drawn taut, then fell abruptly to the track as the plug-in connection broke loose. Telephone service aboard the *Century* was disconnected.

Twenty-two seconds later the *Century* had cleared her dock and was out in the terminal fan. Like a liner on the bay, she lighted up the whole place about her, cheerily; and the gloom was all the blacker when she passed on.

GANDY DANCER

IT WAS GLOOMY all right; and when the *Century*, gathering speed, had disappeared into the tunnel, there seemed to be no light anywhere, for a moment, except from the windows of what appeared to be a far-off house, what was in reality Tower A.

In a weird half-light, the workmen began to roll up the carpet. You saw them bend and tug. You could not have made out their faces, though, at a hundred feet. Still holding the yellow quit-claim papers in his hand, the clerk from the terminal manager's office led the way to the far end of Platform 26. He had a peculiar gait which Ichabod was quick to call attention to.

"He was a bit of a gandy dancer in his day," the tall fellow decided. "If you look into it, you'll probably find that he was once an agent at some unheard-of place where he had to walk the tracks, three miles each way, to get his meals at the nearest farmhouse. . . .

"The trouble is," said Ichabod, "that the cross-ties on American railroads don't fit the stride of men—as they ought to. They're too close together; and you can't walk the tracks in comfort for mile after mile if you step on each one. But you can't keep going either if you step on alternate ones; they're too far apart for that. So railroad men strike a balance by skipping every fourth tie—two mincing steps and a long step with the right foot; two mincing steps and a long step with the left foot; two mincing steps and a long step with the right foot, and so on for mile after mile. It's rather like walking to waltz-time; the rhythm gets in your bones and you develop a kind of prancing gait that sticks to you. . . . It's called the gandy dance.

"Origin obscure," Ichabod declared hastily. "In American railway lore, tramps are said to be ever searching for an El Dorado called the Candy Mountain; so it may have been the Candy dance, originally. Or it may have been the gander dance. . . ."

Ichabod grinned for a moment. Then he asked abruptly: "Do you see the way that fellow's coat-tail is kilting . . . left, right, left, right?"

The fellow stopped at the end of the platform, and waited for us to catch up with him. Then he salved his conscience by giving us a final warning.

"This place," he said, looking very impressive, "ain't healthy. . . . It comes on you all of a sudden. Did you ever read in the newspapers that So-and-so was taken to the hospital 'suffering from shock'? Well, that's one thing can happen to you here. Only they won't take you to the hosp'tal if it does. And did you ever hear your mother say she's run down, and your big sister says it wouldn't a-happened if she'd a-took her vitamins? Well, that's another thing can happen to you here. But if you get run down here, vitamins ain't gonna help you.

"What I mean to say is. . . ." Here the fellow paused for effect; then: "You gotta look out for two things: You don't want to be cut up under the cars, do you? And you don't want to come in contact with the third rail, or by the time the current is shut off, your own mother won't be able to identify the body. So do as I tell you. Keep to the catwalk. Don't step over a third rail except at the catwalk, where it's heavily covered with rubber blankets painted black and white . . . diagonal stripes. And don't cross a track until you look both ways and see a red light each way. Then you can cross.

"But if you see a yellow light, that track has been opened up for a train or a locomotive. So don't try to cross it. Stand back, or duck into a safety hole where the catwalk hugs the wall. We don't have time to hold a route open for more than thirty seconds around here, so if you see a yellow light, you're going to see a train before you know where you're at."

"How about a green light?"

"There aren't any green lights. Nothing goes faster than half-speed inside the terminal limit—that's the rule. So a green light would be out of place. . . . All signals are two-indication light signals . . . mounted on dwarf standards. They show a red light for *Stop* and a yellow light for *Caution;* just them two. And they ain't up high on a mast, like out along the line. They're dwarf signals, down low beside the track. . . . Like the fella said, 'The yard is carpeted with rubies, and the locomotives pounce on yellow lights'—it was kinda that way. . . ."

"Mousing," said Ichabod, helpfully.

"What?"

"Mousing was the word . . . 'the feline Hudsons of the New York Central . . . mousing for green lights among the switch-points.' Lucius Beebe wrote that about the yard at Cleveland. . . ."

"Yeah," said the gandy dancer. "Yeah, that's it. . . . Out in Cleveland, though, you got a very different situation. Here you never get above a yellow light. . . . And they're dwarf signals, like I said.

"They stand eighteen inches high—mostly. I mean, they were all eighteen inches high till 1933, when they streamlined the *Century*. Blueprints were checked . . . showed the low skirts along the sides of the new cars would foul the dwarf signals at Grand Central. Tracks are so close together here there's no space left for signals between-tracks—so you have them close in to the right-hand rail. Really you have them under the overhang of the cars. So we had to lower them a couple inches. . . . That took time, of course, and for awhile there the *Century* didn't have the free run of the place at all but was restricted to a very few tracks at Grand Central. . . . It's different now, though.

"How many? We got here a total of 419 switches and 570 signals, all interlocked and controlled from five different towers. I'll tell you how it is. . . ."

A switch—what the layman calls a switch—is a junction where two routes come together in a single route; and, viewed the opposite way about, it is also a fork where a stem route divides to form the two branch routes. The point is that every switch has three approaches; the two branch routes approach the heel and the stem route approaches the toe. And from this, of course, it follows that every switch must be protected by three different signals, one facing each of the approach tracks.

"Now, then," said the gandy dancer, "you got one switch and three signals. So, in the tower, you got a bank of four levers—push-and-pull levers they are, here at Grand Central. You got four," he repeated, spreading out the fingers of his left hand and pointing to each one separately; "you got three with red bands painted onto the handles, to show they're signal levers, and you got one with a black band painted onto it to show it operates the switch-motor. . . .

"The idea is, you go there and you find all four levers in. That's normal position: Switch closed, all three signals at the *Stop*, which is red. That's normal. No route. . . .

"So you pull out one of them red levers—the No. 1 lever, say. When you do that, the signal guarding the toe of the switch changes from red to yellow. You've opened up a route through the switch. Actually, you've set up orders to the approaching engineman to take his train through to the next signal. . . .

"But that isn't all. When you pulled that lever out, you also threw a series of rods that locked up all three of the other levers. So the switch-motor is out of action, and the switch is locked in position; and the two other signals are red, and they got to stay red, because the levers are locked and you don't have any control over them any more. Why? Because you've established one route through the switch, and you can't set up another route . . . because any other route would foul the one you got already. Two routes through the same switch ain't acceptable. And you can't throw the switch, because no route would be safe if the towerman could still monkey with it after he once raises the signal, thereby calling on a train. . . . That's why everything is interlocked with everything else. That's what an interlocking machine is for.

"All right, then. Now suppose your train has passed through, clearing the route you set up for it. Now you want a different route for the next train to follow. Your first move is to cancel the old route. You go back to normal position, all four levers in, all three signals at the *Stop*. Now you can move the switch, if you want to. You can never move a switch unless all three of the signals are at the *Stop*.

"And now, let's say, you want to line up the No. 3 route. First you throw the switch, by pulling out the black lever. Next, you raise the No. 3 signal, and that's all right because No. 3 signal is acceptable to the open switch. But let's say you make a mistake. Instead of pulling the No. 3 signal lever, like you meant, you grab the No. 2 signal lever instead. Nothing happens . . . because the switch is in the wrong position for the No. 2 route. So the No. 2 signal lever is locked. It won't 'come.' Therefore you have no control over your No. 2 signal. You can't feed electricity into it. None of its working parts are working. It's completely out of action; it's 'dead.' So it's at the *Stop*, because gravity is what keeps a signal at the *Stop*.

"Mechanical or electrical devices of all kinds are bound to fail once in a while; so you depend on them only to raise a signal to the *Caution* or the *Clear*, and everything that works has to be working right, or she just won't rise, that's all. And if any mechanical failure develops when she's up already, the signal collapses—zingo!—just tumbles right back to the *Stop*. Gravity never fails.

"So, with mechanical trouble, you can get a false *Stop* all right. A false *Stop* never did any harm, though, except tie up train movements. But gravity ain't gonna give you a false *Caution* or a false *Clear*. That's the first rule of signal work: equipment failure must always happen on the side of safety. Them signal engineers got it all figured out.

"So you see the way it works out in the case of a single switch. Two out of your three signals are always red. You can't move a switch unless all three are red. You can raise only one signal at a time to yellow. And you can't raise a particular signal to yellow if the switch position is false to that signal. And it's all done simply by threading electric circuits back and forth between the levers, the signals and the switch-motor . . . so that you can't so much as close one circuit but that you break all the conflicting circuits. Science! Know what I mean?"

At Grand Central, however, a single, isolated switch hardly exists. Here we find them in groups and clusters, and great alignments where the terminal tracks peel off the ladder tracks. We find them alike along the edges and at the very heart of the fan. And we find them plain and fancy—turnout, crossover, scissor, slip-switch and double-slip. But the main point is that they exist in masses.

In general, therefore, signals are consolidated, and one may guard the approach to a succession of switches. But this, of course, is only another way of saying that the switches are interlocked in groups. Within the same group they're interlocked with one another all around, and with all the various signals that guard that group. The groups in turn are interlocked; conflicting routes cannot possibly be opened up within them or between them. And all these integrated groups at last coalesce in five great interlockings.

Each interlocking is centered in a tower of its own. Each lies within a frontier of blazing red lights. Each is a territory no engineman may enter unless and until a particular avenue has been laid out for him and, by raising the signal from red to yellow, the towerman orders him forward.

The towers are in close contact with one another, and the tower directors—Dispatcher's local deputies at Grand Central—"swing" the trains along to one another, just as the various Dispatchers swing them back and forth between divisions.

First, as the incoming train arrives at Grand Central, is Tower U, below the sidewalk at Park avenue and Fifty-seventh street. Here the tunnel ends and the four main-line tracks fan out to become ten parallel tracks. Of these ten, four tracks begin burrowing to a level twenty feet lower, where—passing out of the bailiwick of Tower U—they form the throat of the lower-level fan. The remaining six tracks continue on at roughly the same level and form the throat of the upper-level fan.

The upper-level fan is the jurisdiction of Tower A, which is below Park avenue at Forty-ninth street; and the lower-level fan belongs to Tower B, which is directly downstairs below Tower A. Control of the loop tracks is centered in Tower F, which is just off the northeast corner of the Lower Concourse. And Tower C, the fifth and last of the Grand Central towers, governs the yard tracks that lie to the east of the upper-level fan. Of all five, the biggest are A and B.

"And Tower A," said Ichabod, "is right up the track there, where you see the lights in the windows."

"Yeah," said the gandy dancer, good honest fellow that he is.

That settled, he reminded us again that we were taking our lives in our hands. He assured us that he wouldn't care to have the matter troubling his conscience in the years to come. He shrugged. Then, turning about, he abruptly flew down a steep flight of steps, a kind of ship's ladder, to the track level. There were seven steps. On his way down, the soles of his shoes barely tapped the nose of each. And through that Stygian darkness that never knows the sun, he led the crooked way along the catwalk that zigzags between tracks and across tracks to the tower.

"Tower A," said Ichabod in his best pedagogical manner, "has this in common with ancient Gaul, that it's divided into—"

A Yankee locomotive burst into view, hardly a hundred feet away, and Ichabod, already one foot over the third rail, involuntarily drew back.

"Where did she come from?"

"From the— Wait a minute. Let me get my breath. . . . From the parallel track, by the crossover through that opening in the concrete wall."

By the time we asked the question, the jack had already stopped and was abreast of Ichabod, who could have touched her with his elbows. It was terrifying. But Ichabod recovered quickly, and now could think of nothing more soothing to say than that her gears were loose.

The jack had come to a stop in three or four seconds; and almost at once there was a sharp, slapping sound as the switch-points back of her flicked over smartly to a new position. The signal rose to yellow, and the jack was off again, dashing up the track in the general direction of the old Commodore's brick-arch tunnel. In a matter of seconds she was lost in the gloom; only her tail light remained visible. One's breathing benefited appreciably.

"Like ancient Gaul," Ichabod resumed, as if he thought we should go on with our mad scheme. . . .

"Is it safe here?"

"No," said Ichabod promptly. "Cross now, though, and you'll be all right."

"As I was saying: Tower A, like all Gaul, is divided into . . ."

"Hadn't we better get there first?"

"Oh, well. . . ."

It was 6:22.

TOWER WORK

TOWER A is a long, narrow, many-windowed enclosure within brick walls that rise from the track-level to the roof; from the steel deck on which the upper-level tracks are laid to the steel deck that upholds the sidewalk of Park avenue for a block and a half south of the Waldorf-Astoria Hotel. It's a kind of house islanded about by a network of tracks and switches. It's twenty-two feet wide, 230 feet long; and it has a kind of kitchen stoop at the south end. The catwalk that begins at Platform 34 terminates at the tower stoop.

The gandy dancer took hold of both rails and almost hauled himself up the steps; hand over hand, as it were. Then, without a word, he went forward to the lever room at the north end of the tower to announce our arrival. Ichabod stopped short in the dimly lighted corridor, just inside the door.

"As I was about to say," he began, "Tower A is divided into three parts. Here at the south end you have the locker room and the shower baths. . . . At the opposite end you have the lever room. And, in between, you have the relay room.

"You know what a relay is. . . . A relay is a device for making and breaking electric circuits; it's a device, in other words, for turning on and shutting off a flow of electricity. And it works by electricity itself.

"It's absurdly simple. . . . It consists of an electro-magnet, like the magnet in your doorbell; plus a steel armature that corresponds to the bell clapper. The armature is the interesting thing. It's hinged at one end, free at the other; and the free end, a quarter of an inch or so below the magnetic poles, rests upon a contact—an electrical contact. Thus a channel is completed for the passage of electricity through the contact and through the armature itself. . . .

"But if you take a different current of electricity and pass it through the coils of the magnet, the magnet is energized; having had no magnetic properties a moment earlier, it now becomes highly magnetic, and the armature flies upward to the poles and freezes there as long as the magnet continues energized. Thus the armature is drawn away from its contact, and that circuit is broken; that flow of electricity is stopped—to be renewed, however, the instant the armature is released by the magnet and falls back, drawn by gravity alone, to its other position. Simple ninth-grade physics!" said Ichabod.

"And that," he continued, "would be the whole story of the relay if it weren't for the upper contact. The truth is that when the armature flies up it strikes another contact; and so, in exchange for the circuit that's broken, you have a new circuit that's closed.

"And that's that—except that instead of having only one lower contact and one upper contact, you can have a great array of contacts, both upper and lower. And so, in general, everytime a relay 'picks up' a number of contacts are broken, a number of new contacts are made, a number of electrical currents are snuffed out, a number of new currents are established, and set flowing. And, of course, when the relay drops again, the new contacts are broken, the old contacts restored. That's what a single relay does.

"But in the relay room here at Tower A, you have thousands of relays—thousands and thousands of them—and they're all connected and interconnected. Thousands of different circuits are threaded back and forth between them . . . from contact to contact; so that if one relay picks up, it may cause a dozen others to pick up also, and a dozen more to drop. . . .

"This is the heart of the interlocker . . . When a lever is drawn in the lever room," said Ichabod, "the primary effect is to actuate one relay; but instantly a great number of circuits are broken, a great number of new circuits are closed; and the total effect is both to operate a given signal, let us say, and to throw out of operation all conflicting signals and switch-motors."

The tall fellow stopped abruptly.

"I hope," he said, a little testily, "I'm not boring you."

"Oh, no, no! No, indeed! . . . very interesting—when you get the hang of it."

"That's it," said Ichabod, warming up again. "And the beauty of it is that you don't have to be a signal engineer to get the hang of it either. Really," he said—and this time he had the grace to give us a slightly apologetic nod—"all you need is the broad idea. You've got to know roughly how it works, or you'll never understand what the interlocker does, and what a tremendously important thing it is. . . . There are five interlockings at Grand Central and, as I said before, the whole terminal is built around them.

"And now," said Ichabod briskly, "we'll look in at the lever room."

The lighting in the lever room was powerfully concentrated; perhaps for a purpose. Too strong for our eyes at first, it was all upon the levers and upon the tower director's desk at the far end of the room. The rest was deeply shadowed; and from the shaded "boards" the tiny green lights blazed and flashed like jewels.

There was not much talking. There was the frequent roar—and, worse than that, the glare—of passing trains. But even in the intervals of comparative quiet there was hardly any talking. There was an air of concentration that can probably not be matched anywhere else in New York.

There were no introductions. There was no time for any. As we walked forward—the room is 130 feet long—the levermen gazed at us for a moment, but with a strange sort of indifference. True, they could not have seen us very well; could hardly have seen, perhaps, much more than silhouettes moving in the shadows. Even so, they looked at us with the indifference you often see in cats; then turned away, one by one, with a look of almost catlike abstraction.

The tower director looked up from the record sheet, raised his hand in recognition, flashed a smile at Ichabod, seemed about to say something. A white light sprang up on a signal frame beside his desk; a voice came through the automatic telephone; and Tower Director dismissed us with a muttered: "Make yourselves at home."

A look of total absorption came over his face too as he studied the board. A train sped by the tower, barely twelve inches away, and lit up the place with blinding flashes of light; but Director's face betrayed no sign that he was even remotely conscious of it. He still had a minute or so to work his problem out. The white light—a signal from Tower U—showed that a train was speeding down the tunnel for Grand Central. The voice identified her as No. 143–Y. A second light flashed. The Yankee railroad's No. 143 would arrive at the A interlocking in half a minute on Track H. The director of Tower A, of course, would have to "pick her up" there and—

"Track H, Ladder X, Track 40."

Director called out the route in the calmest of conversational tones. The levermen, who had been silently waiting for the call, sprang forward—each upon his own third of the long "piano." You heard the click of brass levers—throwing switches, raising signals to the *Caution*. You heard the voices of the levermen reporting back:

"Track H to X."

"Ladder X out of *H*."

"Ladder X into 40."

Hardly three seconds had gone by since Director called out the route. Now that route was established—a particular avenue clea through the switchwork from Track H to Terminal Track 40.

Upon the sheet before him, a kind of ship's log of tower operations Operator—the tower clerk, who is called Operator because in the ol days he had to be a Morse telegrapher—made a series of entries; an then, with a brass stylus which he used as if it were a pencil, he wrot upon a tiny square of metal: "Y–143 on 40."

This writing was reproduced on the telautograph machine in th Arrival Station; and, reading it, the train cryer would even now b raising his voice to tell the news. We could guess what he was saying "Six-twelve train from Pittsfield arriving on Track 40! (Just over her to the left, Lady. Stand well back, please!) Pittsfield train on Trac 40. (Yes, Ma'am, twenty minutes late—account of snow.) Ne Haven train from Pittsfield, Lenox, Lee, Stockbridge, Housatoni Great Barrington. . . ."

Unlistening, Tower Director was studying his board again. Quietl he called out another route, and signaled Tower U to pick up a outgoing train on Track C. Calmly and steadily the levermen calle back the orders; the route was lined up, and Operator's pen was en tering it on the sheet. A green light flashed on the board, and in stantly Director spoke again. The levers clicked, and a route wa canceled back of an outgoing train which had just pulled clear of th interlocking. That too went O S—on the sheet.

Tower Director kept glancing at the board, kept glancing at th clock in front of him, kept calling out the avenues for trains coming and trains going; and all the while calmly and smoothly, Operator kept signaling Tower U, kept signaling the Arrival Station, kept answering the telephone, kept O S'ing every move to the quarter of a minute. Out of a memory that would be astonishing in a chess player, Director laid out a proper route before each departing train just thirty seconds before that train was due to roll. One after another, in steady procession, he was "pulling" trains out of Grand Central—and Heaven befriend the engineman who was slow to obey his orders!

But he was also ushering in trains, that was the real trouble.

There was nothing to do for a moment but watch him, fascinated —and watch the levermen obey his orders.

"The lever teams at Grand Central," said Ichabod, "are the best trained and probably the most expert in the world. No tower anywhere, I should say, can produce a team to match them for speed and accuracy of performance. . . . You'll hear it said in signal towers all over the country that it takes ten years to train a leverman. These boys at Grand Central are the pick of the whole New York Central System. . . .

"Perhaps he isn't altogether typical," the tall fellow went on to ay, "but take that second man over there—the man in the No. 2 position."

The man in the No. 2 position, a stocky man of middle height, tood with his arms folded, busily gazing into space as he awaited the next order of his chief.

"I'll tell you about him," said Ichabod. . . .

It was 6:37 by the tower clock.

LEVERMAN

His name is Herman Rinke, and he's a relief leverman. He works at Tower A tonight, Tower U tomorrow night, some other tower the night after that; a different job every night, to cover the place of a leverman who has that night off. A regular job would be easier, of course. But Herman doesn't have enough seniority to bid in a regular job. So at thirty-five he's a relief leverman.

He's no ordinary person. From time to time you may have seen some of his letters published on the editorial pages of New York City newspapers. He's a passionate defender of the trolleycar against the motor bus; he accumulates statistics on the subject and writes letters to the editors about it. Weighty with fact and argument, they make it clear as day that any number of American cities are today wisely abandoning bus lines in favor of newer and swifter and bigger and more comfortable trolleycars.

A native of New York, Herman grew up in the Yorkville section of the city—in Little Germany. Therefore he speaks (when he's off duty) in slow and heavy cadences, and with a slight German accent. And if his speech is heavily loaded with statistics, that's understandable too; for he's a graduate engineer with a degree from Stevens Tech. As a youngster he was lucky in landing just the job he wanted, in the general offices of the railroad.

And then, as easily as that, he won the Railroad Fellowship at Yale It provided for a year's study in the School of Transportation at Yale all expenses paid; and over and above that, it gave him an income fo that year.

At Yale he chose for his particular field of study the track layou at Grand Central; his goal was to discover how more trains could b worked in and out of the terminal—not by enlarging the layout, bu by greater efficiency in track employment, by sheer skill of maneuver sheer adroitness of management. And this was the subject of his thesis, which is now in the hands of the terminal engineers. In 1939, he was transferred from general offices to Operations.

Coatless, and with arms bare to the elbow, Herman Rinke went on with his work in the No. 2 position midway down the long piano. To all appearances he was totally unaware of our presence.

"The fact is," said Ichabod, "that the efficiency of the towermen is the one thing essential to the success of the whole Grand Central system; and the company won't stop at anything to improve their training, increase their efficiency. . . . You have here a tradition of extreme efficiency, and that tradition of the towermen represents the main line of Grand Central's development.

"Fundamentally, Grand Central is a track layout . . . and down the years the struggle to make Grand Central work has always centered in the interlocking towers. It was that way in the Eighties and the Nineties, when men by desperate searching learned how to use the tracks ever more and more effectively, and day by day succeeded in getting out of them more than their designers ever consciously put into them. And it's that way today, when a man like Herman Rinke is sent to Yale to cogitate for a whole year on that selfsame problem. . . .

"It's astonishing," said Ichabod, "how much depends upon the sheer tradition of the towermen. If you kept all the tracks just as they are, but lost their skill and all their accumulated knowledge, the finest towermen you could bring in from the outside could not keep Grand Central going. . . . With only a handful of trains moving in and out of the terminal, the crowds would disappear and nothing would be left. . . . In the long run, the whole Grand Central system hangs on one thing; and that one thing is what you see going on in this tower now—the flawless ordering of a succession of train maneuvers so closely integrated with one another that even the slightest dislocation would bring havoc upon the system as a whole. . . .

"When you see that," the tall fellow abruptly added, "perhaps you'll understand what a figure the towerman really is—the tower director and the leverman too; and Herman Rinke along with the others. . . .

"I can tell you more about Herman. He writes letters to the editors in praise of trolleycars; but he also rides them. He's a trolley fan. He belongs to the (amateur) Electric Railway Association, and goes on long week end jaunts by trolleycar. He pores over maps, works out great itineraries. Once he led a group of members of the E. R. A. all the way from New York to Buffalo and back by interconnecting trolley lines. . . . Where the lines don't meet, the boys walked from one car to the next; but their longest walk—near Utica—was less than three miles.

"It isn't that they wanted to go to Buffalo, mind you. For his part Herman, as a railroad man, could have gone there by train without having to pay his fare. But he paid his fare on the trolleys. It's just that he likes to explore the trolley lines and the interurbans. It's his hobby, you see.

"Also," said Ichabod, "Herman is something of a railway historian and something of a model railroader too. . . . If you attend the shows of the New York Society of Model Engineers, you may have seen Herman, perhaps, doing a professional job at one of the interlocking towers on the society's O-gauge railway. . . . On that road," said Ichabod, "the locomotives are just four inches tall. . . ."

Still pouncing upon the piano each time Director spoke, or gazing into space between jobs, Herman Rinke carried on as a leverman, and betrayed no sign of having seen or heard us.

It was 6:46.

TRAIN PROTECTION

TOWER DIRECTOR, too, was still carrying on; still calling the routes, still O S'ing routes and trains alike, still managing the telephone and the telautograph machine, still watching the clock, still studying the board, still ushering trains in and out of the upper-level fan at Grand Central.

There is this to be said for the outgoing trains, that they all follow a schedule, and that if each one will only step off dead-on-the-second, there can be a set program of dovetailing routes methodically established and methodically canceled, minute by minute; and the same program can be followed day after day and night after night. And, in general, that's how it is with outgoing trains.

But the incoming trains cut across and through every program that's ever been devised. Always some are late and others are on time, and they never arrive in the same sequence two days running. So there is no program there, but the tower director must "catch them as fast as they come," and improvise a route for each—without fouling the routes already established, without blocking the routes that will have to be set up a few minutes hence.

To help him, of course, he has the board, with its mass of green lights forever flashing off and on. The board reveals everything; and to know where every train is at any particular moment, to know what tracks are vacant, what routes are available, you only have to look at the board.

"The board," said Ichabod, "is a panel—"

"We got four boards here," said the gandy dancer; "one for the chief and one for each of the levermen. They're hung from the ceiling in a one-and-one-quarter-inch iron yoke . . . so you can tilt it, or turn it around to suit yourself. And it's hooked up to the track circuits so a light goes on—"

"First," said Ichabod, "the board is a panel. Next, a diagram of the track layout is painted on the panel."

"Anybody can see that," said the gandy dancer—a bit contemptuously, it seemed.

"I mean," said Ichabod humbly, "that it's *all* there. Every track and switch in this whole interlocking is represented in the diagram. None is left out. That's important."

"Yeah."

"Another thing you have to know," said Ichabod, "is that every track is broken up into blocks. Block signaling came from England, and *block* is an English term. . . . It means what American engineers call a *space-interval*. Roughly, you can call it the distance from one signal to the next.

"The rails are insulated where each block ends, so that electricity cannot pass from one block to the next. . . . On the board, therefore, each track is represented, not by a continuous line, but by a broken line —by a series of segments. Every segment represents a block of that track."

"So you see," said the gandy dancer, "every block is numbered, so the chief here—"

"The important thing," said Ichabod, stubbornly, "is that you have each block separately represented on the board; and for each block there's a green light. . . . The board is studded with green lights, but if you look closely you'll see one for each block."

"Yeah—and when the light blinks out you got track occupancy, and when the whole board begins getting dark, the chief's got trouble on his hands."

Ichabod conceded the point.

"The arrangement," he said, "is this: For every block you have a track relay, and you also have a track circuit—and through that circuit a current of electricity is forever flowing. It begins at one end of the block. Through the left-hand rail it flows to the other end; it passes through the coils of the relays; it flows back to its source through the right-hand rail. And so the track relay is energized, the armature is up, the signal circuit is closed . . . and on the board a green light, corresponding to that block, is burning.

"But the instant a pair of wheels enters the block, the track relay is short-circuited. . . . Through the wheels and axle, the current flows directly from one rail to the other, without having to pass through the coils of the relay. So the relay is robbed of its power, the armature falls, the signal circuit is broken, and the light on the board goes out."

"When the relay drops," the gandy dancer said severely, "it breaks the switch circuit too—so you can't throw a switch once a train is on the approach track; that's very important."

"So it is," said Ichabod.

"As I was about to say," he continued, "you have one great system of relays controlled by the levermen here in the tower; and you have another system of relays controlled by the track circuits. You have the tower relays, responsive to the push and pull of levers; and you have the track relays, forever dropping and picking up again in response to the movement of trains, forever reflecting track conditions.

"Of themselves alone, the track relays operate the board—for every green light you have a vacant block, and for every dark spot upon the board you have a train. You can trace the movement of that train across the fan as lights blink out and light up again. From Tower A you can see hardly a handful of tracks and trains, but the board reveals everything. . . .

"On the other hand, the entire system of track relays and the entire system of tower relays are interconnected. . . . Circuits are woven back and forth between them. . . . It's a simple hookup in every instance. But the simple thing is repeated over and over again till it looks appallingly complex. If you could see all the wiring at once, it would look like a cobweb that only ten thousand spiders could have spun—and the wonder would be," said Ichabod, "how the signal engineers ever got so many spiders to work together."

The gandy dancer was not amused.

"Anyhow, the wires are threaded back and forth, from one set of relays to the other, and the result of that," said Ichabod, "is that the towerman cannot do certain things unless the track conditions are favorable. For example, he cannot throw a switch if a train is passing over it, or even if a train is already on the approach track."

"Right!" said the gandy dancer.

Ichabod was silent for a moment. Then he turned again to his favorite subject of history.

"This," he said, "was one of the very earliest electric interlockers, and was quite wonderful for its day; though that, remember, was back in 1912. It permits the setting up of large numbers of mutually acceptable routes, it prevents the setting up of any two routes that foul each other. It protects every established route against all lateral train movements. It prevents any movement of the switch-points under a train. In short, it provides complete protection against any human error on the part of the towermen who work it.

"Suppose, for example, that two trains are coming in, one on Track H, the other on Track D. For the first, the levermen line up a route from *H* to Track 37. Then, in rapid succession, they lay down routes for two outgoing trains, and presently the train arriving on *D* catches them unprepared. In a crisis, the tower chief decides upon an avenue from *D* to Track 40. But there he's made a mistake—for *D*-to-40 crosses *H*-to-37. Nothing happens, though.

"Or nothing much happens. *D*-to-40 opens up only part of the way. Where it approaches *H*-to-37 it comes to an end, for the signal guarding the intersection froze at the Stop when *H*-to-37 was created, and now it can't be raised until the *H*-to-37 train has cleared the switch, and the route is canceled back of her. Then, and only then, it becomes possible to complete the *D*-to-40 route. . . .

"And all this," said Ichabod, "is virtually guaranteed—and I don't use that word lightly. The interlocker is so devised that every working part involved in any given operation must actually work, or that operation won't come off. . . . Remember, every signal in the place is normally at the *Stop*. To open a route you have to raise that signal to the yellow, and you have to raise her against the downward pull of gravity. If a wire breaks, if the current fails, if a relay jams or burns out, if anything at all happens to the equipment, the signal simply tumbles back to the *Stop* . . . thereby canceling the route. Normally that's all that can ever happen. It's what you call a false *Stop*. Its only effect is to tie up traffic. . . .

"It *can* happen, though: On all the railroads of the United States and Canada, the signal engineering books agree, a false *Clear* happens once in fifty million operations. It happens when rats eat away the insulation, and two wires cross, and a dead circuit borrows current from a live circuit.

"But that possibility is carefully guarded against at Grand Central . . . and so, from the point of view of safety, no exception can be taken to the Grand Central interlocking plant. It's as nearly perfect, in this respect, as anything ever built by man. But it isn't true," said Ichabod, "that Grand Central has the world's most modern interlocker—as you may have seen it stated recently."

The gandy dancer, apparently, had been waiting for something like this.

"What's the difference," he demanded, "between this machine and the most modern machine in the world?"

"Only," said Ichabod, "that four times as many men are needed to operate this one."

"It works, doesn't it?"

"So does a Model T Ford."

Still watching the clock and the board, still minding the signal flashes from Tower U, still calling out the routes and O S'ing every move, the director went steadily on with his work—but the work was thinning out now. The worst part of the evening rush was over, and he was beginning to catch odd moments of relaxation; to stretch out a bit, to give a quick rub to the muscles of his legs, to yawn briefly. You noticed these things; but you noticed, too, that he never took his eyes off the board.

Ichabod drew his attention; told him simply: "Downstairs. We'll be back." There was a flashing smile, a wave of the hand. That was all.

We walked back toward the relay room. On the other side of the long piano Herman Rinke and his fellow levermen gazed after us for a moment, but still gave no sign of recognition.

"This tower director," said Ichabod in somewhat of a confidential whisper, "his name is—"

"Does he have a name?"

Ichabod considered that for a moment; then he admitted, "He seems mighty impersonal, I suppose . . . all discipline, concentration, efficiency. But he's human; a fine fellow. . . . And he *does* have a name. It's Strever—J. J. Strever."

Ichabod showed us to a stairway, and led the way down to Tower B.

Directly downstairs under Tower A, Tower B is the biggest at Grand

Central, and it used to be the biggest tower in the world. Every switch and signal on the entire lower level is controlled from Tower B.

It was now 7:02. Things were becoming slack; and the chief of Tower B was already warming up the coffee in his dinner pail on the steam radiator back of him. But he was busy enough. Three or four times he began to say something, only to be stopped in the middle of it by the demands of his exacting job. And silence, you would say, is not precisely natural to this tower director, for he comes of a talkative race. He's a powerfully built man of sixty-odd, with blue eyes and a great shock of unruly white hair.

Things are much the same as in Tower A, save that the somewhat larger piano runs the entire length of the room, and the chief is not far up at the north end, but takes his place amidships, upon a low platform. And it may be on this account, or it may be simply because Mike is Mike, but there seems to be a closer contact between the chief of Tower B and his three levermen. Mike is a pitilessly hard worker himself and, presumably, a severe task master; but tonight he hardly ever called out a route without fitting into the order the additional word or two—if it were only "Boys," used in the vocative case—that somehow conveyed the idea that four men were at work together.

As the minutes wore on, Mike finally found his chance to speak to us.

"Keep your eyes on that board," he said abruptly. "Now do you see that train on Track 105? There's a train there," he hurried on to explain, "because the light's out on the board; every green light on the board is an open track, and every dark spot is a train. . . . Keep watching her, then—the train on Track 105. She's gonna roll in four seconds. Now keep your eye on her! And see how damn' fast I yank her out of New York!"

Ichabod chuckled.

"That's the way with towermen," he said a little later. "The enginemen don't get much credit—they're only the hired help who do as the towermen tell them to do."

The tall fellow looked thoughtful for a moment. Then, as if the recollection gave him a certain pleasure, he added, "Sometimes, though, the enginemen get their own back. . . . Sometimes the towermen makes a mistake. It can't be serious, of course; the only result is that the engineman is confronted by a *Stop* indication—proof that the route wasn't laid out in front of him correctly.

"In such a case, the engineman reaches for the whistle cord, sounds the *Call-for-signals*. . . . They have a way of manipulating things, they play upon the whistle, they call it *feathering*. . . . They can make the *Call-for-signals* sound very insulting."

We were upstairs again in Tower A. Tower Director signaled us over —J. J. Strever. He had a moment's freedom. He shook hands with Ichabod—and was abruptly called to the telephone.

It was Trainmaster speaking; and the substance of what he said was that the third or fourth car of a particular train had a flat wheel. The train was already on her departure track, far over to the west, and was due to leave in twenty minutes. Tower Director, without interfering with his elaborate schedule of arrivals and departures, would have to provide the routes clear across the fan that would enable Trainmaster to withdraw the crippled car and put another in her place within ten minutes flat.

Tower Director sat down and began to think. Ichabod signaled us away. Tower Director looked up.

"I was going to tell you," he said, "that No. 68 was washed off the board at Albany, and No. 26 left Harmon only two minutes ago—10 hours and 27 minutes late—looks like an all-time record. . . . Thought you might like to know. . . ."

It was a silent, sulky gandy dancer who led the way back from Tower A to the Concourse. We hurried; where we could, we ran along the catwalk.

"Tower A," said Ichabod, "is no place to visit for a friendly chat during business hours. . . ."

It was 7:08 P. M.

TENOR

ITCHING TO find out why No. 68 had been washed off at Albany, Ichabod deserted us—left us standing at the foot of the ramp that leads down to the Concourse from the Waiting Room. But he was thoughtful enough to introduce us first to a friend of his, one of Captain O'Neill's men, Patrolman George Bednarchick; and so we stood there, for a time, listening to this tall, thin, grave policeman, whose brown eyes never rested but kept roving over the crowd, scrutinizing every face, while he talked to us in a quiet, almost absent-minded way.

He was telling us about his music; for under his blue policeman's uniform, George nurses the heart of a singer. The Third Napoleon, in his early years, was a London policeman, who never ceased assuring his fellow Bobbies that one day they would see him at the Palace of the Tuilleries. George is less assertive; but what he hopes for is that one day we shall all see him at the Metropolitan. That's why he became a policeman. A short while out of the army at the close of the First World War—he was in the Battle of the Argonne Forest at the age of eighteen—he joined the force because the comparatively high starting wage enabled him to pay for singing lessons. He spent several years at the New York School of Music. Then he studied for years more under Paradise at Carnegie Hall. And now, still at it, he's working under Albano.

"Maestro Eduardo Albano," said George, still watching the crowd, still peering into every face with those alert brown eyes of his—he stopped abruptly to watch a half-tipsy fellow recover his balance after nearly slipping on the marble floor.

"Albano," he resumed, "is the world's greatest baritone."

George, though, is a tenor. With appealing dignity he told us that he knows, in Italian, the tenor role of every Italian opera ever produced at the Metropolitan during the regime of the late Giulio Gatti-Casazza.

It's been a hard life; a life of unending study. But there have been compensations. They stand out like bright lights along the way and shed upon all else a warm and genial glow. There was that night, for example, when he made his debut as a concert singer at Town Hall; and there was that other night when he sang at Carnegie Hall. On each occasion the critics were quite favorably disposed. But the times, of course, were bad, and George wasn't the only artist who has had to pay dearly for the Great Depression. Since then he's appeared as soloist at the Hotel Astor, at the MacAlpin, at other places. In particular, he's been quite a favorite at the annual banquets of the New York Society of Daughters of the American Revolution. That's a long way from the Metropolitan, of course.

"Meanwhile—"

George never finished that sentence, but what he meant to say was obvious enough. His thin, eager face was thrust forward, his roving eyes were still, as it were, combing the crowds, picking out each face, apparently taking in everything, missing nothing. It was obvious that, meanwhile, George is a policeman.

Bednarchick? It's a Slavic name. "My people came from Silesia." George, though, was born in Yonkers. He spent his boyhood in Philadelphia where he was graduated from Saint Malachy's Parochial School back in 1917. A fortnight later he joined the regulars: Thirty-ninth Infantry, Fourth Division. Now he lives in Mount Vernon—with a wife "who loves music too."

"I was the tenor soloist at the Lutheran Church of the Good Shepherd, up in Mount Vernon, and she was a member of the choir. That's how we met," said George. "Because of my ambition, I didn't want to get married. But one day . . . we were passing the City Hall, and she said: 'Well, we may as well get it over with.' So, just like that, we had a quiet, peaceful wedding.

"She had a newspaper job at the time; she was assistant-manager of the Mount Vernon *Daily Argus*. . . . Now she's an executive with a publishing house here in New York. . . . She's a lovely woman, always smiling, always helping me on with my music."

That's the way the talk was going while those watchful brown eyes of his kept noticing everything.

"If you're interested in railway music," he said, "you mustn't overlook a choral piece called 'The New York Central.' It was published by a music house here in New York. . . . It has a very interesting rhythm—the rhythm of train wheels going over the joints. We sang it once—it broke up a number of years ago, but we used to have a choral society here at Grand Central, and we sang it—"

It wasn't that George again stopped short. He was gone. He had spotted the girl in the green coat, and he was off. She was an attractive youngster—eighteen, or possibly nineteen; redhaired, nervous, highly excitable. We caught sight of her as she was coming down the ramp. Her eyes were bright with elation. We heard her exclaim: "What an exciting place this is!" And that was precisely it. She was too excited.

You saw this all in a flash; and, without any telling, you realized why George was now sauntering toward her. With some harsh question, he would bring the girl to earth—if he reached her soon enough. . . . But he didn't reach her soon enough. So he looked after her till the Travelers Aid took charge.

There's a tenseness in the air of every railway terminal; and there's a type of mind acutely sensitive to it. You may not know this; but the welfare agencies do, and so do the terminal police. The girl in the green coat was a typical case. Trains and travel, the thought of breaking free of the trammels of every-day life and of being whisked away to new worlds and new adventures, all this—in the very presence of departing trains—is pleasurably stirring to most minds. To others it's terribly exciting; and if the excitement goes too far, it takes only a second for the rest to follow. Excitement gives way to a sudden transport of ecstasy, and ecstasy in turn gives way to acute depression.

Before George Bednarchick could intervene with his "arresting" remark, the girl in the green coat was crying—crying for no reason that she could understand, but crying just the same, and crying uncontrollably.

The Travelers Aid is always on hand to take care of such cases. Welfare workers have a name for it. They call it "station hysteria."

At Grand Central, the Travelers Aid Society is represented by a staff of fifteen professional welfare workers and thirty-two volunteer aids. From 8 A. M. to 9 P. M., seven days a week, you can always find two or three of them on duty in the Concourse; they have a large desk with three telephones at the northeast corner of the room, beside the luggage counter; and they have a smaller desk with two telephones just under the balcony at the northwest corner. And after ten o'clock at night, you've only to telephone, or step across the street, to find a worker always ready to answer a call for help.

It isn't precisely across the street. Travelers Aid headquarters are at 144 East Forty-fourth street, just a few doors in from Lexington avenue; and back-to-back with it, facing Forty-third street, is the guest house, where temporary shelter is provided for out-of-town girls and women, and boys up to twelve years old, who are the "casualties" of present-day travel.

Some arrive friendless and penniless in the big city—the teen-age girl whose mother never "understood" her, and who therefore ran away from home; and the young war widow with her two babes, who had come three-fourths of the way around the world in a fierce struggle to reach Detroit and the home of a couple she had never seen—the parents of her dead husband. Others, stricken by sudden tragedy, or simply failing after a time to establish themselves in New York, are cared for till tickets can be provided to take them back to a new start in their old home towns. Roughly a thousand girls and women are received at the guest house every year, and each one stays, on the average, three nights; so that every night, from one year's end to the other, an average of eight or nine guests are being cared for. Thousands of others are there for only a few hours; and every year fifteen thousand meals are served free at the guest house.

The Travelers Aid Society dates from 1907; but so faithful has it been to a single task, endlessly performed, that it hardly has a history. So they incline to tell you at headquarters what is, strictly speaking, quite another story. It begins, as so many other stories begin, with an Irishman—this time, Bryan Mullanphy. Mullanphy founded the Saint Vincent de Paul Society in Saint Louis, Missouri, at a moment—back in 1849—when that city was overrun with families deserted by husbands and fathers who had joined the Gold Rush to California. For the next two years Mullanphy and his followers carried out one of the greatest works of pure charity in all American history; and thereupon the old gentleman wrote a famous will bequeathing a million dollars in trust to the city of Saint Louis, to be known as the Bryan Mullanphy Fund for Travelers, and to be used for the alleviation of distress among families traveling westward, in covered wagons, through Saint Louis. That was the beginning of the modern travelers' aid movement in America.

It was an unconscionably long time before the movement spread, however. In 1866, the Young Women's Christian Association of Boston "distributed warning notices," and in 1885, in New York, the "protection" of unaccompanied women travelers was taken up by the Quakers, who for this purpose retained the services of the city's first professional welfare worker. Almost at once, however, the Female Auxiliary Bible Society put two workers in the field; and in Boston, two years later, the Y. W. C. A. engaged a worker for service at the piers; and the Girls' Friendly Society organized the Young Travelers Aid, a volunteer group who carried on the same sort of work at the railway stations. The next year, 1888, the Chicago Y. M. C. A. organized a travelers' aid department; and in 1890, in New York, the Council of Jewish Women engaged workers to assist Jewish families arriving on the immigrant ships from Russia.

It was 1905 before any serious effort was made to co-ordinate the work of these and other sectarian groups. In May of that year Grace Hoadley Dodge, a wealthy spinster and leader of the Y. W. C. A. in New York, organized the nonsectarian Travelers Aid Committee, and two months later the committee, absorbing some of the earlier groups, began active work at Grand Central and at the piers and ferry houses of New York. Notably, the new organization had the backing of the city's two most influential citizens, the Episcopal bishop and the Catholic archbishop. After two years, a sort of shake-down period in which aims were clarified and methods were agreed upon, the Travelers Aid Committee resolved itself into the present-day Travelers Aid Society, a nonprofit corporation chartered by Legislature "to provide information, advice, guidance and protection to travelers . . . particularly women and girls . . . without charge of any kind for its services and without reference to race, nationality, religious creed, or political beliefs or affiliations."

And ever since 1907 Travelers Aid has been doing just that. From New York—from Grand Central, in fact—the movement spread rapidly over the whole country, as affiliated societies sprang up in other states. Today they form a network reaching from coast to coast and touching every city of importance in between. And all the work is paid for out of the dues and volunteer subscriptions of the members—and such others as wish to give. Others do give; in a recent report, for example, the New York society dutifully sets forth a contribution from Detroit—a matter of thirty-five dollars—advanced to a young woman from overseas, a war widow with two babes, to enable her to reach the home of her in-laws.

And that, briefly, is the story of the Travelers Aid.

"But what happened to the little redhead in the green coat?"

She was all right. Ten minutes' rest and quiet is all those cases need. And the workers know just what to do. So you don't have to worry about the girl in green.

It was 7:28 by the Golden Clock. At the far side of the Concourse Patrolman George Bednarchick was slowly, unobtrusively, pacing his beat and—you could be sure of it—looking at everybody, seeing everything, missing nothing; and dreaming dreams of the Metropolitan.

"And now," said Ichabod—

"Where did you come from?"

The tall fellow ignored the question.

"Now," he said, "there's somebody else I want you to meet—fellow over in the Stationmaster's office. He works the evening trick," said Ichabod, and chuckled softly, as if he looked forward to this meeting with special delight. "He works the four-to-midnight trick, so he's just about back from dinner now. . . ."

NIGHT CLERK

FROM THE Concourse it's only a few steps to the Stationmaster's office; and we arrived there just ahead of Ichabod's friend.

He was a grim, unsmiling little man with quick movements and flashing brown eyes; and at first glance you would have said that he was a testy-tempered little man if ever there was one. To the most civil inquiries of half a dozen red caps and gatemen—who had apparently been waiting for him—he barked the gruffest kind of replies; and when he had answered all their questions, he brusquely ordered the lot of them to "get out—and stay out." When Ichabod hailed him with "Hello, Bill," he glared up at the tall fellow truculently, then turned on his heel and marched off to the far end of the office where he proceeded, with elaborate gravity, to hang up his hat and coat. At last he condescended to reply.

"You're one of the adwice gratis order," he announced in a regular Cockney accent, "or you wouldn't be so werry fond o' *me* all at once."

Then he came forward again, a trim little man in a trim little suit of brown. He went through all his pockets as if organizing himself for what remained of the night's work. He ignored us studiously; and you had a chance to see how right handsome the little gentleman is. Bill, as Ichabod had called him, is a man of fifty or so, with the kind of face that used to be called Victorian. It's a type in which principally a well-developed nose and a well-developed chin are found in combination with a firm and slightly recessive mouth. Caricatured, it becomes, you know, the face of Punch; but no artist has ever struck off anything finer than a really handsome Victorian face. And Bill, lean and nervous, is handsome.

You might have noticed, too, what a well-proportioned little man he is. You might have seen—

"Now, young man, wot do you want?" he snapped suddenly; and

with the utmost good humor Ichabod told him, in effect, that we had spent the day in seeing the rest of Grand Central and that now we had come to see him.

The little man looked us all over, appraisingly.

"I'll try and bear up," he said acidly, "agin such a regular knock-down o' talent."

Ichabod considered that for a moment, but apparently had no comment ready, for he said nothing; and with a strange look in his eye, Bill went over to his desk and began examining a sheaf of papers. Conversation was stalled almost as it began. You could think what you pleased.

One thing, perhaps, you could hardly help thinking: Bill is one of those beautifully proportioned little men who, in photographs, often look heroic. Built upon a larger scale, they'd astonish the world with their good looks. But, being small, they're overlooked; and so, of course, they have the choice at the one extreme of turning sour, at the other of turning upon the world every now and again with a savage toot upon the horn of challenge. Bill would seem very savage indeed, if it were not for those bright eyes of his that somehow, in spite of him, make his anger seem unreal.

A young trainman burst into the office demanding to know where his conductor might be found, and Bill barked at him furiously that the conductor was not there, "and whoever says or has said he is, says that which is not the truth, but so far from it, on the contrairy, quite the rewerse."

Dumbfounded by such a rapid flow of words that, apparently, meant nothing at all, the trainman hesitated for a moment, then slowly pronounced his verdict: "You're nuts!"

Bill rose from his desk at that and went straight to him. He began by presuming that the youngster knew "the time o' day." Severely, then, he demanded to know what the "ghosts of mail coaches carry in their bags," but before the trainman could say a word, Bill dismissed him—looking grimmer than ever—with an abrupt: "The dead letters, of course."

"You're plumb crazy!" the young man shouted louder than before, and was about to expand upon the subject when a gateman arrived and told him his conductor was on the platform, where he belonged, watching the loading of his train. And to this Bill added swiftly: "Coaches, Sammy, is like guns—they requires to be loaded with werry great care afore they go off."

The trainman was about to express himself a third time when Ichabod broke in almost with a yell: "*Pickwick!* It's the *Pickwick Papers!*" Whereupon the little man, who had seemed such a mountain of uncompromising anger half a minute earlier, was seized with a sudden fit of uproarious laughter. He smacked his thighs, he bent over double, he held his ribs as if they were in danger of bursting.

"Crazy as a bedbug!" the trainman roared and dashed out of the office.

"He's been quoting from the *Pickwick Papers,*" Ichabod said. "Bill knows most of Dickens by heart; can quote chapter after chapter, word perfect. Tonight he's been giving us *Pickwick.* Every time he opened his mouth, he was quoting something—and it was pretty much to the point, too."

"Did you see the look on the face of that trainman?" Bill demanded; and promptly doubled up again with a new paroxysm of laughter. So it turned out, finally, that ferocity is only an affectation, and that really the bright-eyed little gentleman, to quote again from Dickens, is "in the comic line."

"Well," he said, becoming abruptly serious, "we don't get a lot of money on this job, but we have a lot of fun. . . . Most of them think I'm crazy. Well, that's all right, too."

"Tell me, Bill," said Ichabod, "how many times have you read through the complete works of Dickens?"

"I couldn't answer that question," said Bill, who now seemed very amiable indeed; "more times than I can remember. From two to four or five o'clock in the morning each day it's my habit to read; I get a great deal of contentment from reading. But I've not limited myself to Dickens. . . .

"Who? Steinbeck? Never heard of him. *The Grapes of Wrath?* I looked it over. I wouldn't waste my time reading trash like that," the little man declared.

"This morning, about two o'clock, I took up the *Decline and Fall* . . . after a lapse of about five years. Now there's a writer for you—Gibbon. . . . Take Winston Churchill, for example. I've read his

Nile Campaign, and I've read his history of the First World War, and, in fact, nearly everything he's ever written; and the touch of Gibbon runs through all of it. . . . That's about the only education Winston Churchill ever had, reading Gibbon in his tent in India when he was a subaltern. . . .

"His father, Lord Randolph Churchill, never had much hope for Winnie; never saw much promise in the lad. . . . Lord Randy—there was a man for you. He was the only true successor of Disraeli, and Young England was the Tory Democracy of Dizzy's era."

Ichabod broke in upon this to ask: "Aren't you in your own right one of the most widely known experts on the history of the United States Navy?"

"Not so widely known," was the quick reply; "but I have assisted in settling some difficult problems of American naval history."

This is the sort of man Bill is. When he isn't dishing out Dickens by the jugful, and worrying the lives out of untutored trainmen, he's building up a reputation for himself as a naval historian or talking learnedly of books and authors.

Smith is the name the little gentleman revels in—William L. Smith. It's an English name (though it appears only once or twice in Dickens); and William L. comes of a well-known English family established in the Delaware valley for more than two centuries. They fought in the American Revolution, which was a thoroughly English thing to do, says Bill; and they've fought in every succeeding war this country has engaged in. They belong to that whole region between the Water Gap and Trenton, New Jersey, where Bill himself still lives. (He spends four hours a day commuting.) They're equally numerous on the Jersey and the Pennsylvania side of the river; and Bill tells us he's also related to the Getty family of Gettysburg.

For more than two hundred years the Smiths of the Delaware valley have, in general, been farmers. But Bill is a member of the Brotherhood of Railway Clerks. He is, in fact, the night clerk in charge of the Stationmaster's office at Grand Central.

"And that's the story of Bill Smith," said Ichabod.

But Bill himself had the last word: "Vether it's worth while goin' through so much to learn so little, as the charity boy said ven he got to the end of the alphabet, is a matter o' taste."

It was 7:42, and we ought to be hurrying away, especially since Bill had rounded out the interview so beautifully for us; but a red cap, with a bag of tools laid out before him on the counter, was fitting a pair of spectacles on a woman, and that called for attention, didn't it?

She was a clerk employed at Grand Central. She had needed a new pair of glasses; and, as many another Grand Central clerk has done, she had gone for them to Red Cap No. 130—Rudolph J. Foster, who in 1925 took his degree in optometry at Columbia University. And now Rudy was delivering them, adjusting them to fit more snugly, and having the patient read the various sizes of type upon the card he placed before her.

Except for a few brief periods when he tried to live wholly by his profession, Rudy Foster has been a red cap at Grand Central ever since 1921. It was thus he paid his way through the university in the first place. A tall and rather handsome man, a light-colored Negro, he has a regular office in Mount Vernon, where he sees his patients daily from 9 A. M. to 3 P. M. And when that day's work is done, he takes the train to Grand Central where he does a second day's work as a red cap from 4 P. M. to 11 P. M.

"And there's many another red cap like him," said Ichabod.

Rudy, packing up his tools, assented.

"On the night side," he said, "you'll find a number of college men who by day are trying to get themselves established in some profession or other. I wouldn't know them all, but there's Frank Bradley, with two degrees, B. A. and D. D. S.; he's been a practicing dentist now for nine years, but he's still here nights doing red-cap work. There's Percy Verwayne; he was a captain in the Army Air Force during the war. There's Sylvester Crothers, Jr.; his father's the acting Bishop of Long Island, Afro-Methodist Episcopal Church, and one of his sisters is head of the Department of Psychology at Teachers' College, Washington, D. C. Sylvester himself went to Howard University, but he got into trade-union work—and he was the man who organized the red caps for the CIO. . . ."

"Is Newman around?"

"Just outside the door," said Rudy; "or he ought to be . . . I'll look him up."

Rudy went out, and almost immediately Milton Newman, Red Cap No. 148, came in—the last of the white porters and the only Jewish porter, it is believed, in the whole history of Grand Central. He's a white man all right; he's blue-eyed, and in his youth he must have been a blond. His uniform coat was unbuttoned—that would hardly have been tolerated in a Negro—and his cap rested upon his ears. The last of the white porters, he was also the last man ever to raise the American flag over the Commodore's Grand Central.

"I was a conductor on the Forty-second street horse-car line," he said; "and you know the old saying, 'Once on the railroad, always on the railroad.' So I took a job at the old Grand Central as a red cap—that was just the year before they rebuilt it. As I was the youngest of the lot, they made me the night man. . . .

"Every night they used to close up that old Grand Central at 1 A. M., and it was my job to go around and lock all the doors. Everybody had to get out—even people who had tickets had to stay out in the street till the station opened up again at six o'clock. And I was the guy used to open up the station again at 6 A. M. . . .

"At 5 A. M. on the last Washington's Birthday before that station was done over, I went up to the roof to raise the flags. There should have been five flags up that day, but a hurricane was blowing, and before I had the first flag all the way up, a gust came along and took me off my feet. I hung onto the rope, though, with both hands. The wind swung me out over Forty-second street, and I just stayed there, almost level with the top of the flagpole. I hung on. I was afraid the rope would break. Then I was afraid the pole would break. But I hung on anyway. . . .

"Then that wind stopped, and I swung back to the foot of the flagpole. And do you know what I did then? I could have jumped right down through the scuttle in the roof. . . . But I stayed there till I got the flag all the way to the top and made her fast. . . . And that was the last flag ever raised over that building."

Newman frowned for a moment, as if trying to remember; then he said with finality: "No, I didn't raise the four other flags. Only one flag went up that day. I told them it was dangerous."

TARDY ARRIVAL

It was 7:46.

The Concourse was in a gay mood now. It was the brightest hour of the day. It was the hour of the white scarf, the occasional opera hat; it was the hour of the long skirt, the glittering slipper and the ermine wrap. It was the hour when wives and daughters come trooping in from the suburbs, and city girls in their party dresses come surging up from the subway platforms. In short, it was the hour before the curtain rises. The theater crowds were passing through Grand Central—laughing, carefree crowds.

Near the Golden Clock a young woman with small eyes and a sharp face, a brazen article, stood with her legs spread wide apart, sketching some of the evening cloaks; a fashion writer in quest of ideas, perhaps. Near the luggage counter, under East Balcony, a tipsy gentleman slipped on the marble floor; and there was an uproarious burst of laughter as he got quickly to his feet again and began drinking out of what was left of the bottle he had had on his hip. At the northwest corner of the Concourse, opposite Track 29, a gateman was calling the *Cleveland Limited*; at the approach of a clergyman, a tall man with white hair and rosy cheeks, the gateman forgot to say *please*, and also forgot to lower his voice, and so you heard him halfway across the floor: "All tickets good evening, Father!" The crowd laughed at that, too. The gateman raised his cap. The priest laid down his bag and took the gateman's hand; stood talking for a moment, then hurried through the gate. The gateman again raised his cap and his voice: "All tickets, please! Have your tickets ready!"

Laughing and talking eagerly, sometimes calling aloud to friends, the crowds pressed on:

"I'm waiting for Daisy."

"It's according to the time of day you were born, maybe!"

"Darling, don't pay more than two dollars."

"It's a verra seemple question: *whur is the Caledonian Club?*"

"I'd rather sit in the gallery, anyhow."

"I see you got your glad rags on. Steppin' out tonight, hey?"

"There's a theater ticket agency here in Grand Central—right next to the Baggagemaster's office."

"Maybe Daisy ain't comin'."

"Stand here quietly. Father will get us a taxicab, and we have plenty of time."

Other crowds were coming in—for it was now the time of day when most travelers leave the big city for New England, Upstate New York and the Middle West. And then too, of course, there were the usual number of tardy commuters going home to the suburbs after working overtime, or taking their dinners in the city. They chattered too as they cut across the theater crowds:

"There's our train over there!"

"It's getting cooler this evening."

"Only slaves would spend a day like this locked up in an office."

"Our train leaves from the Lower Concourse."

"We've got a lot of freezing weather still ahead of us."

"Good night. And remember all of us to the folks over at your house, won't you?"

"Hey! Do you know our train leaves in half a minute?"

A squad of gatemen hurried in from the general direction of the Arrival Station; hurried to the gateway opposite Track 26. Swiftly they set down standards upon the marble floor of the Concourse; they strung lines from one to another; they erected cordons to keep back the crowds. Then a light went on, and a loud voice raised the cry of "*Twentieth Century Limited!* Train from Chicago! Arriving on Track 26!"

There was a rush of people to the cords. There's always a rush to see the *Century* come in. But this time the crowds were taken by surprise —or most of them were. A few, tired to death, had been around Grand Central, waiting for this moment, since nine o'clock this morning. Wearily one of these walked between the cordons, but was quickly appraised of the error: "Back of the line, Lady! Everybody back of the line, where you'll all be sure to see your friends . . . just as soon as they come through the doorway."

There were those who were weary with waiting. But the crowd for the most part was made up of those who had simply happened to be passing by, and had had this unexpected pleasure thrust upon them. For a glad few minutes, they'd forget what brought them here. They'd wait, tensely poised against the ropes, in the hope of seeing close at hand a few romantic beings out of Hollywood. As if by a miracle, half a dozen autograph books appeared, half a dozen fountain pens were out and ready.

Two Catholic nuns—tall women in the lofty headgear of the Josephite order—looked down from a vantage point in the West Balcony, north of the staircase. A fussy little man with a clubfoot came hurrying down the stairs; he had a cane and he moved rapidly enough, but it wasn't good to watch him. The fashion writer stationed herself where nothing could escape her. The tipsy gentleman who had broken his flask wandered over to see what the commotion was all about. A gateman told him, and he promptly demanded: "How much you wanna bet?"

He was eminently reasonable about it.

"I know the *Century's* time," he said. "She comes in here at 9 A. M., and A. M.—that means in the morning. Now it's night-time. The stars are out!"

He made a sweeping gesture toward Paul Helleu's great ceiling above the Concourse. And then he realized what a splendid joke he had there and laughed till the tears came to his eyes.

The little fellow with the clubfoot darted every which way, as if looking for somebody. He was worried. He was the picture of despair.

After a swift look through the doorway, the gateman again lifted his voice, announcing the arrival of the *Century*. It was 7:55. An excited chatter went up among the crowd. Then there was silence. And when a cross-looking traveler came through the gate, a tall man in a hurry, the silence was unbroken—till the tipsy one gallantly saved the situation by shouting: "Hurray! First man ashore!"

Then others came; but they were all unknown. The notables, it was whispered, were holding back. A tall woman, wearing an Easter outfit in January, had the air of a notable; flashing a professional smile, she bowed to the left and right as she marched along the widening corridor between the ropes; but nobody seemed to recognize her, except the little man with the clubfoot. He cheered her for all he was worth; pointed her out to all around him and—in a shrill, almost effeminate voice—shouted her name. But within the bosoms of the crowd no spark leapt up to greet the flame of his enthusiasm, and to the end he was the only one who raised a voice on the lady's behalf.

She addressed him angrily, in what was meant to be an undertone. She used a word not often heard on a woman's lips; and the little fellow wilted. In that high piping voice of his he protested that the newspaper people had been here all day, but. . . . And then it became obvious what was wrong. Probably for the first time in twenty-five years, the *Century* was in without benefit of reporters and popping flash-bulbs.

In the end, nobody of eminence came through the gate. The notables—if any such, indeed, were aboard the train—apparently slipped out quietly by following the outer concourse along to some other door, where nobody was waiting. There was one, brief, thrilling moment when a woman appeared who looked, at a distance, as if she might have stepped out of Hollywood. She was swathed in furs and was clutching a Pekinese while a corps of red caps carried her thirty hat boxes. But she turned out to be fat and florid—"the chorus girl," said Ichabod, "that somebody married when he was young."

The door was closed, the gatemen gathered up their lines and standards, the crowds broke up. The *Century* had pulled in ten hours and twenty-five minutes late.

"Be sure of it," said Ichabod, "that's an all-time record—for the *Century*, that is. It's because of the snow; remember what I told you this morning. When the gales are up, and the blizzards are blowing in across the lakes, it's a matter of bucking the snow all the way from Chicago to the Adirondacks. The snow has been falling for three weeks now," said Ichabod.

"In consequence, the best trains on the board run late. . . . How late? Mathematically, it varies from half a minute to infinity—as in the case of No. 68 today . . . or any train that doesn't arrive at all. I'll tell you about No. 68. . . .

"No. 68 is the company's second-best train, eastbound. She's the *Commodore Vanderbilt*. She leaves Chicago at 2:30 P. M., and she's due in here at 9:30 the next morning. . . .

"But—when the snow is bad—the trains run late, and the effect of late arrivals is twofold: they cause terminal traffic congestions that, sometimes, are critical . . . merely by coming in when they have no right to be coming in; but, what's worse, they also upset the balance of cars in the equipment pool.

"The point is that, normally, a train arrives from Chicago, let us say, in the morning, and the cars go directly to the coaching yard at Mott Haven to be cleaned and scrubbed, ready to leave for Chicago that afternoon. But, with delays, the westbound *Commodore* may have to draw upon the floating reserve of cars on hand in the equipment pool.

"But late arrivals, continued over a period of many days, have the effect of wiping out that reserve. The cars accumulate in Chicago, and New York is short; the pools are out of balance. Or, on the other hand, four trains instead of two may be on the road at once, and both pools are short. And then, of course, the train that arrives from Chicago in the morning has to be cleaned in a very great hurry and sent back to Chicago the same afternoon. . . .

"That was the condition the *Commodore* got herself into more than two weeks ago. . . . And then storm followed storm, and she began arriving so late that the men weren't able to clean her out in time, and the result of that was that she began *leaving* late. Things had got to the point at which No. 68, the eastbound *Commodore*, was tying up No. 67, the westbound *Commodore*. The mischief was becoming cumulative . . . and, of course, that sort of thing can't continue long.

"Today, like the *Century*, the *Commodore* was running later than ever . . . and it became evident that she could not arrive at New York till four or five hours after she was due to leave again for Chicago. . . . And so No. 68 was canceled at Albany; washed right off the board. Her passengers were transferred to a train of ordinary day coaches that ran *Special* from Albany to Grand Central. . . .

"And another train of day coaches ran out of Grand Central on No.

67's time at 4:15 o'clock this afternoon. . . . She made the run to Albany in the normal 2 hours and 40 minutes, and transferred her people to the *Commodore* . . . which had only arrived at Albany half an hour earlier, to be turned around and cleaned and scrubbed, apparently in record time.

"So you see," said Ichabod, "it's been a great day in the history of Grand Central. The *Century* came in later than ever before, and the *Commodore* never got here at all. . . .

"You saw the *Century* arrive. You saw the crowds. It may have occurred to you," said Ichabod, "that the small-town folks are not the only ones—that the rustic habit of watching the trains come in is pretty firmly established at Grand Central. . . ."

The crowds were thinning out now. It was 8:03. Except for a few stragglers—"*Daisy!* Now ain't you awful!"—the early theater crowds had gone, and the quiet of evening was settling over the Concourse. No. 21, the *Ontarian*, was pulling out at 8:15 from Track 37, and at 8:50 No. 29, the *Niagara*, would be pulling out from Track 34, over at the northwest corner of the room. We strolled over that way.

Ichabod was quiet for a moment, as if he had something on his mind but was not quite certain how to say it. Suddenly he cleared his throat and began.

"You mustn't forget," he said, "that what we've been looking at all day long is the third Grand Central. The Commodore built the first. The second resulted from an effort to cope with a new and staggering problem—a mass migration of people out of New York to the suburbs. . . . As I said before, the second Grand Central was completed at a cost of five million dollars in 1901, and she was only one year old when—"

Ichabod stopped short, and a look of surprise passed over his face. Perhaps, too, there was a look of recognition. There was that tilted smile once more, and once more that strange light came into his glittering green eyes.

"Fact is," he said abruptly—and it seemed almost like a burst of confidence. But then he recovered himself, and all he said was: "Well, it may seem too fanciful."

At the gateway leading to Track 34 stood a white-haired old woman and a white-haired old man. They were going away; that was obvious. And their family was there to see them off—a son and two daughters, daughter-in-law and one son-in-law, and half a dozen grandchildren already in their teens. The old gentleman was smiling broadly. His wife was elated. Her cheeks were flushed, her eyes sparkled, she spoke rapidly—and louder, probably, than she realized.

"We were married in the morning, and Papa went back to work that afternoon, and they docked him half a day's pay. . . . When I found that out, I cried. But . . . fifty years don't seem long when you're looking forward to the honeymoon you never had."

CIVIL ENGINEER

"As I was about to say," said Ichabod—tired out, we were now sitting down in the Philosophers' Gallery—"the second Grand Central was only one year old when . . .

"It was the twenty-second of January, 1902. The morning rush was near its peak; the smoke in the Park avenue tunnel was particularly bad. . . . Deep in the tunnel a New Haven commuter train was 'in the color'—standing stock-still, that is to say, in front of a red light. Back of her, on the same track, a Central-Hudson train was moving through the smoke by dead reckoning. . . . It was a mean crash; 'at least' seventeen people were killed. It was a major disaster; and, of course, it was no excuse that in all the history of the Park avenue tunnel such a thing had never happened before.

"Newspaper men," said Ichabod, "were kept out of the tunnel, in spite of the *New York Journal* man's historic '*I* am the public.' And, affronted, the newspapers played up the wreck for all it was worth. They said the smoke was what caused all the mischief. They made themselves at least the spokesmen for the public. They raised a protest, they lifted it to a crusade. And, up in Albany, Legislature passed a law.

"It was decreed that after the first of July, 1910, no steam locomotive might enter Manhattan on any track employed predominantly for passenger service. That meant that steam power might still be used for hauling freight trains down the West Side of Manhattan; but it also meant that the railroad would have but eight years to electrify Grand Central. . . .

"And that," said Ichabod, "was the beginning of many things. . . ."

It was a day in September, 1902; the wreck, the outcry in the newspapers, the uproar in Legislature culminating in the order to electrify, all this had come to pass in less than eight months. It was toward the middle of the afternoon; a tallish fellow—a lithe and rugged out-of-doors man with a brown beard and a keen face—was gravely turning these matters over in his mind. He was a young man, barely forty, but he was the chief engineer of the Central-Hudson Railroad. Appointed to that post in 1899, it was he who had swiftly reorganized the terminal, had redesigned and rebuilt and reopened within two years the new Grand Central Station—at a cost, remember, of five million dollars. And it was he, William J. Wilgus, who now had to worry about the electrification project. And so on that September afternoon he sat thinking, cogitating, beside the window of his fourth-floor office on the north side of Grand Central Station.

Then he stood up—not so very tall at that; possibly 5 feet 10, possibly 170 pounds—and gazed across the fan, where half a dozen yard goats were tugging wasp-like at their work, and a score of road engines were belching enormous quantities of smoke as they lazily backed in, ready for their evening race to the suburbs. It was a devilishly noisy place, full of a wild cacophony of sounds—the shrieking of the whistles, the crashing of the couplers, the eternal screeching of the wheels where the curves were too tight and the rails gripped the flanges. And it was a grimy place, appropriately closed in upon the east, and upon the north, by the backs of grimy tenement houses—where teeming thousands of people lived and were cheerful, and hung out their wash on Mondays, under a heavy pall of smoke and soot.

It was not beautiful; it was a place robbed of all those elements that somehow fall together, in other places, to make beauty. Track, for example, can be laid out in the most graceful curves; and should be, if it's to be good track. And we all know, perhaps, that beauty that was so admired by Pennell—a triumphant kind of beauty that's all the more poignant because it inhabits, and glorifies, and won't be denied by, the smoke and grime of men's working-places. But here there was none of that. Here there was only noise and dirt; unadulterated dirt. Here the trackage was not graceful, but had a hunched and twisted look, and the fan was so unnaturally short that you were oppressed by it. Pennell himself, had he been standing there beside

Wilgus that day in September, 1902, would have turned away in despair.

Wilgus turned back to his desk—he was alone at the time—and began idly sketching as he had many times done before. With a few swift strokes he roughed in the main outline of the fan, then framed it within the "limiting factors" of Vanderbilt and Lexington avenues to the west and east, and Forty-second and Forty-ninth streets to the south and north. Then he fixed his eyes upon the lower right-hand corner of the sketch, the northwest corner of Forty-second street and Lexington avenue; and there his skimming pencil began to work in a new structure, immediately to the east of Grand Central Station. This was to be a station annex; for above all else, at that moment, the railroad needed office space, thousands and thousands of square feet of office space.

No matter what came next, this annex, this office building, would have to be erected first. It would have to be tall; there wasn't any choice about that. With proper allowance for future needs, it would have to be eighteen or twenty stories high. And, of course, it would be modern, perhaps beautiful. The bearded fellow with the keen face—a remarkably intelligent face—worked faster and faster as the lines began developing under his fingers, as the picture began taking shape, began emerging ever more clearly out of a haze of tentative lines.

It was a tall tower, when he had finished it. He looked at it critically; and was rather more pleased with it than not. It would require a great deal of development, but the idea was there, and so it was a beginning well made. To see the whole effect, however, he drew beside it the six-story Grand Central Station—and decided that the contrast was ludicrous.

He took a new sheet of paper, and again drew in the fan, again fixed the boundaries within which his plan would have to be contained. He cast about, then, for a place to put the tall new tower, convenient to the station yet not so close as to cause a clash. He tried it here—there—everywhere. But here, there, everywhere were tracks; tracks crowded together, tracks covering every inch of ground clear over to the courtyards of the tenements.

"I continued working," he said some forty-two years later on, "and then, suddenly, there came a flash of light."

It was tracks, bridges, buildings all in a single structural entity; not separate things any longer, but integral parts of an immense new whole.

"It was the most daring idea that ever occurred to me," the old gentleman said in 1944.

First and foremost, of course, it was tracks. It was tracks laid upon the bedrock of Manhattan, forty feet below the surface; it was more tracks, laid upon steel bridgework twenty feet above the lower tracks; and it was that same sturdy bridgework rising twenty feet more to carry city streets, or soaring onward to the clouds to become the skeletons of skyscrapers. That was the idea. It was as simple, and as bold, as that.

To drive the fan below ground, as part of the electrification project, would not of itself be such a breath-taking venture—though it would be difficult and costly to carve out of almost solid granite the enormous gallery, forty feet deep, in which the tracks would lie. And to double-deck the fan—though no one before had even attempted such a thing—would again be feasible though costly; it would amount, essentially, to building an elevated railroad above another railroad.

But a great deal more than this was involved in Wilgus's idea; for if skyscrapers could be erected over the fan, then it stood to reason that the fan could just as well underlie Vanderbilt avenue, Park avenue, Lexington avenue and even Grand Central Station itself. In other words, there would no longer be any question of closing off city streets—which the city had steadfastly refused to do—and, under ground, the fan could spread.

It could be made much broader at the base, and, to give it altitude, the tunnel could be "cut back" from the portals at Forty-ninth street almost any distance at all. Though the cost would be staggering, the tracks could begin fanning out far up the avenue, the present crumpled-up fan could be discarded in favor of two immensely larger and much more smoothly tapered fans, and—what was of the highest order of importance—the introduction of loop tracks, which had not been possible before, would be possible now. And so it was. The idea that came to Wilgus so abruptly that September afternoon, was so all-embracing that it took in its grasp all the railroad problems which had plagued Grand Central for a generation; and it found a solution that would last, or so it seemed at the time, for a century to come.

And yet that was only a single aspect of the whole idea; turn it about and you would find a second aspect which, in the end, was equally important. There would be bridges carried on the same steel-work that carried the upper deck of the fan. Instead of high foot bridges across the thirty-year-old open fan—bridges that for years now had connected the separated parts of Forty-fifth, Forty-sixth, Forty-seventh and Forty-eighth streets—instead of those high, narrow, soot-laden foot bridges, there would be flat steel bridges; and these would be at street level, they would be street-wide, they would have concrete sidewalks and roadways paved with asphalt. They would be in line with, they would restore the continuity of, those crosstown streets. And a fifth bridge, perpendicular to the others, would carry Park avenue on down from Forty-ninth to Forty-second street. Like the double-decked fan, it was a bold and daring concept. Thus far, in fact, it was only too bold, too romantic, in the light of an engineer's first duty, which is to restrict his imagination to what is financially possible.

But there was still a third aspect of Wilgus's idea—an idea that was so completely integrated in itself, so internally organized, that it could hardly have been said to have parts. And that third aspect was represented, for the moment, by the spaces left between the bridges. These were rectangular openings, where the upper-level fan would lie, twenty feet below street-level, exposed to the sun and rain. But they were immensely more than just openings. They were nothing less than building sites. And they could be leased to the Government for a new post office, or to private real estate operators for great hotels and office buildings. Somebody else would erect those many sky-scrapers—and, for the privilege of doing so, would pay enormous rentals to the railroad.

Not directly founded upon bedrock, the buildings, of course, would ride upon the steel-work bridging over the fan; they would literally complete the roofing of the fan. But, above all, they would transform the railroad's land from a dead-weight holding, on which taxes had to be paid, to a revenue-producing property. And so the net result of Wilgus's idea would be to create a huge source of income, that would justify—perhaps—the cost of the whole scheme.

And there was the vital principle that made the idea live. The railroad would build its fan, would also build the bridges that would underlie the streets. And then somebody else would "develop" the building sites, and pay the railroad—ground rent? Not quite. The rights pertaining to the ownership of land are three: First, there are the surface rights; the owner, that is to say, has an exclusive right to fence in, to grow crops upon, to play tennis upon, or otherwise to use the surface of his land. Second, there are the sub-surface rights; the owner has a right, for example, to excavate, to build cellars, to lay foundations as far below the surface as he pleases. And, third, there are the air rights; the owner has a right to erect buildings into the air above the surface of his land. It was not usual, perhaps, but Wilgus knew from the start that, legally, the railroad had a right to retain the sub-surface rights and to lease the air rights above its fan. And that was precisely what he intended that the railroad should do. "Air rights" became his battle cry.

But if the building of skyscrapers would be left to other enterprisers, the whole scheme, from the engineering point of view, would nevertheless be of a single piece. The steelwork that carried the upper-level trackage would rise another twenty feet, both to carry the bridges and to receive the steel frames of those tall buildings that ultimately were going to stand cellarless above the tracks. Those buildings, of course, would face upon the bridges—so that a stranger wandering through that region would never know that he was upon a bridge, but would see only a roadway, curbing and sidewalks, and stores, hotels and building entrances facing the sidewalks. Inevitably, the bridges would come first, and the buildings later—perhaps even several years later. But the buildings would be provided for in the first instance; that was the point. And, in the end, the double-decked fan below the surface, the bridges at the surface and the tall buildings above the surface would all be parts of a single structural entity—a revenue-producing entity that would cover a dozen city blocks.

You can say that the elements had all been present in his mind for years; and that would be most probable, for Wilgus had for years been brooding upon this problem. But, however long considered, the elements fused in a single instant, and the scheme—we have Wilgus's own word for it—was complete in every essential aspect when it came to him in that flash of light as he was sketching in his office that September day in 1902.

He stayed at the office late that night; and the next day found him there earlier than usual. He wanted to explore to the utmost the possibilities of his plan; he wanted to probe out the weak spots. He threw the routine work of his office into the laps of his lieutenants, told them he would be busy for the next three months. Then he began tramping back and forth across the fan and through the city streets that immediately surrounded the terminal property.

He meant to carry Park avenue all the way down to Forty-second street; to unite that avenue for the first time with Fourth avenue, of which it once had been a part—though only in theory. He meant to tear down the five-million-dollar Grand Central Station, which he had completed only two years earlier. He decided now to erect in its place a combination hotel and station that would straddle Park avenue from Forty-second to Forty-fourth street, and that would tower twenty-two stories high.

He built up a great draughting force, he began work on a great series of drawings. He began by designing the new terminal fan—the first, and in all probability the last, double-decked fan in the whole history of railroading. He located many of the buildings: the new office building that was needed so urgently; the station-hotel with its heroic archway spanning two whole blocks of Park avenue; the new post office—the Government could always be relied on to spend a little money. He developed every last detail of the work below ground-level; he equipped himself with blueprints in which all the track-work and all the bridging stood complete to the last rail and the last girder. And so he was able to estimate the cost to the last few hundreds of dollars.

He took advice of lawyers, he studied the opinion of real estate operators, he "saw his way through." And, notably, he hedged on one point. The skyscrapers, he decided, could be carried on the same bridgework as the upper-level tracks, or—if it seemed advisable—on independent columns striking down to bedrock between tracks; without anywhere touching the railroad bridge.

By the middle of December, all this preliminary work had been completed, and on the twenty-second—eleven months to a day after the tunnel disaster—Wilgus presented his plan to William H. Newman the president of the Central-Hudson Railroad. He described it as a general scheme for electrification, depression of the tracks, enlargement of all the terminal facilities, and utilization of the air rights pertaining to the company's real property. He laid down all the figures. He declared that the five million dollars expended on Grand Central Station would have to be sacrificed. He announced that the cost of his new project would be $34,360,000, of which $4,500,000 would be required at once to begin the work of blasting out of the rock the enormous gallery tha would contain all the track-work.

But he also laid it down that the air rights, at a fair rental, shoul yield enough revenue to pay an annual return of 3½ per cent upon the total cost of the project, plus a return of 10 per cent upon the company's real estate. So in the end it was not simply an engineering project tha he laid before Newman; it was a profit-making enterprise.

Newman, though he had been prepared for something on the heroi scale, was astounded; and "raised all kinds of objections." At a hastily summoned meeting of the board of directors, however, Wilgus outlined the problem. He set forth one by one the controlling factors of a complex situation; and then he outlined the plan, displayed its grasp and management of all those operating, engineering and financia factors. Most of the objections melted away and disappeared as he continued talking; and the board sat silent all through the performance—fascinated by the crystal-clarity of his presentation and the swift confident calculations of one of the acutest minds that ever wandere into the field of engineering.

Most of the objections disappeared; but one remained. Railroa hotels, Newman declared, were never successful ventures; all ove Europe they were definitely second class.

And the reason for that, said Wilgus, was noise and smoke. With electrification, both of these would be eliminated, and the hotel a Grand Central would prosper because of its very nearness to the sta tion.

"But the cabbies," Newman persisted—"the cabbies would neve take up a stand at the entrance to any hotel of ours. Nothing could pe suade them to leave the sunshine of Fifth avenue. The horses need th sunshine, and the cabbies know it."

"Mr. Newman," Wilgus replied, "I don't think you need worry about hat. I predict that before our hotel is completed, motor-cabs will be in peration all over New York."

After all, said Newman, the hotel was not a vital feature of the plan, nd before it was built there would still be time to argue its merits. Meanwhile, were there any questions? There were none. The board of irectors accepted Wilgus's proposal at once—unanimously.

Wilgus became a colonel in the First World War; became Director f Military Railways of the American Expeditionary Force in France. And he was the fastest man I ever knew at sizing up a situation," says Colonel Frederic A. Snyder, late of the 103rd United States Engineers. In his first look round he saw everything, and he saw everything in its xact relation to everything else."

Others have noted—what is perhaps the same thing—his ability to um up a situation.

The story goes that upon a day in September, 1918, he was summoned y Pershing to attend a council of officers at general headquarters. He vas late in arriving, however, and Pershing decided to go on without im. Pershing announced that the Americans were about to take over sector of their own—the San Mihiel sector which, up to then, they had een sharing with the British. And Pershing was determined to attack t once; the purpose of the council, he said, was to plan the attack.

According to one who was present at the council, the talk had been oing on for two hours, and not any too profitably, when Wilgus arrived. n that abrupt way of his, Pershing told Wilgus the bare purpose of the ouncil, then immediately called upon him to speak. And without nowing what any of the others might have said previously, without ven waiting to remove his dripping raincoat, Wilgus began.

He spoke for an hour and a half without a pause: There was a swift nfolding of the whole situation at San Mihiel—the terrain, the bstacles, the troops, the guns, the whole state of readiness for an dvance; even the names, the experience, and the reputation of the German regiments blocking the way. There was a careful weighing of ne factor against another; as if Wilgus were delivering a prepared ecture. There was a mapping out of steps to be taken in a given equence; not as if those steps were part of a concocted scheme, but as

if each in turn were dictated—as in fact they were—by things inheren
in the situation itself. And there was a forecast that the battle would b
won in forty-eight hours.

Then Wilgus sat down; and there was the silence of men who had no
the breath to speak.

It was Pershing who broke the silence. In effect, he said that tha
was it; that they would do as Wilgus had made it plain they must do

The battle of San Mihiel began at midnight of September 11/12
1918. It was ended forty-eight hours later. And it opened up that ga
in the German line that enabled the American divisions to launch thei
great and decisive Meuse-Argonne offensive.

These dates are worth observing: Wilgus laid down his plan for th
present-day Grand Central on the twenty-second of December. Christ
mas came three days later, and all of the following week was a holiday
The board of directors met and approved a thirty-five-million-dolla
scheme at a single sitting immediately after New Year's Day. By th
tenth of January, 1903, Wilgus had been made a vice president of th
Central-Hudson Railroad in charge of New York terminal construction
And by the fifteenth his track and bridge designs—the fundamenta
work of civil engineering—had been distributed among a score of th
nation's foremost architects, who were invited to offer designs for
great new station.

The conditions were severe. The station would have to stand abov
the loop tracks, and would have to be a revenue-producing structure—
either a station combined with a hotel, or a station combined with a
office building. Park avenue and Fourth avenue would have to be linke
up to form a single, continuous thoroughfare. And the competition wa
to close on the first of March; the architects, such was the fierce energ
with which the scheme was being pushed forward, would have but littl
more than five weeks in which to consider the whole problem and offe
sketches for a prize—which was, of course, a contract involving fees that
might conceivably run to a cold half-million dollars.

And why this mad haste? Of course, there was that great and stil
increasing flood of commuters to the suburbs. Their comfort had to be
considered, their train service had to be improved, or they would choos
homes in Jersey, or Long Island, in preference to homes in Westchester.

That was one reason for haste. Again, the builders and real estate agents of Westchester—who had just introduced the word *bungalow* to the every-day vocabulary of Americans—were none too patient. And Wilgus, who never missed a chance, had been to see these gentlemen, had won their approval of a scheme to raise fares, and reduce local taxes on railroad property, in order to help pay for the new Grand Central. And that was a second reason for haste. But a thousand times more urgent, more instant in its whipping effect, was the simple fact that there was a barge out on the Hudson river. The East river tunnels to Brooklyn had just been completed and now, over to the other side of Manhattan, a contractor's barge was slowly moving up and down the river, sounding, probing, exploring. Only one deduction was possible. Burrowing below the lordly Hudson, "the unbridged and unbridgable Hudson," the Pennsylvania Railroad was coming into New York!

So they were not carefully developed plans that the competing architects turned over to Wilgus on the first of March, 1903. Essentially, they were ideas that would still have to be worked out in detail; and they were judged as ideas. They were offered, some of them, by the greatest living architects—Samuel Huckel Jr. of Philadelphia, D. H. Burnham of Chicago, Stanford White of New York. All these accepted Wilgus's idea of a station straddling Park avenue; which was, of course, a station split by the enormous arcade through which the street would run.

White reared above the archway a tower sixty stories high, what would have been the tallest building in the world; and he proposed that from the top of this a jet of steam should be driven three hundred feet higher into the air, so that tower and plume together should rise a full thousand feet above the streets. By day then, as he pointed out, the plume would be visible from every part of the city; would serve as a gigantic advertisement of Grand Central. By night red lights would be played upon it, so that even then it would dominate New York. And by day or night it would also serve as a beacon to ships at sea—the last bit of New York visible to those outward-bound, the first to be descried by those coming in.

It was curious. White had just then completed a new Madison Square Garden, replacing that original Garden that was, as we have seen, the old Twenty-sixth street terminal; and, having done that, he was now bidding to replace the old Forty-second street terminal. At least there were the classic unities to recommend it. But the prize this time was not for him; and the classic unities, by a sardonic fate, were satisfied a little later, when Stanford White was at the Garden he designed and Harry Thaw walked up to him and shot him dead.

And the prize was not for Burnham, who had been the architect of the Chicago World's Fair of 1900. Nor was it for the daring Huckel, who had made men gasp when he designed the Philadelphia City Hall as a pedestal for the gigantic statue of William Penn. The architects who won the prize were comparatively unknown. They were Charles Reed and Allen Stem, partners in the firm of Reed & Stem of Saint Paul, Minnesota.

It was they who suggested ramps for the interior of Grand Central. (Even the word was unknown at that time, or not very widely known, and *Munsey's Magazine*, in telling about them, felt called upon to explain that Julius Caesar when he had laid siege to a city, began at once to build a *ramp*, a long, sloping roadway of earth, clear to the top of the city's wall, to carry his war chariots over the wall and into the heart of the city; while charging up the ramp, the chariots were *rampant*, and on attaining the *rampart*, they began their *rampage*.) But they won the prize because, in addition to the ramps, they had one superb idea, which was to connect Park avenue and Fourth avenue without splitting Grand Central into two parts. They had designed a twenty-two story hotel set well back from the building lines on every side, and they had surrounded this with a broad, elevated roadway—a "circumferential plaza," they called it—that was to form the link between the two avenues. It was to be a full story high above the sidewalks; and, to connect with it, the middle lanes of Fourth avenue were to be continued northward from Fortieth street upon a viaduct clear across Forty-second street. (This would roof over the open cut in Fourth avenue; in effect, it would extend the Murray Hill Tunnel northward the better part of two blocks, and the approach to the Forty-second street viaduct from the south would therefore be along the slowly rising roof of the tunnel.) And the link with Park avenue, north of Grand Central, was likewise to be effected by ramp and viaduct.

A serious traffic problem was solved in this way; for if Wilgus had carried Park avenue at street level southward to Forty-second street—as he had thought to do—it would have had to be a narrow Park avenue where it passed through the building, and then it would not have met the divided roadways of Fourth avenue, but would have struck between them, directly opposite the tunnel approach. Wilgus had been aware of this complication. Reed & Stem side-stepped it beautifully.

Reed & Stem! All the punsters of New York made merry over that name; for what is a reed if it is not the stem of a certain kind of plant? And was it any wonder, then, that together they could stalk fame and fortune? Pleasantly New York decided that, though a reed was not to be leaned upon, this partnership could stem all opposition. And in that there was more than a touch of prophecy, for Reed & Stem were pounced upon quickly enough.

For the moment, though, they had won the prize, and the railroad had signed a contract appointing them architects of the new station—what was to be the third Grand Central, what was to be officially Grand Central *Terminal.* They went to work at once; and it wasn't as if they were strangers, for Reed & Stem had done work for the Central-Hudson Railroad before this, and even at this moment they were engaged in building the new station at Troy. Reed in particular knew how to work with Wilgus; they whipped out their thoughts together, dovetailed their plans. They formed a strangely effective pair, for they knew each other intimately and they completely trusted each other. As a mere point of fact, Reed was Wilgus's brother-in-law.

A new problem lay ahead for Wilgus. The vast project he had devised would have to be approved and authorized by the city. He was responsible for all the engineering blueprints. Reed & Stem contributed the "architectural treatment." Between them, the architects and the engineer worked out a whole inner city that would rise on bridgework over the tracks—station, post office, hotels, office buildings, even an opera house. And it was this great scheme that was laid before the city authorities.

The city approved on the nineteenth of June, 1903—and this date, on which the last preliminary task was completed, is the date usually taken to mark the beginning of Grand Central Terminal. Actual work was begun the next day; but it was twenty-four years before the job was done. The demolition of Grand Central Station was begun on the first of July, 1903, completed on the first of July, 1910; and Grand Central Terminal was thrown open to the public on Sunday, the third of February, 1913. But the loop tracks—which had been the starting point of Wilgus's thinking—had not yet been built in 1913. It was 1917 before the upper-level loop was placed in service; and the lower-level loop, completing the layout as it stands today, was not opened till the twenty-first of May, 1927.

And why was it called Grand Central Terminal? Because the Pennsylvania Railroad was building a bigger station, which was to be, however, a through station; not a terminal. Because the publicity department of the Central-Hudson Railroad had for years been shouting that Grand Central was "the biggest station in the world." And because that same publicity department wanted to continue shouting. Adroitly—and instantly the extent of the Pennsylvania's planning became known at Forty-second street—they altered one word and began yelling that Grand Central was "the biggest terminal in the world." And, of those who noticed any difference at all, the majority of people assumed, apparently, that the alteration was cooked up simply to intensify the phrase, since "terminal" sounds so much bigger than "station."

In point of fact, Pennsylvania Station is entered from the West by the Pennsylvania and from the East by the Long Island Rail Road; and the tracks are continuous. (Indeed, the Long Island is not a separate railroad but merely a division of the Pennsylvania.) Consequently, the train from Chicago, Pittsburgh, Washington or Philadelphia can discharge her passengers and promptly move on, in a forward direction, to the Sunnyside Yards in Long Island City, while the train from Montauk Point, Long Island, can discharge her passengers on the opposite side of the same platform and just as promptly pull out of the station and over to the Meadow Yards in Kearny, New Jersey. This is not, of course, invariable practice, but it discloses the principle on which Pennsylvania Station was designed.

It becomes obvious, then, that Pennsylvania Station at least has the physical form of a through station. And today through trains actually make use of it; for example, the New Haven railroad operates a regular service of several trains daily between Boston and Washington via the Hell Gate Bridge, Sunnyside and Pennsylvania Station. The New Haven, indeed, has now two rights of entry into New York, and you can take a train for Boston either from Grand Central Terminal or from Pennsylvania Station.

It becomes obvious too, perhaps, how beautifully different a through station is from a terminal; and therefore how wrong-headed it would be, as well as churlish, ever to mention that Pennsylvania Station is bigger than Grand Central Terminal.

True, Pennsylvania Station is what the engineers call a "functional terminal"—meaning that it serves the purpose of a terminal—because the overwhelming majority of trains, when they arrive there, are "washed off the board," having completed their runs. But that's only a detail; and the difference still stands, and the difference is abysmal. You remember, for example, the story of the Upstate farmer on his way to the big city by the New York Central. "I say, Conductor," he demanded cautiously, "does this-here train stop at New York?" The conductor eyed him silently for a moment, then: "Be an awful crash if it don't." The point is that you can't tell that story about the Pennsylvania Railroad. Instead you recall the anguished cry of an old *New York Herald* man the day the plans for Pennsylvania Station were first made public: "They're reducing New York to a two-minute stop on the line from Long Island City to Rahway, New Jersey." For years after that, the *Herald* man went about mumbling that New York was on the map at last: "The limited from Boston to Washington whizzes through our town at seventy miles an hour."

TEN YEARS' EXCAVATION

Wilgus had laid out a great plan for Grand Central. Now that plan, transferring itself far into the future, became an objective; and other plans had to be devised, new and totally different plans, for attaining the objective. Wilgus had been at work on these ever since January; the question was now to realize the terminal he had so clearly envisaged—how to carve out of the granite the enormous underground gallery that would contain all the track-work, how to do this without interfering with a very heavy schedule of train arrivals and departures. There was the poser; and, grappling with it, Wilgus found his answer.

He began at the east, just beyond the terminal precinct; he tore down buildings along the westerly side of Lexington avenue from Forty-fourth street to Fiftieth. But he spared—notably—the Grand Central Palace, the great exhibition hall occupied by the Merchants' & Manufacturers' Exchange, at Lexington avenue and Forty-third street.

Then he took down the annex and the Commodore's magnificent train-shed—and this was an engineering work of such magnitude as to attract attention in England, Germany and Italy. Wilgus designed and built a traveling trestle nearly as wide as the train-shed, nearly as high. At the north end he tore out the great glass wall, and, without obstructing a single track, the trestle moved southward into the train-shed as the lesser tube of a telescope moves into the greater. It spanned all the tracks, and the trains passed in and out below it as if it weren't there. Men worked atop of it. It caught the glass and iron they let fall. It protected the trains and the crowds of people on the station platforms below.

Without delay to any train, the men atop the trestle took down the shed—took down 350 tons of cast iron, 1,350 tons of wrought iron, 60,000 square feet of glass, 90,000 square feet of corrugated iron. The debris piled up about them on the trestle by day; by night they lowered it to work trains to be carted away.

They began at the north end. They took down the web of roofing between the first and second of those magnificent iron arches; and with blow torches, simultaneously, they twice cut the isolated first arch. They caught the collapsing middle segment upon their trestle, they caught the other segments as they toppled inward from either side. Then they advanced their trestle to a new position southward, and began the demolition of the second ring; and the third; and the fourth; and so on till nothing remained of what had been the greatest iron-arch structure ever built in America.

Next, where he had cleared away the Lexington avenue tenements, Wilgus blasted and cut—but the city insisted that the elevated foot bridges across the fan be kept open to the public all through the building operations. Wilgus went back to his draughting board, designed a portable bridge 172 feet long with wheels at one end. He built three of these, threw them across the excavation to give access to the foot bridges from Lexington avenue.

Parallel to the avenue, east of the most easterly track, he carved in the earth a long, narrow slot: half a mile long, one hundred feet wide, forty feet deep—except at Forty-fifth street, where it was sixty-five feet deep to provide for a transverse subway, by which all baggage would be carried to and from the train platforms.

From that bottom of the excavation, Wilgus had to build to six-foot drainage sewer to the East river, nearly a mile away. Mostly, of course, he had to cut through granite. But under Third avenue he ran into quicksand, had to quickly shore up the Third avenue elevated railway, had to supply that structure with new supports, founded upon a subterranean bridge he threw across the sand from granite to granite. This was one of the unforeseen things. It delayed the opening of the sewer. Water accumulated in the excavation at Grand Central.

It was only a few days longer, though, before the sewer was in service. The water ran out. And within that long, deep, narrow slot he had carved in the granite, Wilgus erected the steelwork, built all his bridges, laid the tracks each in its final position. And when that was done a portion of the whole Grand Central job was completed.

Immediately, then, these new tracks were placed in service; and in exchange for them Wilgus took over a number of old tracks immediately west of the new installation. He tore them up. He cut back the foot bridges above them. Upon the new steel bridges, crossing the new tracks at street-level, he rolled his portable bridges westward, till they again connected with the elevated foot bridges. Then he blasted and cut a second time; carved out a second long slot beside the first; and again he erected steelwork, bound it to the steelwork east of it. And again he laid down tracks each in its final position, and exchanged them for the next group of tracks to the west.

And so the number of terminal tracks in service remained constant or was gradually increased, as the work of building the new Grand Central in a succession of narrow strips, complete in two levels, was carried steadily westward; as concrete walls and steelwork rose beside and between tracks that every hour of the day and halfway through the night were alive with fast-moving trains.

Over the new tracks the steelwork from Forty-sixth street to Forty-seventh was carried straight on upward for thirteen stories, and a new building came to birth on Lexington avenue. To protect the trains that were already passing under it, a waterproof floor was built at street-level; and after that the builders worked only at night—from 11 P. M. to 7 A. M. But the work advanced with astonishing rapidity. The outer walls were bricked in as fast as the steelwork rose, and the marble was set in all the corridors before the roof was on. And from first to last, from the roofing above the railroad tracks to the roofing above the completed edifice, the job was done in less than six months.

This was the new Grand Central Palace. As soon as it was ready, the Merchants' & Manufacturers' Exchange moved into it, and the old Palace at Forty-third street became the temporary station. To make way for the blasting, the second Grand Central Station was coming down.

Never before, it was said, had such an enterprise been carried out on so vast a scale, or in the face of such enormous odds. At one point, as we have seen, the rock towered forty feet above street-level; and the formation was so varied that blasting became a work of precision. Geologists were brought in, made careful contour maps, laid out the lines; and the drilling had to follow those lines to the quarter of an inch, lest the blasting upset any of the old tracks or injure the new installations. And lest the movement of trains be interfered with, every operation had to be scheduled and carried out to the quarter of a minute.

That was the procedure for blasting and excavating a million cubic yards of earth and two million cubic yards of granite—enough to open a pit 40 feet deep, 770 feet wide, and half a mile long. The work trains hauled it out, and it was used to buttress 150 miles of sea wall where the tracks follow the river's edge from Spuyten Duyvil to Albany. Week after week, month after month, year after year, for ten solid years, an average of four hundred carloads of excavated material was carried out of the workings every single day—and this, too, was a work of precision, for every movement of the work trains in and out of Grand Central had to fall in with the carefully dovetailed movements of the revenue trains.

But if it was thus all very precise, it was never cut and dried; for more than once it became a question of how even to find foot room for a steam shovel. On such occasions Wilgus had to go to the terminal manager, whose answer was always the same: "If I give you that space, what new track can you give me in exchange?" After all, it was now desperately hard to get trains in and out of the terminal; and in the end, as often as not, Wilgus had to build an extra track somewhere. It would be in service, perhaps, for only twenty-four hours, but it required the laying of a switch and it required hours of planning, and it had, of course, to be just as well and sturdily built as if it were to last as long as Grand Central itself.

There was a row; and in 1907 Wilgus quit the service of the Central-Hudson Railroad. But the job was well advanced by then; so much so that his successors had little choice but to follow the lines he had laid down for completing it. They were, in their own right, great and famous engineers—George Harwood, W. F. Jordan, George Kittredge. They met appalling problems day by day and solved them. They corrected the imperfections that experience revealed. But the plan they carried through to the end, without any material change, was the plan laid down by Wilgus.

Wilgus himself went on to other things. He became, as we have seen, Director of Military Railways under Pershing in the First World War, and the story of his virtually dictating the battle plans on the eve of

San Mihiel at least has the flavor of his other exploits. After that first war he became chairman of the board of consulting engineers for the building of the Holland Tunnel under the Hudson river; he became chairman of the board of advisory engineers for the building of the Detroit River Tunnel; he became consulting engineer for the designing of the Narrows Tunnel below the entrance to New York harbor.

THREE ARCHITECTS

After Wilgus, one other man seems to dominate the story; but what his contribution to the building of Grand Central was, what single gift was his and his alone, it would be hard, perhaps impossible, to say. He was Whitney Warren, "architect of Grand Central Terminal."

But Reed & Stem were the architects. Quite so. Charles Reed and Allen Stem were men from the Middle West. They stepped into New York and the most luscious plum the city had up to that time known fell into their hands. They might just as well have stepped into a cage of lions after that. They were cagey enough, though. They hung on to half the plum as long as Reed lived. Then they lost even that, but Stem had gumption enough to go to court about it.

The facts, in briefest outline, appear to be these: Reed & Stem won the contest, received the contract, prepared the drawings that were submitted to the city fathers for approval. They were the architects at work on Grand Central.

On the other hand, William K. Vanderbilt—son of that William H. Vanderbilt who fought the duel against the Pennsylvania Railroad—was "the very highest railroad authority." William H. Newman was, as we have seen, the president of the Central-Hudson, but William K. was chairman of the New York Central Corporation, the higher command which had ruled over all the Vanderbilt railroads, somewhat protected from the public gaze, ever since the "Public-be-damned" episode. Vanderbilt, in short, was the man who mattered.

And Vanderbilt, in private life, was a connoisseur, passionately in love with art. Whitney Warren was his cousin, Whitney Warren was not only an artist but a man magnificently capable of discussing art, and Whitney Warren was Vanderbilt's closest friend.

The firm of Warren & Wetmore—Whitney Warren and Charles D. Wetmore—drew up a rival plan for the new Grand Central and laid it directly before Vanderbilt. It called for a nonrevenue-producing station having a "low monumental effect." Vanderbilt withheld approval, but declared his preference for a "monumental" station, made it quite clear that he opposed the "cheapness" of a profit-making station, and conveyed to Reed & Stem the idea that they ought to take Warren & Wetmore into partnership. The inspiration was at first resisted, but presently the Middle Westerners consented, and the two firms of Reed & Stem and Warren & Wetmore were linked under the title of Associated Architects of the Grand Central Terminal. Notably, Reed became the head of the joint firm.

The station plans were scrapped—the plans which had won the prize. New plans were developed. Perhaps they were largely, perhaps they were even wholly, Warren's. (We can overlook Wetmore in this connection, for Wetmore was not an architect at all but a lawyer, the "business brains" of a partnership to which Warren alone brought any element of artistic ability.) They called for a low, nonrevenue building, without ramps, without the bridge across Forty-second street, without the "exterior circumferential elevated driveways." All this was the work of four years.

And then, in the fall of 1909, Vanderbilt remembered the trouble his grandfather had had with the New Haven Railroad; remembered how those stubborn Yankees had held out on the Commodore, and how they had won their point, which was simply that nothing whatever can be done at Grand Central without the consent of the New York, New Haven & Hartford Railroad. Tardily, he submitted the new plans for their approval. They said No.

In December, Vanderbilt—feeling, perhaps, just how the Commodore felt aforetime—gave the word and the new plans were scrapped in favor of the original plans; the plans developed by Charles Reed and Allen Stem.

But not much time was left now. Wilgus's gigantic pit was almost completed, and the dynamiters were ready to begin blasting below the sidewalk of Forty-second street. There was a great deal of work to be done, for the railroad had meanwhile acquired additional land, and the plan drawn up in 1903 would have to be adjusted to a larger site. But the point is that what was adjusted, what was worked over and punched and pummeled into new proportions, was not Whitney Warren's plan, but Reed & Stem's plan, with its system of ramps instead of staircases, with its bridge across Forty-second street, and with what Reed himself so proudly spoke of as "exterior circumferential elevated driveways."

The readjustment of the plan, however, was not easy, and Warren no doubt contributed to it much that was valuable. Perhaps it was he who made the Concourse "monumental" in character; who kept out of the Concourse, and quite adroitly concealed from the Concourse, all the revenue-producing features of Grand Central, banishing them to the ramps and corridors. He didn't have everything his own way, though. The plan, for example, called for a twenty-two-story structure, to serve partly as a railway station, partly as a hotel or office building. They compromised on that. They put in all the steelwork eight stories high and stopped at that point. So they produced—by, as it were, a sawing-off process—that "low, monumental effect" that Warren demanded; but they also left it to a future generation of railroad officials to decide whether the station should not some day be completed by the addition of that fourteen-story tower directly above the Concourse. When the revision was completed, the plan retained every fundamental feature of the original Reed & Stem plan of 1903.

Then, on the nineteenth of December, 1911—thirteen months before the station was completed and thrown open to the public—Reed died; and on that same nineteenth of December, 1911, Warren & Wetmore severed their connection with Associated Architects, and the railroad signed a new contract under the terms of which Warren & Wetmore became the sole architects in charge of Grand Central.

When Grand Central was opened on the second of February, 1913, it was very generally presented to the world as the work of Whitney Warren; and the Institute of France gave the newspapers a handsome headline by cabling to Warren its congratulations.

But the story doesn't end there. On his own behalf and on behalf of the estate of Charles Reed, Allen Stem sued Warren & Wetmore; and in the Supreme Court of New York County, on the seventeenth of July, 1916, Justice Delehanty excoriated Whitney Warren and Charles D. Wetmore for their breach of trust in negotiating their new contract behind the backs of Reed & Stem, and at the very moment when Reed lay dying. The Court's denunciation was unusually severe: he lectured them on "good faith" and "morality" and "questionable dealing." Some time later a Supreme Court Referee declared Warren & Wetmore liable for more than $200,000 over and above the sum which their "erroneous and improper" accounting showed to be due to Stem and the Reed estate. It was the fourteenth of January, 1922, before the case was finally settled. On that day Justice Delehanty signed an order compelling Whitney Warren and Charles D. Wetmore to disgorge sums aggregating little less than $400,000.

Whitney Warren was a formidable fellow, be sure of that. Tall, burly and handsome as the devil, he had the good fortune also to be rich; he fell heir in his time to well over five million dollars. He was the cousin of Harry Payne Whitney as well as the Vanderbilts. He studied at the Beaux Arts in Paris. He wrote books in French. And, when all is said, he was an artist of undoubted ability.

He was also an amateur pugilist—presumably undefeated; for there were aspects of his character that might have been improved by contact with somebody his own size. He was triumphant in half a dozen sports, but he would seem never to have known the meaning of sport. In 1910, when he was already forty-seven years old, he swam from Bailey's Beach to Narragansett Pier, a distance of twelve miles; and presently was sued, and compelled to pay damages, for manhandling a news photographer and smashing his camera. The man had given him no offense; nor was the camera turned in his direction. The only explanation he could give the court was that he "thought" the man "might" take his picture and he didn't want his picture in the newspapers.

"The standard of success in this country is the making of money," he once declared before a school of architecture; "therefore, the architect should make money and be considered successful." There were other fragments of advice, but this was the cardinal rule he laid down for the students to brood upon. And this was the rule he followed with a passion that bordered on ferocity.

It may be, of course, that he was more than half the time in straits. That's only a suspicion, but it seems a hard one to put down; and it would seem, in some measure, to explain the man. After all, Whitney Warren lived extravagantly; and his manner of doing things involved great expenditures of money.

He made it his business, for example, to know every artist, painter and sculptor, who could ever be of any use to a successful architect; and if the artist was exceptionally worth knowing, Warren kept strings on him by over-paying him for little jobs against the day when he might need him for a big job. In short, Whitney Warren kept a "talent pool" —which in part accounts, by the bye, for his artistic success. Thus it enabled him to reach over to Paris for Paul Helleu when he wanted something astonishing in the way of a ceiling design for Grand Central. But his talent pool must have been a very costly investment.

Again, it was Whitney Warren who organized in New York the annual Beaux Arts Ball for the benefit of his old school, *l'Ecole des Beaux Arts,* in Paris; and it was he, for that matter, who persuaded James A. Stillman to contribute a cold $100,000 to form a student-aid fund at the Beaux Arts. The very next year, curiously, Warren was made a member of the Institute of France; and when Grand Central was opened, the Institute, as we have seen, made a splash in the New York papers by its cabled congratulations to its American member, Whitney Warren. And a few years later on it was the Institute that chose Warren—on Warren's promise to raise in America all the cash that would be needed —to build the new library at Louvain. Perhaps there is room for question whether, in the long run, Warren did not spend as much in getting his wonderful contracts as he ever made out of them. Perhaps that, in part, explains the man.

But he was not without courage. When bullets were trump, after the First World War, he rode into Fiume at the head of the Irridentist army, side by side with his old crony, Gabriele d'Annunzio; and there are those who still suspect that it was not the dream-shot Italian poet, but the belligerent-minded New York money-maker who was the architect of that adventure.

A little later he hailed his new friend, Benito Mussolini, as "the greatest man of the century," and called upon Clemenceau to emulate *il Duce* by setting up a dictatorship in France; and all through the 1930s he stuck to his guns, upholding Mussolini, pointing to Italy's unusual prosperity, and—with admirable impartiality—denouncing the whole anti-Fascist crowd in Italy as "a few obstructionists" and excoriating Adolf Hitler and the whole Fascist crowd in Germany as barbarians. So he had the courage, anyhow, to take his own line, and follow it; and it was not his fault, perhaps, that Mussolini attacked France within the week of Whitney Warren's frantic appeal to him to attack the Germans.

When he took the curtain call at the opening of Grand Central, the world was only too ready to heap its honors upon Whitney Warren. But in the end, of course, he made himself to many minds throughout the world a very symbol of the meanness of mean men; for having built the new library at Louvain in the early 1920s, he spent the next ten years fighting the Bishop of Louvain through all the courts of Belgium in a vain effort to enforce his own wish to inscribe across the face of the library the legend: *Furore Teutonico Diruta: Dono Americano Restituta* (Destroyed by Teutonic Madness: Rebuilt by American Gift). Warren said he had got these words from the gentle-minded Cardinal Mercier. But Mercier, as the Bishop of Louvain pointed out, wrote exquisite verses in Latin, and had been for many years a teacher; he could not have been capable either of such vindictiveness of spirit or of such abominably bad Latin.

So many men shared in the enterprise, so many contributed so much, that it seldom is possible to pick out any one thing at Grand Central and say So-and-so did this. Of course, we know that the statuary out front was the work of Jules Coutan, and that Paul Helleu was responsible for the ceiling above the Concourse. But we know little more than this. And yet we know that it was Whitney Warren who brought here from Paris both Helleu and Coutan. And there is a sound probability that we owe to Paris-trained Whitney Warren the magnificent interior of Grand Central: New York's first example of the Modern French style of architecture.

It was an interesting set of problems that Warren faced. When all is said, the framework of Grand Central Station was determined, first, by the nature of the track development, and next by Reed's exterior circumferential elevated highway and Reed's great system of ramps. Warren's main problem, in the end, was to take the framework as he found it, and to apply to it the exterior envelope of granite and limestone; and likewise to hang upon it the interior finish. In brief, it was to cover the naked steelwork with an outer and an inner veneer.

For his treatment of the exterior he was not quite responsible. It's Flamboyant, as we have seen; it belongs to a period that ended when the Modern French came in. Here, indeed, we see the hand of Charles Reed, working out his plan of 1903 and then hurriedly revising it seven years later; through no fault of his own, stretching it and pulling it to its final state, in which proportion seems to have been thrown to the winds.

Jules Coutan is responsible for the statuary that tops off the Forty-second street façade—a massive group in which a twenty-nine-foot Mercury stands with one foot forward upon the clock like an acrobat with outstretched arms acknowledging the applause of lower Park avenue. It's the great French clock he stands upon; the Big Fellow that Jake is so proud of. Upon his left is Minerva poring over a set of blue-prints; and upon his right is an astonished Vulcan holding his hammer the wrong way about. (The railroad publicity department tells us that this is Hercules, not Vulcan. But when did Hercules exchange his club for a hammer? And are not the iron turnpike, the iron horse, and steam itself the works of that mighty blacksmith who taught men how to master iron with fire?)

Some say the group is supposed to represent the Glory of Commerce; that Mercury here stands for Progress, supported by Mental Power and Physical Strength. And there are those who discern in the clock the symbol of Time, against which Progress must contend, and over which Progress prevails, with the help of Brains and Brawn. For a certainty, Progress tramples upon the clock.

It may have been the experimental nature of the job; for all these figures are of molded concrete inwardly strengthened with great skeletons of steel. Nobody had done that kind of work before; and Coutan did as well, perhaps, as could be expected. Among artists he is remembered for a certain exquisiteness of line. But there is nothing here that's exquisite. He was afraid, apparently, of the "mud" he was working with, and "laid it on thick." When Grand Central was new, the publicity men assured New York that the result was "powerful," or "dynamic," or whatever the fashionable word was. But it was only heavy and clumsy; it was "kolossal," as Elmer Davis said. And below it today, as if maliciously to point a contrast, stands the heroic bronze figure of old Commodore Van Derbilt—but that, as we have seen was only in 1929 translated there from its perch above the freight house over on the Lower West Side.

That use of concrete represents one of the unprecedented problems that had to be dealt with at Grand Central, for the engineers were not sure of the vibration factor. They had long since begun their study of it; they had taken up seismology, the science of earthquakes, they had set up their seismographs, they had recorded the waves that were sent racing through the steelwork as hundreds of trains moved in and out of the upper-level fan.

They laid mattresses of cork between the tracks and the bridgework. And a few years later on, for the fine apartment houses along Park avenue, they sank separate steel columns down to bedrock, and lest the jar of the trains be conducted by the granite itself, they tucked under each column successive layers of asbestos and lead; so that the building "floated" upon these insulating materials. But Grand Central itself they had built upon the same bridgework that carries the track, and so they stipulated that the statuary be of concrete—first, because the job was thought of as temporary, and next because heavily reinforced concrete, though it might chip and crack as a result of severe vibration, would never split suddenly and go down with a crash.

Inside Grand Central, of course, that same problem had also to be dealt with; and it was met one way in respect of the side walls and another way in respect of the great barrel-vaulted ceiling above the Concourse.

For the side walls, Warren decided upon Caen stone; but not the actual stone quarried about Caen in the west of France. There was fear that that would be too heavy, and too brittle. So they compromised on a manufactured product. It's almost indistinguishable from Caen stone (it's said that only an expert can tell the difference), it came in "boards" one inch thick, and—for a building material—it was almost impalpably light. It's soft, however, and not washable; and it was for this last reason that Warren introduced the wainscoting of Botticino marble where crowds may rub against the walls or human hands may touch them. The marble is the hard wearing surface at Grand Central; and it's the marble alone that receives the nightly going over with soap and hot water.

The ceiling above the Concourse is spoken of as barrel-vaulted, but the term is used here loosely, intended only to describe shape. The ceiling is not vaulted. And it is, in fact, but a great thing of steel and plaster that mainly hangs above the walls and the cornices; tied into and receiving some support from the walls, but mainly suspended from high steel trusses below a still higher "monitor" roof. Shaped like half a cylinder and pierced for six low dormer windows, it was built of steel girders and a vast network of steel "channels" and steel angles and steel laths, upon which was laid the under-surface of plaster—common house plaster.

In suspending the ceiling from above, the engineers intended in some measure to stiffen it against vibration; and it's the mark of their triumph over the whole problem of vibration at Grand Central that in thirty-two years, though a few cracks appeared, none of the plaster ever fell. At the end of that period, in 1944, the ceiling was resurfaced with boards of pressed asbestos. This material, chosen for its high tensile strength, is counted on to last for at least a hundred years without repair.

"Well," said Ichabod, "I've told you now almost all there is to tell . . . and if you're disappointed to learn that these buff-colored walls are not made of stone at all, but excelsior and glue and perhaps a bit of sawdust—well . . . the stonework of every steel building is essentially false; it's only a veneer, and it doesn't even bear its own weight, but imposes the heaviest load the steelwork has to carry. There may be a few exceptions; I'm speaking of the average steel building in New York.

"And if it's a false veneer to begin with, why not go the one step further and reduce the load upon your steelwork by using, where it's safely protected from the weather, an imitation stone? . . .

"Just the same," he added, "it's one of the triumphs of Grand Central that not one person in a million realizes that these walls are not of genuine stone.

"And you may like to know," he continued, "that some of those early engineers have lived to realize how well they solved the problem of vibration . . . for example, old Colonel Wilgus himself. He's still alive. He was up here looking the place over as recently as 1940. . . . He walked up to a building on Park avenue near Forty-seventh street, and stood for a moment with one foot upon the sidewalk, the other foot upon one of the doorsills of the building. As a train roared by less than twenty feet below him, the old gentleman felt the sidewalk tremble, but there was no discernible vibration in the building—which was founded, you remember, on insulated, independent columns. . . .

"Colonel Wilgus loved it. . . . He's retired now . . . living down in Carolina."

The tall fellow consulted his watch.

It was 9:47.

GLORY TO THE MEN OF OLD

In that drowsy undertone in which men talk in the dark, or when they are very tired, Ichabod went on with his story.

"After Wilgus and Warren," he said, "the next big name is Paul Helleu's. As I said before, Helleu was responsible for the ceiling at Grand Central—the great painted sky above the Concourse, that everybody knows about because it's all in reverse. . . ."

You may not remember Paul Helleu; but you can see his portrait at the Boston Public Library, where he appears as Malachi in Sargent's frieze of the Hebrew Prophets. The likeness is excellent—the thin, sensitive face, the black hair and pointed beard, the dark skin, the deep-set, luminous eyes, the almost Oriental cast of feature. But he wasn't an Oriental; Helleu was a Frenchman, and he was an artist whose portrait of Whistler won the approval of that irascible old fellow himself. He was happiest when he was painting, but the world remembers him as an etcher—a dry-point etcher, who incised his lines directly in the copper plate with a diamond needle and without the use of acid. No erasures were possible, no corrections could be made; yet he worked with amazing rapidity, and the story goes that he was the first etcher since Rembrandt to work directly from living models, without any preliminary sketching, without any preparation whatever.

He was an artist's artist, and yet was immensely popular. His quest of "the most beautiful face" was followed by the newspapers of two continents—in the years before the First World War—as if the salvation of men depended on it. In an age when those commodities were appreciated, he was "the epitome of elegance, refinement, and graceful technique." And, by the same token, his sitters, his "beautiful women," were always lovely, always dainty of feature, always gracious of manner, always just a trifle unbelievable. But his work was remarkable for all that, and as recently as 1943 the etchings were again exhibited in New York. Light and remarkably delicate, they gave a fleeting glimpse of that fascinating age that died when the First World War began.

But hardly anybody remembered, in 1943, that Paul Helleu was the man responsible for the ceiling at Grand Central. A few did, of course. Frederick Mordaunt-Hall recalled a frosty morning thirty years earlier when he had met Helleu in the barber shop at the Ritz. The work on the ceiling had been completed the night before, and Helleu was in high glee. "*J'ai eu des ennuis, qui m'ont presque bouleversé,*" he said, "*mais maintenant tout est bien—car les étoiles brillent au firmament!*" "I have been nearly bowled over with worries, but now all is well—for the stars shine in the firmament!"

The facts of the case, then, are rather simple. To begin with, Paul Helleu had become famous overnight for his portrait of a beautiful woman. That woman, the American-born Duchess of Marlborough, was the former Consuelo Vanderbilt, daughter of that William K. Vanderbilt who was the "very highest" railroad authority. And perhaps he laid himself out to repay Helleu; anyhow, Grand Central was building at the time, and Helleu was commissioned to design a ceiling for the Concourse. He was back almost immediately—some say it was the very next morning—with a leaf torn out of a medieval manuscript volume, a book on the science of astronomy. It was a large leaf, folio size; and upon it, limned in blue and gold by some old monk in some ancient monastery of Italy or France, was a remarkable presentment of the zodiac and the whole middle region of the heavens. Unlike the wooden diagram of a modern textbook, this was the work of a scientist who was also an artist. It was accurate; or accurate enough. But it was also drawn with dash and stunning power. It was one of those astonishingly beautiful things that nobody but an artist would have thought of using to decorate a railway station.

Helleu presented it—just as it stood, presumably—as his design for the ceiling at Grand Central, and received for it a right handsome fee. Had not his friend Whistler only a few years earlier established the point in law that an artist is paid, not for what he does, but for what he knows?

As a matter of fact, Helleu did a great deal of work before the job was finished. To begin with, the design was immensely too large. Helleu put his finger upon the most dramatic part. They could take just half the zodiac. And the zodiac, it may bear telling, is the central band of the heavens; it embraces the orbits of the planets, it lies eight degrees on either side of the ecliptic, which is the apparent path of the sun among the stars. Relatively it's a rather small part of the whole sky. But even so, Helleu chose only half of it. He put his finger where the great golden bands of the equator and the ecliptic cross at the vernal equinox. Discarding the rest, he said, they could take just that.

But the engineers raised a serious objection. They tried to make themselves plain. On the inner surface of a dome, where such a ceiling as this belongs, the intersection of the equator and the ecliptic might seem dramatic enough; but on a cylindrical surface it would more than probably become absurd. They made the point that if you project a spherical surface upon a cylinder, as Mercator did, the equator remains a circle, but all the meridians become straight lines, parallel to one another; and every other great-circle reverses itself and becomes an S-curve. At Grand Central, with an east-and-west axis, the equator and the ecliptic would both reverse themselves at that very point of intersection which Helleu found so interesting on paper.

The engineers worked for weeks over this problem; and solved it by reducing further the amount of sky to be depicted, and by so arranging things that the point of intersection fell close to the southwest corner of the ceiling, where the distortion would be slight. Also, possibly, the equator was "bent" a little the other way, to create an illusion of regularity. Helleu had a finger in all of this, and when it was a question of weighing one effect against another, it was his judgment that prevailed. Also it was his idea to light up the major stars; and it was his angry, tenacious battle for good taste that prevented a mere banal display of electricity.

And then something happened—and nobody seems to know why. It was uncalled for, it served no possible purpose, it was utterly wanton. It made Orion left-handed instead of right-handed, it spoiled the balance of a fine picture. It took away from its integrity. Orion was lifted out of his proper place in the heavens, reversed, and placed in a position several degrees north of where he belongs.

But this stupid piece of tampering was fortunately not repeated; and there was little else to criticize in the ceiling that was finally disclosed to the public on the second of February, 1913. Helleu said sadly that the painters had made a botch job of it. Overruling Helleu, it would seem, the publicity men declared it, as we have seen, "the most beautiful ceiling in the world." That, of course, was absurd; but Helleu was overly critical. Few would deny the unusual beauty of the ceiling.

And then came the discovery, the anguished outcry, that the whole ceiling was in reverse. (Orion was not.) The stars were put on backwards; those that belonged in the east were in the west, and those that belonged in the west were in the east.

As to this there was great arguing in New York for more than thirty years. Some said that the artist copied the stars from a celestial globe, without knowing, however, that on such a globe the stars do not appear as we see them from the earth, the center of the celestial bowl; but appear, rather, as they would be seen from a vantage point outside the bowl—beyond the stars. Others argued that the artist, being an educated man, must have known this, but simply forgot to reverse the tracing he had made. And still others contended that it was not the artist at all but the painters who were to blame; declared flatly, and professed to know, that these fellows, instead of putting it where it belonged, laid out the design upon the floor of the Concourse, and transferred it from there to the ceiling point by point, using a transit to erect a perpendicular from each point on the floor to the corresponding point on the ceiling. As the years went by the rival theories multiplied, and the bickering overflowed into the correspondence columns of half a dozen New York City newspapers. Every explanation put forward was wrong.

And the railroad authorities themselves were as much in the dark, apparently, as anybody else. For a long time the publicity department was silent on the subject; then it became touchy, and in the long run lost its temper. "The ceiling is purely decorative," the department was saying in 1924; "it was never intended that a mariner should set his course by the stars at Grand Central." Some years later another explanation was offered, to the general effect that the constellations are more "beautiful" in reverse than they are in their "correct" form. And by the summer of 1946 the flat assertion was made that the sky at Grand Central had had to be reversed, because "it would not fit the ceiling unless it *was* reversed." Why? No answer. Of course, no answer was possible, for the assertion was absurd.

But if the publicity department never dreamed why it was in reverse, it learned quickly enough that "the most beautiful ceiling in the world" was going rapidly to the devil. It was perhaps never intended to be more than temporary. It was a beautiful thing; but the fact remains that it was painted in water color on plaster. It remained in tolerably good condition for hardly five years, and by 1922 it was definitely not what it used to be.

And then, in 1924, a mysterious thing happened. New and unidentified stars appeared, and comets flashed their way across the painted sky, reproducing at Grand Central all the celestial phenomena that foretold the death of Caesar. There was a great to-do about this in the newspapers, and—as it was a Presidential year—there were those New Yorkers who betrayed alarm; all the more so because the Democratic National Convention was coming to New York (of all places!), and because the Governor of New York, in his brown derby hat, was the outstanding candidate for the Democratic nomination for President. There were rumors galore, and all kinds of theories about what was happening to the wonderful ceiling, but nobody knew. Chinese scholars were reminded of Li Tai Po, who twelve centuries earlier sang the "Song of the Wandering Stars."

It was discovered, finally, that the ceiling had become wet, and that mold and mildew had run riot over large areas, transforming its appearance. It was reported that cracks had developed, that the moisture had entered from the outside. But this was not true. The moisture came from below; from the breathing of so many hundreds of millions of people, from the water they tracked in on rainy days, from their wet clothes. The moisture had been carried up in warm air which the ventilators had not drawn off swiftly enough; and then the spores of fungi had found their way to the ceiling, had taken root. The ventilators were easily adjusted; and—since the damage was so widespread—the repainting of the ceiling was decided upon.

The decorators began, however, by offering new designs. Helleu's design, they said, was "not a balanced creation." So they submitted new, and (presumably) balanced, creations of their own; and while the merits of one were laboriously weighed against the merits of another, the days fled by. And the weeks and the months and the years fled by. And the mildew and the mold continued spreading. By 1930 more than half the ceiling had been devastated. But by that time the railroad, fast in the grip of an ever-deepening depression, had not the wherewithal to pay for having it painted over again.

It was the summer of 1944 before that work was undertaken. This time the problem of moisture was dealt with first. The ventilating system was not changed, but to prevent future condensation of moist air upon a cold plaster surface, the entire cylinder was lined with pressed asbestos; and the sky was painted afresh—this time in oils—upon this new material. Knowing the characteristics of the building, and having regard for the quality of all the materials used, the terminal engineers say that the new ceiling will require cleaning in 1970 and perhaps repainting at about the turn of the twenty-first century.

"For a long time," said Ernest B. Moorhouse, the assistant terminal manager, "we considered changing the design, and a number of interior decorators came forward with plans. Most of these, however, were unimpressive. And then for a long time we considered keeping the original design but reversing it, so as to put an end to criticism. It's taken up a lot of our time, you know; a day never goes by around here but some zealot, bursting with excitement, goes rushing into the Stationmaster's office to tell us that the stars are backwards. So we thought we'd turn the thing about. But to do this, to reverse the positions of the stars, would have involved changing about all the electrical installations; and that was out of the question. The decisive argument against it was that the old wiring could not be torn out and used again, and under the wartime restrictions on the use of copper, we were not allowed to buy new wire.

"On the other hand, we talked the matter over at great length, and from all possible points of view; and we concluded that it might be a good thing after all to follow the old design, just as it stood—for its legendary value. It's a legend by now, you know. Millions of people know that the sky at Grand Central is backwards; if they know nothing else about Grand Central, at least they know that. So, we thought, why not let it stay that way?"

And that's how it came to pass that this great ceiling was preserved —"this majestical roof, fretted with golden fire"—this stunning page torn out of a medieval manuscript.

That's what it is, of course, and that's the whole point of the story. You remember where Helleu got his design. He tore a leaf out of a book. And so this painted sky at Grand Central is not a New York sky, but a Mediterranean sky. It is not even a modern sky, but a medieval sky. And the manner of its presentment is wholly medieval. Therefore Orion is armed with a club instead of a sword. And therefore the whole chart is in reverse.

Were not the heavens, in medieval times, always represented in reverse? As we of the West have known it, astronomy traces back six thousand years to Babylonia, and to a time when it seemed as plain as day that man dwelt upon a flat earth beneath a great blue vault; and that the vault was translucent, and the stars in their courses moved upon its slippery outer surface. To find the secret of that movement, men considered the vault from the outside; upon its outer surface they located the constellations, traced the pathways of the planets.

All their calculations, thus, were founded upon a system which regarded the heavens from, as it were, the reverse side. And this habit, the established way of the ancient world, continued unbroken down to a mere three hundred years ago. In the course of ages, man's concept of the universe passed through revolutionary changes, but every generation of men clung to the habit—indeed, to the standard practice—of viewing the universe from a vantage point exterior to itself. After all, it made no difference, mathematically; and, as long as the practice lasted, the charts and the celestial globes accorded with each other as they do not accord today. It was in the seventeenth century that Johann Bayer, celestial cartographer, turned against the whole stream of tradition and became the first of his profession to depict the stars as we see them from the earth.

As a mere matter of fact, Helleu's design was in reverse; but the point is that it was rightly so. It was therefore faithful to its day and age; or, as the antique dealers say, it was on that account "all the more authentic." And we can assume that the architects were aware of this, for they called in Professor Harold Jacoby, the Columbia University astronomer, to check on the accuracy of the antique design. We can assume that he knew it was in reverse, and that he called the fact to their attention. And so the question is, in the end, whether the architects were not right when they forbore to produce a "correct" sky by reversing Helleu's design.

Once its origin is known, the sky at Grand Central partakes of the interest of an historic document. . . . Orion? Well, let's say the document has been abused and mutilated. Let's say a portion of the page has been cut out and pasted in again rather badly. It remains an historic document just the same.

And in this instance, this page from an ancient manuscript conveys to us a special meaning. Grand Central, as we have seen, is very French; and in its day this Concourse was very new. It was Modern; it marked a turning away from that traditional style which had evolved slowly out of Renaissance into Flamboyant.

But the French will never deny their past; and so, to each thing new, they'll always add a touch of something old—as a mark of the essential continuity of things and of their own integrity; as a filial tribute to their sires. The Modern French architecture was very new, and so was this Concourse at Grand Central; and Paul Helleu was never more profoundly French than when he matched the very new with something very old.

"It's the one valid touch of symbolism at Grand Central," said Ichabod.

"There's a story too," he added, "that Helleu in the first place chose the heavens to symbolize the vastness of the railroad; and, after that, selected the antique presentment of the heavens. . . . Perhaps too it was Helleu's idea—and perhaps it's only a recent fancy—that the stars in their courses represent the orderly procession of the trains, all moving together and all 'on time'; and that the various constellations represent the many departments of the railroad, which fit together in a single system. . . .

"It's a magnificent ceiling," he repeated. "Nearly 2,500 stars are painted in gold leaf upon a field of Cerulean blue 25,728 square feet in area. Only the sixty-odd major stars are lighted up. . . ."

Ichabod fell silent. He yawned wearily.

The daytime crowds had all deserted, and the great Concourse was, comparatively, quiet. The *Fast Mail* was on Track 32, receiving passengers for Chicago. The *Iroquois* was on Track 35. The *Owl*, the Yankee railroad's famous night train to Boston, was on Track 22. Passengers stood about the gates, laughing and chatting, sometimes weeping a little, with those who had come to see them off.

Somebody was whistling, or was trying to whistle, the "Rhapsody in Blue." Heatedly, two men raised their voices in dispute—and set the echoes flying. Unsteadily, a sailor wove his long and winding way across the floor.

"When the after-theater crowds come through," said Ichabod, "everything will come to life again, for a little while. . . .

"After that, the cleaners come trooping in, dead on the stroke of 1 A. M., with their ladders and their sponges, their mops and their drying cloths and their pails of steaming water. Fifty-nine of them come in, all at once. They're always fifty-nine," and Ichabod; "never fifty-eight . . . never sixty . . . just fifty-nine. . . ."

The tall fellow was actually falling asleep. But he caught and roused himself; and went on with the story a little more brightly.

"They swarm over the wainscoting around the lower walls, they swarm over the balustrades of staircase and balcony, washing down the marble with soap and clean hot water . . . then polishing it dry. With all mops working, they advance across the marble floor in a kind of battalion-front formation. . . . It's one of the sights of New York," said Ichabod.

A gateman raised his voice; and a few stragglers of the late commuter crowd made a quick dash for the gate. Other lingerers remained, waiting for other trains. A pair of youngsters stood riveting their eyes upon each other; a girl of twenty or so, a boy of twenty-one, about to leave the big city, perhaps, at the close of their honeymoon. The old woman in the velvet hat—tradition says it's been the same hat now for thirty years—moved furtively across the Concourse. The coppers call her Molly; when they pay any attention to her at all. But nobody knows her name. She "works" the telephone booths; goes from one to another, placing her fingers in the coin-return boxes, finding a few forgotten nickels.

Wearily Ichabod pulled himself to his feet.

"The point is," he said, "that there isn't any end of this." He gestured toward the Concourse. "It just goes on and on. . . . It's been going on now for more than a generation. It began when Taft was still in the White House. . . ."

He paused for a moment. He smiled that tilted smile again, and again there was a light in those green eyes of his. He slowly buttoned up his loosely-fitting coat. He bowed, a little awkwardly. It was 10:22 P. M. Almost shyly, Ichabod said:

"Good night!"

INDEX

A, Tower, 196, 201, 203 *et seq.*
Air rights, 242
Albany, race to, 41
night express from, 177
Aldermen, 61
American Society for the Prevention of Cruelty to Animals, 95
Andy (chief dispatcher), 78 *et seq.*
Animal traction, 21, 23, 95, 96, 99
Annex, the, 178
Architects, 248, 249, 257 *et seq.*
competition of, 246
Arrival Station, 16, 27 *et seq.*
Art gallery, 8, 55
school, 56
Automatic switchboard, 109
telephone, 82

B, Tower, 201, 216
Bachtold, Jacob, 35 *et seq.*
Baltimore & Ohio Railroad, 21, 163
Bar, oyster, 124 *et seq.*
Barnard, Justice, 68
Bednarchick, George, 218 *et seq.*
Bergh, Henry, 95
Big Fellow, 37
Big Shed, 109
Biltmore, Hotel, 16, 29, 70
Blizzard Belt, 27
Broadway, 3
Broadway Limited, the, 192 *et seq.*
Brotherhood of Railway Clerks, 102, 156
Burnham, D. H., 247

C, Tower, 201
Campbell, John W., 56
Capacity of station, 188
Carey, J. P., 92
CBS television studio, 8, 55
Central-Hudson railroad, 68 *et seq.*
Central Railroad of New Jersey, 163
Century, the, 189 *et seq.*; 231 *et seq.*
Chambers street, 19
Chatham street, 24
Chief dispatcher, 78 *et seq.*
Churchill, Lady Randolph, 64, 70
Winston, 64
City Hall, 19
City map, 19
Cleaners, 275
Clockmaster, 35 *et seq.*
Commodore, Hotel, 70, 128
Commodore Van Derbilt, 22, 60 *et seq.*; 149 *et seq.*
Commuters, 45 *et seq.*; 181, 185 *et seq.*
Competition, architects', 246
Concourse, 5, 13, 14, 15, 51, 77, 117, 185, 186, 187
Lower, 15, 47, 187
Concrete statuary, 4, 263
Connors, Edward J., 119, 120
Corners, Harlem, 61 *et seq.*
Courtelyou, Jacques, 46
Coutan, Jules, 263
Crime cycles, 138 *et seq.*
Crowd control, 73, 74
patterns, 186, 187
Crowds, average, 1, 7
record, 188

Davis, Elmer, 4
Dedication, 174
Depew, Chauncey, 150, 160
Depot, Grand Central, 6, 14, 68, 69, 97, 98, 99
Harlem, 95, 96, 99
Dispatchers, 78 *et seq.*
Drew, Daniel, 61, 63, 65 *et seq.*
Durkin, Andrew F., 78 *et seq.*
Duchess of Marlborough, 10, 71, 268
Dwarf signals, 198

Eagle-eye, 126
Echoes, Concourse, 77

Emmet, Robert, 22
Thomas, 22
Erie Canal, 21, 65
Railroad, 67, 68
Stock frauds, 67, 68

F, Tower, 201
Fan, terminal, 178
Fans, railway history, 9
FBI, 142
Fisk, Jim, 67
Fly-switching, 135, 178
Forms, architectural, 96, 97
French architecture, 4
clock, 37
Fronts, cast-iron, 96
Funeral party, 117

Gahagen, Michael, 216
Gallery, art, 8, 55
Kissing, 16, 33
Philosophers', 72
Gandy dancer, 196
Gatemen, 132 *et seq.*
Gates, Concourse, 168
Lower Concourse, 47, 48
Ghost stories, 58, 59, 149
Gil, Anthony, 123
Golden Clock, 1, 38, 48
Gould, Jay, 67, 68
Granite, 18 *et seq.*; 25, 26
Grant, President, 134
"Gridiron" plan of New York, 19, 25
Guardino, Joseph, 52, 119, 120, 129

Hall, Anne, 118
Harlem corners, 61 *et seq.*
Depot, 95, 96, 99
Railroad, 22 *et seq.*; 40
Head-waiter, 123
Helleu, Paul, 9, 267 *et seq.*
High iron, 79
Hood, Robin, 71
Thomas, 146
William M. (Bill), 144 *et seq.*
Hospital, 8
Huckel, Samuel Jr., 247
Hudson-River Rail-Road, 42, 62, 64

Information chief, 89, 107 *et seq.*; 168
service, 102 *et seq.*
Inquiry booth, Lower Concourse, 47
Inscription, 174
Interlockings, 178
Irish, the, 92
Iron fronts, 96

Jacques, George, 126 *et seq.*
Jake (clockmaster), 35 *et seq.*
Jerome, Leonard, 61, 63, 64, 70
Jersey Central Railroad, 163
Jewish merchants, 93, 94
red cap, 89
Jimmy (red-cap chief), 88 *et seq.*; 109

Keogh, William, 30
Kissing Gallery, 16, 33

Lease, New Haven's, 41 *et seq.*; 98, 179, 258
Legislators, 62 *et seq.*
L'Enfant, Pierre, 18, 19
Levermen, 205 *et seq.*
Library, Public, 3
Line, 79
Living-room, 8, 56, 57
Locomotive No. 999, 9
Lower Concourse, 15, 47, 187
Low iron, 79

MacGowan, Benson, 22
Madison Square Garden, original, 96
Stanford White's, 247, 248
Mahoney, James, 171 *et seq.*
Main line, 79
Map of New York, L'Enfant's, 19, 25
Marlborough, Duchess of, 10, 71, 268
Mason, John, 22
McAvoy, Joseph, 119
Metzman, Gustav, 71
Moorhouse, Ernest B., 272
Morgan, J. P., 165
Morgue, 8
Mullady, Kathleen, 158
Mullanphy, Bryan, 221
Murray Hill, 2, 19

New Fourth Avenue Tunnel, 150
New Haven's lease, 41 *et seq.*
New-York Central & Hudson-River Rail-Road, 68
New-York Central Rail-Road, 65 *et seq.*
New York Central Railroad, present-day, 69
New York & Harlem Railroad, 22 *et seq.*; 40
New York & New Haven Railroad, 41

New York, New Haven & Hartford Railroad, 39, 41, 258
New York, West Shore & Buffalo Railroad, 163 *et seq.*
Newman, Milton, 89, 229
  William H., 244
News butcher, first, 126
News-reel theater, 2, 8, 55
Nicholas, John S., 94, 99, 100
Nick (oyster chef), 124 *et seq.*

O'Connor, Andy, 81
  May, 145
Official map of New York, 19
O'Neill, William V., 132, 141 *et seq.*
Open-wire telephone, 82
Operator, tower, 206
Organist, 115 *et seq.*
Oyster bar, 124 *et seq.*

Park avenue, 3, 150
Passengers, average number of, 1
Patterns, crowd, 186, 187
Pennsylvania Rairoad, 161 *et seq.*; 250
  Station, 5, 250, 251
Philadelphia & Reading Railroad, 162
Philips, George, 144
Philosophers' Gallery, 72 *et seq.*
Police alarm, 142
  captain, 132, 141 *et seq.*
  force, 8, 132
Policy, renting, 94
Preacher, red-cap, 111 *et seq.*
Public Library, 3

Railroad Fellowship, 208
  Museum, 34, 39
Railway gatemen, 132 *et seq.*
  uniforms, 132, 133
Ralston (red-cap preacher), 111 *et seq.*
Ramps, 73, 74
Read, Mary Lee, 115 *et seq.*
Reception hall, 8, 56, 57
Red-cap chief, 88 *et seq.*
  force, 51, 89, 90
  optometrist, 228
Red cap, white, 89
Reed, Charles, 248, 249, 257, 258
Renting policy, 94
Restaurant, 123
Rinke, Herman, 208 *et seq.*
Rocket, the, 21
Rossetos, Nicholas, 124 *et seq.*
Royal Stock Exchange, 68

Scandalios, Michael, 126
Schultz, Solomon, 79 *et seq.*
Singer, 218 *et seq.*
Smith, William L., 224 *et seq.*
Snow, 27
South Pennsylvania Railway, 163 *et seq.*
"Star-Spangled Banner," 8, 115
Station capacity, 188
Stationmaster, 119, 120, 136, 137
Statuary, concrete, 4, 263
Statue of the Commodore, 68
Stegman, Harold, 79 *et seq.*
Stem, Allen, 248, 249, 257, 258
Street number, 3
Strever, J. J., 215, 217
Studio, television, 8, 55
Sunrise, 12
Sweeney, Mary, 154 *et seq.*
Symbolism, 274

Taft, Chief Justice, 123
Telautograph, 30
Teletype, 30
Television studio, 8, 55
Terminal Office Building, 17, 78
Ticket agents, 144
Tienken, Charles, 144
Tower A, 196, 201, 203 *et seq.*
  B, 201, 216
  C, 201
  director, 205 *et seq.*; 211 *et seq.*
  F, 201
  operator, 206
  U, 201
Train butcher, first, 101
Train-shed, 97, 134 *et seq.*
  annex, 178
Trains, average number of, 1
Travelers Aid, 220 *et seq.*
Twentieth Century Limited, 189 *et seq.*; 231 *et seq.*
Twenty-sixth street station, 95, 96, 99

U, Tower, 201
Uniforms, railway, 132, 133
Union News Company, 93, 100, 101, 124 *et seq.*
United States Railroad Administration, 146

Vanderbilt, Consuelo, 10, 268
Van Derbilt, Cornelius, 22, 60 *et seq.*; 169 *et seq.*
Van der Bilt, Jan, 70
Vanderbilt, William H., 160 *et seq.*; 169 *et seq.*
  William K., 257, 258, 268

Van Loon, Hendrik, 126
Viktor (oyster chef), 124, 125
Voice of the Concourse, 77

Waiting-room, 54, 55
Walsh, William P., 89, 107 *et seq.*; 168
Warren, Whitney, 257 *et seq.*
West Shore Railroad, 166
Wetmore, Charles D., 257, 258, 260
White red cap, 89
White, Stanford, 247, 248
Wilgus, William J., 8, 238 *et seq.*; 248, 252 *et seq.*; 266
Williams, James H., 88 *et seq.*

Yale Club, 160
  graduates, 150
  Railroad Fellowship, 208
Yankee railroad, 39, 40
Yard, 79
Yesensky, Viktor, 124, 125
Young, Ralston Crosbie, 111 *et seq.*